Rolf H~ ...~ ~, VVes~ ~~~~ ~lia.
Aft ~~~y yea~s on stage and sc~~en, he ~ ~iow one of Britain's best-loved show-business stars. We have grown up watching him draw cartoons, paint big pictures, wobble his board and talk to animals and their owners. He had the Beatles singing 'Tie Me Kangaroo Down, Sport' with their own words specially written by Rolf. He has won the National Television Award five times for his *Animal Hospital* series, and he painted a portrait of HM Queen Elizabeth II to celebrate her eightieth birthday.

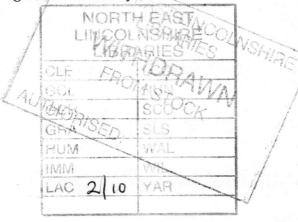

www.quickreads.org.uk

www.rbooks.co.uk

Buster Fleabags

Rolf Harris

CORGI BOOKS

TRANSWORLD PUBLISHERS
61–63 Uxbridge Road, London W5 5SA
A Random House Group Company
www.rbooks.co.uk

BUSTER FLEABAGS
A CORGI BOOK: 9780552160599

First publication in Great Britain
Corgi edition published 2010

Addresses for Random House Group Ltd companies outside the UK
can be found at: www.randomhouse.co.uk
The Random House Group Reg. No. 954009

The Random House Group Limited supports The Forest Stewardship
Council (FSC), the leading international forest certification
organisation. All our titles that are printed on Greenpeace approved
FSC certified paper carry the FSC logo. Our paper procurement
policy can be found at www.rbooks.co.uk/environment

Typeset in 12/16pt Stone Serif by
Kestrel Data, Exeter, Devon.
Printed in the UK by
CPI Cox & Wyman, Reading, RG1 8EX.

2 4 6 8 10 9 7 5 3 1

I would like to dedicate this book to my very dear friend Ross Latham. We were friends from the time we met at the age of nine in primary school. Our friendship was so loving and secure that it lasted through huge separations, firstly when his family moved about thirty miles away from my home town of Bassendean. Ross and I were in our early teens then, and thirty miles was a long way in those far-off days.

Then I sailed for England (an even greater distance) when we were in our early twenties. We lost touch for a very long time, only to meet again, when I was doing concert tours all over Australia. Both of us were married by that time, and Ross and his wife were very successful school teachers back in my home state of Western Australia.

The years rolled by, and every time I returned to Perth I'd look them up and meet their growing family. Then, in later years, I became aware that Ross was not in very good health.

This ill health led to a series of frightening

brushes with death for Ross. When I started writing this book, Ross was once again fighting for his life in hospital in Perth. I was in constant contact with his lovely wife, Maisie, and I took to sending huge sections of the book to her by email as I wrote it. She would take them in to the hospital and read the developing story to Ross each time she visited him. I like to think it was a great boost to Ross, as it featured him very strongly from the time he and I together made up the long, complicated name for my little dog.

I was looking forward to sending Ross and Maisie the very first copy of the book, once it was printed, but earlier this year, just as I'd done the painting of 'Buster' for the cover, I had sad news. Ross had suffered a stroke, was in a coma and was not expected to live. On the 28th of July, 2009, my dear friend passed away.

I dedicate this book to my lifelong friend Ross Latham, and marvel at the strength of the loving friendship that tied us together over ten thousand miles for well over sixty years.

I love you, Ross.

Rolf

Buster Fleabags

Chapter One

Enter Buster

His name was Buster Fleabags. He was my dog, and I was his human.

Buster came into my life in 1942, when I was twelve years old. He was a mongrel, and the same sort of shape as the small Australian sheepdog called a kelpie. His alert ears were always sticking up to catch the next exciting sound. His tail curled up and round to one side and was always ready to wag. In colour he was mostly black, with blurred bits of brown and little white highlights sprinkled here and there.

One of the things I loved about him was that above each eye, where you would expect to see eyebrows on a human, he had a little round light brown spot. From a distance, you couldn't see his eyes among the black fur. You only saw those two pale brown spots. They looked for all the world like they were his eyes, moving up and down as he looked this way and that.

We lived in a house by the Swan River in Bassendean, which is a town about seven miles from the city of Perth in Western Australia. The house had a long driveway. It was really only a track, just wide enough to take a single car, and it came down to the house from Bassendean Parade. Parade was a very grand name for what was in fact just an unpaved dirt road.

On either side of our drive Dad had planted New South Wales box trees and jacarandas. The jacarandas only started to bloom after they were about seven years old. From then on they blossomed with beautiful mauve flowers, and each year the drive was a carpet of fallen purple blooms. The house, which Dad had built himself, stood in more than an acre of land. At the end of the house the land sloped steeply down to the River Swan.

Our family consisted of my mum and dad, my brother Bruce and me. We two lads slept in separate beds out on the veranda. Our family always seemed to have a random collection of animals. It was well known locally that we would take in dogs, cats, any animal really, and throughout my childhood our house was home to all sorts of creatures, large and small. There was a stupid old collie dog named Puppledy who, as her name suggested, was always producing puppies. There were cats and kittens wherever you looked. We had one cat that lived to the grand old age of twenty, producing kittens every year. And there was my brother's favourite dog, Poochie, who sort of became my dog when Bruce went off to join the army. Whenever I went out on my bike, dear old Poochie loved to trot alongside. He was such an obedient dog that if he drifted away, a sharp word from me would always bring him back.

Instinct wrecked all that.

One fateful Saturday I decided that we would go and have a look at Guildford airport. It was quite a trip, as we had to cross to the other side of the river. We went over the Guildford road bridge, then turned right at a T-junction onto the main road. Finally Poochie and I got to the turning for the airport. This was wartime, and there were all sorts of soldiers guarding the airport entrance, but that just added to the excitement. With luck the soldiers might let a kid like me go up and talk to them. Then maybe

I would get a bit of chocolate from one of them. Wartime rationing meant that ordinary folks like me hardly ever saw chocolate.

On that Saturday, Poochie and I had gone over the bridge and reached the main road. I was waiting for a break in the line of cars so that we could cross over and turn right. Poochie had been quietly trotting alongside me until then, but suddenly he spotted another dog on the far side of the road. Instantly the hackles on his back went up and, before I knew it, he'd dashed at full speed across the busy line of traffic to get to the other hound. There was a squeal of brakes and an awful dull thump. The next thing I knew, Poochie was lying dead in a pool of blood in the middle of the road.

The driver of the car, to give him credit, got out as soon as he managed to stop. He came running back towards me, his face as white as a sheet. He picked up dear Poochie and laid him down in the gutter at my feet, shaking his head and saying something. But I couldn't hear anything he said. I was like a zombie. I couldn't hear a thing. The whole world seemed to have gone silent.

I pretended I was in a sad film, playing the role of the brave hero who undid his faithful dog's collar and walked away. I never saw the driver leave.

The next thing I knew, I had left poor Poochie's body by the side of the road and walked all the way home, pushing my bike. It seemed too uncaring to ride. I was determined not to cry, as that was seen as a sign of weakness in a boy when I was a youngster. I knew Dad was at work and Mum was practising for one of the plays she loved to appear in. So when I got home I walked straight into the house – no one locked their doors in those days. I wrote a highly dramatic letter, telling them what had happened to our dear dog. I left his collar sitting on top of the letter on the table and crept into my bed fully clothed. Once curled up and hidden safely under the bedclothes, I finally let the tears come and sobbed myself to sleep.

It wasn't long after that dreadful day that a man from up the road came round to our house, and said that their dog had just had a litter of six puppies. He wondered if we could take one when the litter had been weaned. I was still deeply upset by what had happened to Poochie, but here was the chance to have a brand-new puppy of my own. I've always loved the breath of a tiny puppy. It's all warm and creamy from taking in its mother's milk, and I love the way a puppy snuffles around your ears. Mum and Dad didn't take much persuading. As soon as the pup was old enough to leave his mother, which was about four weeks, he came to live with us. I loved cuddling the tiny little bundle of fluff as the puppy, soon to be known as Buster Fleabags, licked at my hand.

The first thing the new arrival needed was a name. Ross Latham was my best mate. We went everywhere together and talked about everything, and we came up with the idea that the new puppy should have the longest name of any dog in the history of the world. After a great deal of talk we ended up with a name that sounded like a poem with its sing-song rhythm. That name in full was:

Buster Fleabags
Chop-Chop
Aldi Boranto
Fosco Fornio
Poochie Acka Flipp Flopp
Pie Cruncher Biscuit Basher
Bumble Puppy Pimple Head
Hambone Harris!

That's some name, isn't it? And to this day I can still recite it in full at the drop of a hat!

You'll have noticed that Poochie's name was included right in the middle of Buster's flowery title. We did this as a sort of loving link, but of course we didn't often address the new puppy by his complete name. He was just Buster Fleabags for short. If I was calling him in from anywhere, 'Buster! Buster! Buster!' worked wonders, as it was an easy name to shout out loud and fast.

Chapter Two

Buster's Bacon

All through that summer holiday of 1942, Buster Fleabags and I were inseparable.

I played with him constantly, and when I picked him up he was always trying to nip me with his needle-sharp puppy teeth. I had a little red rubber ball that I'd throw for him. He'd go charging off after it, snatch it up in his mouth, then bring it back to me. When he was very little, he would soon get exhausted by this game and flop down on the ground, seeming to fall asleep instantly.

Buster constantly wanted to be picked up, and would bounce up into my arms from the ground without warning. If I was walking somewhere or riding on my bike, he'd hop alongside me. He bounced upright on his hind legs for as long as he could, until at last I'd have to pick him up. He was as tough and strong as any dog

I've ever known, a complete bundle of energy and fun.

Like all dogs, Buster's eating habits left a great deal to be desired. For much of the time he was fed household scraps, such as the fat and leftovers from the Sunday roast-beef lunch. He would wolf down his food, guzzling as much as he could as quickly as he could, and after each meal he'd be given the plates to lick clean before they were washed up. Very little went to waste in our house.

My dad used to play a trick to take advantage of Buster's greedy eating style. He'd get a rasher of greasy cooked bacon, make a hole in one end, thread a length of string through it and tie it on. Then he'd offer the bacon to Buster, who would swallow it in one gulp. Just as the bacon disappeared down Buster's throat, Dad would pull the string, and yank the bacon back up out of his mouth. It was done so quickly and neatly that Buster never saw it go back past him.

Then Dad would offer Buster the same piece of bacon again. Buster would wolf it down, and once again Dad would yank it back out. Laughter bubbled up out of him, even though he tried to keep a straight face. At first I was horrified, thinking how cruel it was, but then

Dad's laughter would get to me and I'd realize how comical it was. Buster just didn't seem to realize what was happening.

Again and again and again the string would jerk the bacon out. Buster, bless him, was never any the wiser. He didn't seem to remember what he thought he had just eaten. As far as he was concerned, he'd eaten about thirty-seven lovely slices of greasy bacon, one after the other. Eventually Dad would remove the string from the bacon and let Buster eat it for real. Dad said it showed that dogs have absolutely no memory of what's gone down their throats. He'd go away chuckling to himself, and so would I, leaving a very bloated pup with a stomach full of imaginary bacon.

All too soon the summer holidays came to an end and I had to go back to school.

But Buster was never far from my mind, and every day he'd be waiting for me when I came home. As soon as he heard my whistle as I walked down the long driveway from the road, he'd come tearing along like a rocket. He would jump up into my arms, licking my face all over.

We had a magical relationship, Buster and I. Every spare minute I was home he'd be there with me, following my every move with his eyes and going everywhere I went. We really loved each other.

I was lucky to have got Buster Fleabags in the summer of 1942, as it was a very carefree time in my childhood. The war was on, but it didn't seem to affect us much in Western Australia. The high school we went to was a short train ride away in Midland Junction, but that summer it was taken over by the army. School became part-time and it was like being on a marvellous holiday. Our local primary school took all the high school kids back. The primary school kids did their schoolwork from nine in the morning until twelve, and we had our lessons from one o'clock in the afternoon. It gave me plenty of time to spend with Buster and my mates.

Buster was as smart as paint from the moment he came to us, and he learned tricks really easily. In no time at all he could trot beside my bike on his hind legs while staring up at me. Then, when I put my left hand behind his head, he'd push back against it and climb up my leg. I used to swing him round my body and place his hind legs on the luggage carrier at the back of the bike.

Buster used to stand there, curved sideways around me, with his body pushed hard against my waist. He put his front paws on my left leg and his chest was held in place by my left elbow.

That became his mode of travel whenever I went anywhere by bike. We became a familiar sight up and down our local roads. He really loved climbing up on the bike, and I loved having him there.

Chapter Three

Buster The Swimmer and Buster The Singer

Like me, Buster was a mad-keen swimmer.

Living as I did on the banks of the Swan River, I was never out of the water. I'd have swum all day with my mates if I'd had the chance. A short bike ride would take us to Guildford Bridge, where we would dive off and do 'bombshells' as we hit the water below, sending huge jets of spray in every direction. We had a great life!

I don't think the war impacted on us at all that summer. It was just something that was happening to other people, over there somewhere. Mum and Dad used to pin up maps of Europe from the newspapers and we'd follow the progress of 'our' forces, but it didn't seem real in our minds. We never experienced any of it first hand.

Apart from having my lovely little bouncing

dog to come home to, there were two things that brightened up my early high school days, and Buster Fleabags featured in both.

The first was that I was very good at art. My art master, Frank Mills, was thrilled to find someone who not only understood what he was talking about, but who was already painting fairly good watercolours and oil paintings. He took me under his wing and I rapidly became the teacher's pet in our art lessons. I loved being taught how to make and print multi-coloured lino cuts. I found it quite easy and could tackle everything Mr Mills threw at me in the art line. I loved those lessons, especially when I had the chance to make the great Buster Fleabags the subject of one of my paintings or lino cuts.

The second thing started with a large typed piece of paper on the school noticeboard. It told of the approaching school swimming carnival and listed all the many events. There were spaces for students to write down their names if they wanted to enter. Quite innocently I entered my name for all the boys' events except breast-stroke. I was useless at that as I couldn't do the frog-kick at all.

The day after I'd written my name down for most of the races I was hauled up before Mr

Calcutt, the sports master. He marched me out to the noticeboard and said, 'This is not a joke, Harris. You've entered your name in almost every event.'

'It wasn't meant as a joke, sir,' I replied.

'You intend to swim in all these races?'

'Yes, sir,' I answered.

Somehow I convinced him I was serious.

'You realize that some of these races will start the minute you've finished swimming the previous race?'

'I suppose so, sir,' I replied.

'And you think you can cope with that?'

'I'm really quite a good swimmer, sir,' I said.

Mr Calcutt muttered, 'Hmm,' and went away frowning and massaging his chin.

Even though I say so myself, that swimming carnival was a sensation for the whole school. They did have to wait on two occasions for me to get out of the pool after one race and head to the other end of the pool to start the next event, but I did really well. I certainly put my name on the school map that day. I won several races and came second in quite a few more. The thing that amazed everyone, though, was that this skinny first-year student had entered the big event, the open 440 yards freestyle.

The top swimmer in the school, a final-year seventeen-year-old called Ray Strauss, was expected to win, but I came in ten yards ahead of him. I had won my school colours in swimming by winning an open event in my first year!

Much of my success at the swimming event was down to the constant swimming I'd done in the river at the back of our house, and that's where Buster Fleabags comes in. He liked nothing better than to leap into the Swan River with me and my mates from the local swimming club and be part of our training sessions.

The river was about sixty yards wide by our house, so we'd swim back and forth until we were exhausted, all the time avoiding Buster if we could. He would rush out and plunge into the river as soon as the first of us dived in, then he'd try and doggy-paddle to keep up with us.

We were much faster than Buster, so he would meet us when we were halfway back. We would avoid him and he would turn and follow us back to the other bank, his front legs going up and down like steam hammers. If any of the swimmers weren't careful, Buster would give them huge scratches from his front feet as he flailed into them.

Eventually, Buster would be exhausted, and

I'd have to swim round behind him to avoid his feet and cuddle him under one arm as I doggy-paddled us back to shore. He would see the sense of being hoisted out of the river then, and stayed on the jetty with his nose down close to the water, watching our every move.

When we'd finished swimming, we'd go to the front room where our piano stood. There, with the kids gathered around, still in their bathing suits and dripping water on the floor, I'd sing songs we'd heard on the radio. I'd work out simple chords on the piano to go with them, and if we couldn't remember the words, I'd make up new ones. Quite often we'd finish up with a totally different comedy version of the song.

Every now and again, Buster Fleabags would point his nose to the ceiling and join in with his own 'singing', eyes closed, head in the air and howling away, much to everyone's delight.

I had inherited a little eight-bass piano accordion, and it was a wonderful instrument for taking with me wherever I went. I could accompany myself on any song, as long as it was in the limited range of those bass notes and in the key of C or G. I was such a show-off. I remember riding up and down on my bike, no hands on the handlebars, playing that squeeze-box, as we called it, and singing songs to all the kids in our street as Buster Fleabags galloped along beside me. If I had any balance problems, I'd grab the handlebar with my right hand to get me out of trouble.

Every now and again Buster would hop up on his hind legs, begging to be hoisted up on the carrier at the back. But that would have been too much for me to manage with the accordion as well, so in the end he'd give up and stay down on the ground. He trotted along in the normal way, until the next time he decided to try and get hoisted up on to the carrier. I'm sure Buster was absolutely thrilled when I would finally turn round and head for home. At last he would see me unstrap the dreaded accordion and if I wasn't going to hoist him up on to the bike, at least I might get him something to eat.

Chapter Four

Buster and The Bamboo Spear

Quite near the house, Dad put up a frame with a horizontal bar. The bar was about four feet long and eight feet above the ground. The idea was for me to use it for gymnastic exercises, but I soon found other uses for it.

I took lengths of bamboo, about five feet long, which were growing down near the river. I shaped them into my idea of what aboriginal spears would look like. Then I'd stand about twenty yards from the frame and practise throwing the spears so they would bounce off the shiny horizontal bar and go whooshing off into the distance. For hours on end I tried to get this just right so that every spear bounced off the bar.

Buster Fleabags was never far from my side when I was at home, and it wasn't long before he decided to join in. You can imagine what a great game this looked like to him! After watching me throw two or three bamboo spears, he worked out how he could join in the game. He'd sit beside me, watching intently as I eased my arm back and prepared to throw the spear. Then at the precise moment I hurled it towards the frame he'd charge off after it. It took him a while to get it just right, as he had to let the spear bounce off the bar. But before long he'd worked out the routine and used to grab the spear as it landed and bring it straight back to me.

The trouble was that the spears were longer than the space between the uprights that supported the horizontal bar, so when Buster Fleabags raced back towards me with the spear clasped between his teeth, he'd whack it against the two wooden supports, stopping himself dead! Every time he did this, he seemed stunned and surprised that his rapid progress had been halted, but he never seemed to learn.

Buster and I got into a sort of rhythm:

Whoosh! went the spear through the air.

Wang! vibrated the bar as the spear clipped the top of it.

Splonge! went the spear as it hit the grass and the bushes.

Rustle, rustle! went Buster as he grabbed the spear from the bushes.

Whack! went the spear against the uprights as Buster Fleabags charged back with it clenched in his teeth.

Whoosh! Wang! Splonge! Rustle, rustle! Whack!
Whoosh! Wang! Splonge! Rustle, rustle! Whack!

I can still hear those noises, and I can still see Buster Fleabags tirelessly racing off after the spear, grabbing it in one deft move, then tearing back towards me.

But even Buster Fleabags got tired of doing the same thing over and over and over. After a while he took to crunching the bamboo spear up in his teeth after he'd grabbed it, rather than bringing it back at all, which rather spoiled the game!

Chapter Five

Buster and The Lemons

There was one pastime Buster really loved, and that was chasing a tennis ball and bringing it back to drop it at my feet. Then he would wait, expecting me to throw it for him again. It was a never-ending pastime. He looked as if he would be happy waiting for ever, just on the off-chance that I would throw it. His tail would wag furiously and he would look down at the ball and then back up to me, as if I hadn't noticed the ball resting between his feet. Of course, the minute I threw it he'd be off like a shot to race it back from wherever he'd found it, drop it at my feet and go through the whole process again.

He was always exercising his jaws on the springy tennis ball, crunching it with all his might. Then one day, one of his teeth must have burst through the rubbery surface of the ball. I can imagine that moment, when Buster found that he'd broken through. He must have felt like a conquering hero. Of course, he wasn't happy then until he'd ripped the tennis ball to shreds.

Why don't dogs understand that once they've destroyed a tennis ball, there is no new tennis ball to replace it? Buster Fleabags would be completely forlorn until Mum, a very keen tennis player, came back with an old ball from one of her weekend matches. The 'fetch it' game was then instantly on again, until the new ball was destroyed, which wasn't long in most cases!

One day I had what I felt was a brilliant idea. We had lots of fruit trees growing in our garden. Dad had planted an orange tree, two lemon trees, a fig tree, about four grapefruit trees, half a dozen almond trees and grapevines. I thought, 'Throw Buster a ripe lemon from the tree instead of a tennis ball. When he chews into that, the viciously sour lemon juice will put him off chewing tennis balls for ever.'

I'll never forget the day I put my brilliant plan into action. I casually picked a ripe lemon from the tree and, pretending to pick up the tennis ball from Buster's feet, I did a quick switch and threw the lemon for him instead. He was off and back in a flash with the lemon in his mouth, proceeding to chew away as hard as he could, trying to break the surface of what he thought was a tennis ball.

I wish I'd owned a movie camera as it would have made a marvellous bit of comedy film. I watched Buster crunch into the lemon, which gave way with hardly any resistance. Then there was a moment when he froze with shock at the sour lemon juice in his mouth. It was comical watching his reactions, which were very human. First he squinted with one eye, as if he was closing it to stop the sourness in his mouth, then he slowly chewed on the lemon again. This time he closed both eyes in a panicky attempt to ward off the sourness. More chewing and more narrowing of the eyes followed, until he'd totally mashed up the lemon. Then he licked his lips as he stared at the mess of lemon rind through half-closed eyes.

I must confess that my amazing idea back-fired completely. We had the only dog in the whole area, probably in the whole world, that went round picking lemons off the lemon trees and chewing them to shreds on a regular basis. He obviously got a great charge out of the instant rush of lemon juice available whenever he wanted it. No lemon at dog height was safe from the little terror. At times I even saw him jumping to get to lemons well above his reach. I don't think Mum or Dad were very pleased with my invention for stopping the odd tennis ball being destroyed!

I guess I was a pest of a kid when I was in my early teens. Our main room, the one with the piano in it, had a shiny polished wooden floor. I would sit with my back against the wall, my legs wide astride, and call Buster to come to me, which he did with great joy, his tail wagging from side to side with pleasure.

Quick as a flash, I'd slide my legs together, taking his feet out from under him. I thought it was hysterically funny watching him being dumped on his side. He'd leap to his feet and I'd spread my legs wide and call him to me again. He'd come rushing in and 'bang', down he'd go again as I shut my legs together. He kept repeating the process over and over again, while I laughed at his discomfort. I don't know whether it was being laughed at, or the constant dumping on his side, but eventually he started to get very ratty with the game. He would lose his temper and start growling and biting at my hands and wrists.

When he got too annoyed with me and started drawing blood with his needle-sharp teeth as he yelped with fury, I would stop laughing and fold him up with hugely loving cuddles and lots of soothing sounds. He'd always forgive me. Eventually, however, he got wise and wouldn't play a game that saw him tricked so regularly. No amount of sweet-talking would convince him to gallop in, only to be swiped off his feet once more. He would stand out of range of my feet, his head cocked on one side and his tail wagging furiously. It was as if he were saying, 'Not on your life!'

What a dog!

I feel very guilty when I think of that cruel game now, but at the time it seemed like a lot of fun, and as a child I felt I could do no wrong. An animal's feelings never seemed to enter into it.

Chapter Six

Buster Catches Distemper

My life with Buster Fleabags wasn't all fun and games. Far from it.

One day when he was still a young puppy and I was tearing round on my bike during the summer holidays, I noticed that he wasn't keeping up with me in his usual determined, energetic way. Then he started to cough, and it gradually became louder, more rasping and more frequent. When we reached home I offered him food, but he wasn't interested, a sure sign that something was badly wrong.

Before long he developed a runny nose and felt very hot to the touch. Worst of all, he just lay around and wasn't in the slightest bit interested in anything around him.

Then I noticed his eyes were all wet and running, and over the next day or so the discharge round his eyes became crusty. It was awful to watch. Soon he started vomiting, and all the time he got hotter and hotter. Poor old Buster Fleabags was in a terrible state.

It was Dad who first said the word 'distemper'. I'd never heard it before, but Dad explained that it was a nasty, very contagious disease that could last for several weeks. He said that it was almost always fatal in puppies and that the odds were stacked against Buster surviving. There was no point in going to a vet with him. We couldn't afford a vet anyway, and in those days I don't think they had the drugs that are available now. All we could do to get him through the ordeal was try to keep him comfortable.

Although Dad thought the chances of Buster Fleabags surviving were very slim, he told me quietly that the magic number I had to keep in my mind was six. If I could keep my beloved puppy alive for six weeks, the fever might just pass.

So every single day for six weeks I nursed Buster. I tried to tempt him with morsels of the food he loved most, but he showed no interest in it. Every night I slept with him in his kennel, which was just outside our house, next to the veranda. I'd sleep curled up round Buster to make him comfortable. All the time I bathed his face, wiped his eyes, cleaned his nose and stroked him with a cold wet cloth to try to keep him cool. I'd keep a very close eye on his breathing, watching him puff his cheeks out with every breath, terrified that he would get worse.

Day followed day, week followed week, and all too soon I had to go back to school, still unsure whether Buster Fleabags would pull through or not.

Dad thought I was mad to nurse Buster as I did. He was sure that it would all end in tears. In his opinion, if a dog caught distemper he was going to die, and that was all there was to it. It was tough, but he felt you had to be realistic.

Mum and Dad promised to keep a close eye on Buster while I was at school, but I felt very bad about deserting him.

During those weeks when I was out in Buster's kennel, curled up round him, I got very little sleep and my school work suffered like mad. I would fall asleep during lessons and dream about poor Buster with his rasping cough and runny nose, only to be lurched awake by a different sort of rasping noise.

'*Harris!*'

'Oh, sorry, sir!'

I couldn't tell my teachers why I was so tired all the time.

As soon as school was over, I'd rush home as fast as I could to nurse Buster, and slowly, ever so slowly, we got closer to the magic six-week goal. Sure enough, just as I was ticking off the sixth week in my mind, I felt Buster's tummy and found, to my joy, that he wasn't as hot as he had been.

Slowly his appetite came back, and this time there was no thought of teasing Buster with a rasher of bacon on a string. He started nibbling at the food I offered him more and more keenly. Then, when he started wolfing it down like the Buster Fleabags of old, I realized that he was almost completely recovered. It was one of the most wonderful feelings of my life.

Chapter Seven

Buster's Broken Leg

One day in 1945, not long after the end of the war, I had borrowed my mother's bike to go on a long ride. This was great for Buster, because Mum had a shopping basket on the front handlebars, which he could sit in. He could survey the world in comfort while being pedalled everywhere. Perfect!

It was a solo expedition, as my friend Ross Latham had moved away with his parents to Fremantle, miles and miles away, so I was on my own with my trusty dog.

When we came to the junction where my brother's dog Poochie had been knocked down and killed by a car all those years earlier, I kept a firm grip on Buster's collar with my left hand. I wasn't going to have that awful Poochie scene repeated *this* Saturday.

I managed to get across the traffic, which was

moving in both directions, then I turned right, and was soon pedalling along at a good lick.

We eventually came to the turning to the airport, and I had forgotten that there was one of those cattle grids across the road to stop livestock wandering onto airport land. You know the sort of thing: a dark and deep trough across the width of the road, with parallel, rotating metal pipes set in it. It was a device that made it impossible for animals to walk any further along that piece of road. On either side of the grid there was a fence, so the only way through was over those dreaded bars. I imagine that the moving metal and the gloomy depth of the trough would have been quite scary for a horse or cow.

You know how thoughts flash through your head much quicker than you could describe them? Well, I'd read somewhere that badly corrugated roads, which made you feel as if your car was being rattled to pieces at slow speeds, would feel really smooth if you made your car go faster, not slower. Get the speed up to about 45 miles per hour and, so I understood, you hardly felt a thing.

That information whizzed through my brain as Buster and I came to the cattle grid. In a split second, I decided to go as fast as I could on the bike in order to 'smooth out' the corrugations caused by the grid's metal pipes.

It was a *wrong* decision. Very wrong.

All these years later I can still hear the bone-shattering *rug-a-dug-a-dug* sound, and feel the vibrations that hit me from my crazy spur-of-the-moment attempt.

As we hit the cattle grid, my mother's bike seemed to fall apart before my eyes. Anything that was in any way movable came off. The first thing I saw was the headlight flying away in bits. The metal rim that clipped the glass on flew off, leaving the glass to fall and shatter on the metal pipes and tinkle into the trough beneath. The reflector holding the tiny light bulb went swinging away, still attached by the wires that carried the current from the generator beside the wheel. That, with its bulky little body and wheel, flew off too, and I never saw it again.

I felt as if I myself was falling apart. My teeth were clicking and banging against each other, like castanets accompanying the awful *rug-a-dug-a-dug*, which felt as if it was going right through my body.

Buster must have decided to bale out of the sinking bicycle just as the basket flew off the handlebars. I didn't see him go, because I was busy watching in despair as Mum's bicycle pump came unclipped from the crossbar and disappeared into the cattle grid.

I had both feet off the pedals and my legs were sticking out sideways like a cartoon drawing as I clutched the handlebars with a death-like grip.

I heard a yelp from Buster, but I was so busy trying to stay on that I didn't realize what had happened to him.

Eventually I crossed the dreaded cattle grid and fell off the bike onto the grass verge. It was then that I became aware of Buster's pitiful whine. He was hurt.

I rushed back and picked my way across the bars to where Buster was trapped between two of the metal pipes. I lifted him up and he let out a piercing yelp. He seemed to have badly hurt his left front leg, which was hanging down in an unnatural way. I carried him back over the cattle grid and put him down near Mum's bike on the grass. He immediately stood up on his three good legs, holding his injured one out in front of him.

I touched it gently and he pulled back his lips to show his teeth. Then he growled at me, something he'd only ever done before when I was playing silly games with him and he lost his temper with me. But this time his growling was really serious. He *must* be badly hurt, I thought.

Leaving Buster standing awkwardly, I went to see if I could fix anything on the bike. It was really pointless. The headlight was in bits and most of the bits were down in the cattle grid, as was the pump. I could see it, but I couldn't get my hand down between the pipes to grasp it. Dad's going to be really pleased with me, I remember thinking.

I couldn't find the generator anywhere, but at least the basket was lying on its side at the edge of the road, although the clips that held it on to the handlebars were nowhere to be seen. Still, the bike seemed to be working, so I undid the top few buttons on my shirt, picked Buster up and jammed his hind legs and bottom inside my shirt, leaving his head and two front paws sticking out. I thought that this would keep him safe and warm and as comfortable as possible while I cycled home.

It was going to be a long trip, but at least Buster didn't struggle. He seemed to know I was doing the best I could for him. I wheeled the bike back over the cattle grid and, clutching the basket with one hand, I held the handlebar with the other and started riding home. Thank goodness it was a ladies' bike. I probably wouldn't have been able to get on if I'd had to throw my leg over the crossbar of a man's bike.

I didn't know what I was going to do when I got home. Dad was working the afternoon shift at the power station and Mum was playing her weekly Saturday afternoon game of tennis at Ford's Place. She was a great tennis player, with a really tricky underarm serve that foxed most people the first time they saw it!

After what seemed like hours of awkward cycling, holding the basket, steering one-handed and trying to keep Buster comfortable as he let out low-pitched whines, I reached Ford's Place. It was only a short walk from our house, and Mum immediately abandoned her match and set off home, with me walking and her on the bike. I was so tired I put the upturned basket on my head like a huge sunhat. I tried to comfort Buster as best I could, but his whining was non-stop.

Mum boiled the kettle when we got home and bathed his paw in warm water. Any touch she made drew an agonized yelp. He had certainly hurt himself pretty badly.

My mother hadn't been too pleased with me when she rode home from tennis and saw all the bits missing from her bike. Still, accounting for that would have to come later. Buster Fleabags was the priority now.

Mum tried to dry off Buster's paw, but he wouldn't be touched. At any approach to his injured leg, he would bare his teeth and growl. It wasn't like Buster Fleabags at all . . .

As Buster's whining went on and on, Mum told me where the local vet's practice was. We'd never been before as we couldn't afford to, but this time we had no choice.

I held Buster's mouth so he wouldn't bite while Mum used some ripped-up cloth to bandage his paw. Within minutes, Buster was back in his place in my shirt, peering ahead as I cycled down the road to see if the vet's was open.

The trip into Bassendean seemed to take for ever, and dear old Buster cried all the way. Eventually I got to the clinic, only to find it closed as it was a Saturday afternoon. There was a sign that read 'Emergencies', with a home address and a phone number. No one we knew in those days had a phone, and I'd never heard of the street where the vet lived. Still, I set off to try and find it.

I asked as many people as I could, and at last I found someone who'd heard of the street and was able to point me in the right direction.

As I approached the vet's house I realized, to my horror, that I was crying. That was the height of embarrassment for a boy when I was growing up! It was all the tension, I suppose, and the guilt I felt at having hurt my dear little dog. I wiped my nose on my sleeve and dried my eyes with the palms of my hands before I rang the bell. I heard it echo inside the house, and eventually a kindly-looking grey-haired man opened the door. He took one look at Buster's bandaged leg and said, 'Come in.'

I went in and dug Buster out of my shirt, and the vet said, 'Take a seat. Now, how did it happen?'

I explained about the accident, and as I was trying to tell the story without making myself look too stupid, he took a thermometer and stuck it in the dog's bottom. I'd used a thermometer myself, but Mum always stuck it under my tongue!

When I asked him about this, he explained that he would get exactly the same reading this way, but putting it in a dog's mouth risked him biting it and breaking the glass. 'He could cut himself,' said the vet, 'but the worst thing would be if the dog swallowed the poisonous mercury inside the thermometer. That could kill him.'

After he had checked Buster's temperature, he told me that it wasn't too high, which was a relief. Then he took a small pair of scissors and cut off the bandage Mum had put on. At this, Buster did a bit of teeth-baring and growling, so the vet asked me to hold Buster's mouth and wrap my other arm firmly round his body to hold him still while his paw was checked over.

Just as I was getting used to this, I nearly jumped out of my skin as poor Buster let out a huge yelp when the vet moved his paw about. 'It's definitely broken,' the vet announced. 'I can feel the bones grating against each other.' Then he added, 'I think it's both bones gone. I'm going to have to put a splint on.' He turned to me and asked, 'Would you be happy to be my nurse while I do this?'

I quickly sat up straight, thinking this was an insult. I'd imagined all nurses were women, but the vet explained that there *were* male nurses and that he needed my help.

I agreed, and the vet allowed Buster to wander around on the floor with his paw held up while he got everything he needed. The vet went off to another room and returned with a bottle and an open jar, a big roll of cotton wool, a roll of bandage and a couple of bits of wood about the same width and thickness as my school ruler, but a bit shorter.

'If you lift him up and hold him,' he said, 'I'll knock him out.'

I did as I was told, but I was very nervous. 'Knock him out', sounded like he was going to hit Buster on the head with something, and both my dear dog and I looked round anxiously to see what would happen next.

I must say it surprised me when the vet ripped off a wad of cotton wool from the roll. He then unscrewed the lid from the bottle, poured a small amount of sickly, sweet-smelling liquid onto the cotton wool and dropped it in the open jar. 'Hold him tight and hold your breath,' he said. Then quick as a flash he shoved the open mouth of the jar up over Buster's nose. With his other hand, he held Buster's head from behind to stop him pulling away. The little dog tried to thrash about, but the vet held his nose in the jar and very soon Buster relaxed and went limp.

'Is he all right?' I asked in a panic as Buster appeared to die in my arms.

'He's fine, just unconscious,' replied the vet.

'That was ether, and he'll stay out for long enough for me to splint him up.' The vet worked rapidly while he was talking. He held the two wooden splints in place at the top and bottom of Buster's leg, and wrapped cotton wool around them. Then he bandaged over the cotton wool with 'proper' bandages, not Mum's ripped-up old cloths. When he got to the end of the bandage roll Buster's leg looked mummified, like the corpse I'd seen in a scary movie the year before.

The vet cut down the middle of the last bit of the bandage, tied a knot in it and then used the two ends to secure the bandage over Buster's splint. Sure enough, my little dog suddenly shook his head and started to move about. I could still smell the sickly-sweet smell everywhere.

The vet said, 'You'd better take him outside for a bit. He'll be fine, but he'll probably be sick. Most pets are after they've had ether. Bring him back in as soon as he's been ill.'

I took little Buster outside, and to my surprise he could walk about normally, putting his full weight on his bandaged leg. He looked up at me at one stage and wagged his tail, almost as if to say, 'Thanks. I'm OK now.' Then he was sick on the grass. There wasn't much in his stomach to bring up, and it was soon over, so I took him back inside.

The vet wiped Buster's mouth with a bit of wet cotton wool. He told me the dog would need to wear the splint for six weeks while the bones knitted together again.

'You can bring him in every couple of weeks to make sure he's OK,' said the vet. 'And if it's raining you can put an old sock over his bandaged leg to keep it dry and clean. Stick an elastic band round the sock to hold it on. He'll be as right as rain.' Then he added, 'And thank you for your help. You did a good job there!'

He gave me an envelope to give to my parents, and away I went with Buster back in my shirt front. I didn't want to risk him running alongside the bike, although he looked quite fit again and well up for it.

To make sure he didn't fall out on to the road again I held him firmly in place with my left hand, and by the time I got home he was fast asleep. I looked down at him as I carried him into the house and thought, What a great little dog!

I gave Mum the vet's envelope. She opened it and read it, and it was clearly a bit of a shock. That little trip to the vet's had cost us four pounds! I believe that Dad went up to see the vet to explain that we really couldn't afford it, and the vet halved the bill, which Dad reluctantly paid in bits and pieces as and when he could manage it.

A couple of weeks after the splint had been applied, I took Buster back to see the vet, who said that it was looking good. As long as I kept the bandage as clean as it was so far, I didn't need to come back again until the six weeks were up.

I was very pleased. It had been a hugely difficult job to keep Buster clean, and the worst bit was keeping him locked inside the house when we went swimming every day. I'd stick notes on the front door with bits of Plasticine saying, 'BUSTER LOCKED IN. DON'T LET HIM OUT OR HE'LL COME IN THE RIVER AND SPOIL HIS BANDAGE.'

At last the six weeks were up, and when I took him back, the vet said, 'This is just a formality,' as he snipped through the bandages and removed the splints and cotton wool. 'He's absolutely fine. Feel the leg. Can you feel that slight bump? That's where the bones have grown and bridged the gap between the broken ends. Nature is a marvellous thing, young man.'

He told me that Buster would be a bit stiff for a couple of days, but after that he would be fine.

I thanked the vet and set off on Mum's bike. Dad still hadn't fixed the shopping basket back on the front, so Buster hopped up and stood his hind legs on the rear luggage rack, while I hooked my arm around him, holding him in place by my side. Buster Fleabags had been restored to me as good as new. It felt *marvellous*!

Chapter Eight

Buster and The Poison Bait

I was about seventeen and about to go off to university. One Saturday afternoon, Dad had gone off to work on his bike, as usual, leaving me and Buster Fleabags alone in the house. It was nearly seven miles by road to the East Perth Power Station where Dad worked, but he resisted taking his Matchless motorcycle and sidecar. He maintained that it kept him fitter if he took his pushbike back and forth (and of course it also meant he didn't have to spend his hard-earned money on petrol).

I had put the kettle on, but I can't remember now exactly why. I might have been going to make Dad a cup of tea before he left and then forgotten all about it. Whatever the reason, it was very lucky that I had, for while I was in the kitchen I heard a strange noise, a sort of soft thump from the front room, where we kept the piano. I couldn't work out what the noise might have been, so I wandered in to have a look.

There, by the piano, was Buster Fleabags lying on his side. That mysterious sound I'd heard was him falling off the piano stool. His four legs were held out ramrod stiff in front of him, and his whole body was shuddering.

My brain flashed back to when I must have been about ten years old and we'd all gone out on the river in our boat. Mum was there; my friend Ross Latham; me; Dad, who was rowing; and our beautiful cocker spaniel Ginger, who'd been so excited to come with us. We'd been over to the fields on the other side of the river, looking for mushrooms, and we were heading back with what we'd collected.

Suddenly Ginger started acting very strangely. He jumped half up on the side of the boat, with his front legs stiff as a board and he shook all over. Then he jerked backwards and fell onto his side, rigid, shuddering and looking just awful.

The farmer who owned the land bordering the river ran a lot of pedigree horses there. He was concerned that they were being 'worried' by stray dogs who delighted in chasing them up and down and biting their legs if they could get near enough. He had obviously decided to put poison inside bits of meat and leave it there for the dogs to eat. Dad immediately guessed that Ginger must have eaten a poisoned bait. He dropped the oars, grabbed Ginger by the head and hauled him over the side, trying to open his mouth in order to force water down his throat. Suddenly Dad swore out loud. I'd never heard him say, let alone shout, that word before, but it seemed to have been forced out of him like a gunshot.

Ginger was in such agony he'd bitten right through Dad's thumb, and there was dark red blood oozing thickly through the hole in his thumbnail. Dad started flicking his hand back and forth, trying to take his mind off the pain, I guess. As he did so, dear old Ginge dropped to the bottom of the boat, his awful shuddering slowing down and then finally stopping. I couldn't believe he was lying there dead. None of us could believe it.

The rest of the trip passed by in stunned silence. Dad couldn't hold the oar in his right hand because he was in such pain, so I took over one oar and rowed with both hands. I sat close to Dad on the seat as he pulled left-handed on the other oar, his wounded right thumb jammed firmly in his mouth.

We buried Ginger in our garden with lots of tears. Much later, after Ross had ridden off on his bike, silent and stunned as he headed home, I asked Dad why Ginger had bitten him.

'He didn't know he was doing it,' he explained. 'He never would have bitten me normally, but he was in such agony.'

Dad had been trying to open the dog's mouth to get some river water down his throat. 'The water's quite salty this time of year,' he said, 'and if I could have got enough salt water into him, I was hoping I could have massaged his stomach and the salt might have made him sick. There was a chance we could have brought up the poison and saved him. If you ever have to make yourself sick for any reason,' he said in his lovely soft voice, 'a couple of fingers pushed down your throat will do the trick, but lots of salt in a cup, mixed with water as hot as you can take it, is the best way. That'll bring up everything that's making you feel ill.'

It was the memory of that awful day, and more to the point the memory of Dad's advice, that raced through my mind's eye as I saw Buster Fleabags laid out beside the piano. Quick as a flash I picked Buster up. He was such a small dog that even with his legs all stiff I could carry him easily. I took him into the kitchen and laid him on the draining board. Then I ripped the lid off the salt cellar and poured the lot in the bottom of a mug. The kettle had boiled a short while before, so it took no time at all to mix the water to a drinkable temperature with cold water from the tap.

Then I discovered that I couldn't open Buster's mouth. The terrible pain was forcing him to clench it closed. I pulled his lips back and up to one side to reveal a space by his back teeth, and as soon as I could, I poured the salt water down there and into his throat. I had to hold his nose to make him swallow, but I knew that I would do anything to save his life.

Then, exactly as my Dad had told me all those years ago, I massaged Buster's gut. I practically pummelled it, I was so anxious to make him sick and get the poison out of him. I rubbed and rubbed and rubbed. I just wouldn't give up.

And it worked! Suddenly I was holding the little dog's head over the sink, and he was retching and heaving and throwing up everything in his stomach. I kept going with more and more salt water until I was sure there was nothing awful left down there.

All the rigid stiffness slowly eased away and

I realized with great joy that my lovely little Buster Fleabags was alive. *ALIVE!*

I felt such a thrill at having saved him. I said a huge thank you in my mind to my dad for taking the time to explain what he'd tried to do for Ginger all those years earlier.

I wrapped my little Buster in the biggest towel I could find and held him warm against me for the rest of the afternoon. At one stage I remember he lifted his chin and weakly licked my face. I burst into tears of love and relief.

Relief was the greatest emotion I felt that afternoon. I was alone in the house. Dad had gone off to work on his afternoon shift and Mum was out rehearsing for one of her plays, and all alone I had managed to save my dear little dog's life.

I was still basking in the warm glow of achievement when I thought I should clean up the sink where Buster had been sick. A thrill of terror went through me as I realized that all the muck and poison that had come out of his stomach was still there in the sink. I imagined one of us, or all of us, being killed by it.

I wrapped the towel tightly round Buster Fleabags and tucked him into my bed on the veranda. From there he could see me hard at work in the kitchen. Dad had built our house as and when he could afford it. We all lived, ate and slept in one big square room for two years when I was very young. Then Dad attached a veranda on one side of the square of the house with fly wire instead of windows, and big shutters against any rain. My brother and I slept there from then on, and when the purpose-built kitchen was added to the next side of the square some years later, I could lie in my bed and see the goings on in the kitchen very clearly.

First I cleaned up with sheets and sheets of newspaper, which went straight into the rubbish bin. Then I boiled the kettle and well and truly scalded out the sink.

After that I scrubbed my hands with soap and water as hot as I could stand it, over and over again. I was terrified that there would be traces of poison left somewhere.

All this time, Buster's bright little eyes followed my every move from his warm safe spot, wrapped in the towel and under my bedclothes. I loved that dog, and the feeling was obviously mutual.

I'd just got the place all cleaned up when I heard my mum cycling down the long drive from the road. Mum was doing the rhythmic tuneless whistle she always did when she felt very happy, but also when she was really annoyed. I guessed she'd had a great day rehearsing her play. She was, by all accounts, a very talented actress. No good asking me. I couldn't tell. To me she was just Mum.

Mum was stunned by my news, and this latest drama took her straight back to that day on the river with Ginger seven long years ago. She fussed around me and Buster, and kept patting me on the back and hugging me and telling me how well I'd done. I tried to explain to her that, at the grand old age of seventeen, I was really a bit too old for hugs from my mother, but luckily she paid no attention.

Mum soon got to work and made her good old standby for both of us: eggs boiled just right and spread on buttered toast. We offered Buster some left-over scraps, but he wouldn't look at food. You can understand why.

By then it was already dark and I was exhausted by all the tension and panic. I said goodnight to Mum, got undressed, moved Buster over a bit and climbed into bed alongside him, on the veranda.

It might strike you as odd that a fellow's mum

would allow him to have his pet dog lying in bed with him, but I must say she didn't mind. Mum wasn't house-proud. Dad often used to proudly say to my brother Bruce and me, 'Your mother would sit on a pile of rubbish six foot high as long as she had a book to read.' I guess I must have inherited that attitude from Mum.

The following Sunday I missed swimming club. I wouldn't leave Buster, who was still very weak and wouldn't eat anything. When Dad woke up in the middle of the afternoon, he was very warm in his praise for me. Mum had told him all about it when he got in from work after midnight. I must say it was heady stuff having my dad praise me out loud. I knew in my heart that he approved of many of the things I'd done, like my painting, my swimming and the fun I had singing and playing the piano, but to have him pat me on the back and say what a wonderful thing I'd done almost filled my eyes with tears.

Chapter Nine

Buster In The Car

Not long before that terrible episode I'd got my first car, a 1928 Singer that Dad had found for me. I'd raised the money to buy a car with two exhibitions of my paintings, but having checked all the second-hand cars advertised in the paper, Dad went off and bought one for me. It was a funny-looking old thing with no side windows. It was open to the weather on both sides, with only the front windscreen and a tiny little window in the back. We'd been planning to spend the Sunday afternoon painting it, to make it look slightly less old-fashioned and stuffy, but making sure that Buster Fleabags was fit and well again was the most important thing that day.

Needless to say, he slept alongside me in my bed again that night, and by the next morning he was up, tail wagging and ready to go again. Marvellous!

What a great dog he was. As with the distemper he'd caught when he was a pup, after this latest near-death experience the bond between us was even stronger, if that were possible.

My new – actually very old – car, was eventually painted a dreadful brown colour, with any trimmings in a lighter brown and a really pale brown, which I made by adding a bit of white to the lighter colour. I was determined to name the car, though not with a name as long as the one Ross and I had made up for Buster Fleabags. There was a big blank curved expanse on the back of the car, so I painted a beautiful lady's face from a book I had on figure drawing, and I printed the name 'Chloe' there. CHL on the left of the face, and a big O E on the right in Art Deco lettering. It was all in different tones of the same dismal brown colour, but the fun of the portrait and the painted name gave it a terrific lift.

My driving lessons went very well. I'd partly taught myself to drive by sitting immediately behind the driver on the school bus and copying his gear changes and foot movements on the pedals. So when I took my driving test I breezed through first time. What a thrill it was to be the only seventeen-year-old in school with their own car! When I finally had the nerve to drive it to school in our last week before going on to university, I nearly burst with pride. I think the comedy lettering and portrait of the glamorous lady on the back took a bit of the pomp and splendour out of the whole thing, and made it seem more acceptable to my schoolmates.

My little Buster Fleabags was in his element in that car. He happily swapped standing on the carrier at the back of my bike for leaping in over the top of the closed car door and roaming all over the seats as I drove around. It was a very difficult job convincing him he wasn't coming with me every time I took the car out, especially if I was planning to drive into the city. The lack of windows helped him to leap in and out any time he wished.

I had one very scary moment when I allowed him to come with me on the seven-mile trip into Perth, which convinced me that he should stay home next time.

I was going up a steep hill on the main road into Perth. I still wasn't that familiar with driving or with the fact that if the car went too slowly in top gear I might stall the engine. I got slower and slower as I struggled up Agony Hill, as we called it locally. Then I realized in a slight panic that I'd have to change down to second gear. This was very awkward with the car slowing down while going uphill. I had to get the revs exactly right as I double-declutched or I'd stall the car. That meant that the engine would stop and I'd have to jam the handbrake on, restart the engine and start driving again in first gear.

This was very tricky. It would involve gently easing the handbrake off as I slowly let out the clutch and revved the engine at the same time.

As I was trying to avoid this awful 'hill start', as it was called, by successfully changing down into second gear, my dear little dog was jumping from front seat to back seat with excitement, barking like mad. He decided the car was going slowly enough for him to get out and walk, so he bounded out of the open window onto the road on the right-hand side! This put him directly in the path of all the cars speeding downhill on the other side of the road.

In my mind's eye I saw him being killed outright. I was still trying to cope with the gear change when I let out a terrified scream, 'BUSTER!' at the top of my voice. He must have heard the panic in my voice, because he bounced straight back in from the road, and out of the path of some rapidly approaching cars. He was like a jack-in-the-box on springs, and he carried on barking from the back seat with the joy of it all. He kept looking back across to me as if to say, 'What were you worrying about?'

Luckily I made the gear change, but that near-thing convinced me I couldn't take Buster Fleabags everywhere I went in the car. I had to be very cruel and refuse to let him come with me if I was going on a long trip.

It was fine if I was just tootling around Bassendean, to the swimming club or wherever, but if I was going on a longer and perhaps more dangerous trip, I had to send him away with his tail between his legs. It seemed as if he thought he'd done something wrong when I had to refuse him a jaunt in the car, but I was only worried about his safety. He would stand miserably at the bottom of the drive, watching me move away.

Chapter Ten

Postman Buster

In 1947 I left school and went off to university, so the time I could spend with Buster Fleabags was more limited. Every time I was at home, though, Buster was with me. He was like my shadow.

One of the most joyful times I spent with him was during my first university vacation. It was, to me, an amazingly long holiday, and to fill the time I took on a temporary job as a postman, delivering mail around my home town.

From the first day, Buster came with me. It was an ideal set-up. I was given a bike with a basket on the front to hold the letters, and of course Buster took his place beside them. He loved it! We became a common sight around the town. I'd whistle and sing songs I'd heard on the radio and my alert little dog would stand in the basket, his paws over the front edge, checking out everything that was happening and barking like mad at other dogs from his lofty position.

I delivered letters to all the houses on my route, chatting to anyone who was home at the time, but it didn't feel like a job at all. It was fun, and even more so because Buster Fleabags was there with me. Nobody ever complained about having dog's paw prints on their letters. Buster and I doing our rounds became one of the great sights of the district, and people would rush out to greet us when they saw us coming, or heard Buster's bark as we approached.

It must have been around this time that my dear mum suddenly, and for no apparent reason, lost the hearing in her left ear. It just went completely and she was totally deaf on that side. It was a terrible blow to her, because she could no longer be sure of exactly where sounds were coming from. This meant that she couldn't pinpoint people's positions on stage, or know from which side they were making their entrances. It ended her acting career overnight, much to her sorrow. She couldn't cope with the loss at all. It was a sad day for her, and for us all really, as her acting in plays had filled a huge space in her life with great joy.

Luckily she was able to ride as a passenger

in my old rattle-trap of a car and hear my conversation from her good ear on her right-hand side. Any time I was going anywhere local, she took to coming with me, which relegated Buster to the back seat. I'm not sure whether Buster ever forgave me for demoting him to the back seat.

Chapter Eleven

Bye Bye, Buster

By the time I was in my early twenties I had a job as a teacher and was very busy on two fronts, music and art. I'd done plenty of musical 'gigs' locally and had had several exhibitions of my paintings.

For a long while I'd had a burning desire to go to London and study art, and by the time I was twenty-one I'd saved enough to buy a ticket. I couldn't really believe it, but with what I considered a fortune – £300 in the bank – I was granted a one-year leave from teaching. I was on my way.

It was all right with my parents, because they knew that by that age I needed to see if I could stand on my own two feet. We were able to talk about it and discuss the various aspects of my move, and I knew we would keep in touch by mail on a regular basis.

The problem was, how was I going to tell Buster I'd be away for a year?

There was no way to explain away the awful crippling sense of loss that would come over him when day after day I didn't come rolling down the drive in my old car. I tried to put myself in his place, but there was no way I could avoid the fact that, to him, it would be as if I had died and gone for ever.

I consoled myself with the fact that it would only be a year and then I'd be back. Mum and Dad would keep him company until then. 'It will be all right,' I said to myself.

When it came to saying goodbye, it was awful leaving him there at the end of the drive, knowing that he thought I'd be home again that evening, and knowing that Dad would drive Mum back in my old car without me. I couldn't imagine what Buster would make of it, but I hoped it would be all right.

I had been in England for about six months when I heard of a studio where you could make your own record. It sounded like a marvellous idea and a great way to send a very personal message to Mum and Dad, and of course Buster, back in Australia, 10,000 miles away. At that point my earnings were tiny, but I figured I could just about afford the two pounds ten shillings that it was going to cost. I had a million great ideas as to what I would record.

The man in charge of the studio warned me that the recording was cut directly onto a hard wax disc, and that there was no way to edit, or redo any of it once it was made, or indeed once we'd started recording. I must have been an awful know-it-all pain in the neck in those days, because I almost cut him off mid-sentence as he tried to explain it.

I knew exactly what I was going to do once we got going. Even in those very early days, I had a great idea of how to get 'sound perspective' into a recording. I was going to start whistling very softly, in my recognizable way, with my back to the microphone, which was standing next to the grand piano. Then I planned to move slowly across the studio, making soft footstep sounds, as if I was walking down our drive. All the while I'd get closer to the piano and the microphone, maybe singing bits of a few of my favourite songs in a casual way.

Then I planned to use my hands on top of the piano to make the sounds of my feet, as if I was coming up the four steps outside our home. I'd gradually make them sound louder, as if I was walking across the hollow front step. I'd knock on the piano with my knuckles, as if I was knocking on the door at home in Bassendean, shouting out (as everybody did), 'Anybody home?'

I intended to make all this sound as real as possible, making sounds in my throat of the door handle turning, then sounds like a creaking old door opening, then imitating the catch closing with a click. I was confident that it would all sound totally real.

Finally, I planned to sing some of the songs Mum and Dad knew well, accompanying myself on the piano. I hoped to time it perfectly to say a fond and loving farewell just as the record came to an end. I asked the man if he would give me some sign as to how long I had left and if he would visually count me down to the finish of my time. He agreed, but once again warned me that once we started, I owed him the two pounds ten shillings whatever happened. False starts, disasters, whatever.

I can't tell you how wonderfully well it went. There wasn't a single hitch. The man played it back to me afterwards, and I felt a fantastic warm glow of love for Mum, Dad and Buster as

I imagined them in our main room, listening to it on their little record player.

It was so real that I believed it myself. It was me on the recording, and the geography was exactly right. I was walking down our path, whistling and singing and getting slightly louder as I got closer. The knocking on the door, and the opening and closing of it, were followed by the really personal, gentle level of voice, as well as the singing and piano playing. I knew it would get straight to my parents' hearts.

Stupidly, I hadn't thought through the effect it might have on Buster Fleabags. I was just being a show-off and imagining the praise I'd get from them for my incredible bit of recording.

I sent the record off by air mail the next day, and prepared to wait the two weeks or so that it took to get a reply to any of my letters in those days. The delay was annoying, but it would be worth it to have a letter back telling me what a great idea it had been, and how brilliant and thoughtful I was.

When Mum next wrote to me, though, there was no mention of the record at all, which I thought very strange. I thought of writing back instantly to ask whether it had arrived, but I decided not to, because if it hadn't yet arrived, that would spoil the surprise. I felt very disappointed that my fantastic idea had so far, it seemed, come to nothing, but I thought it best to keep quiet.

And in truth, I had enough to distract me at the time, not least Alwen Hughes, a stunning blonde student from Devon who I met in 1953 during my earliest days at the art school where I'd enrolled.

I was quite disappointed with the learning, or rather the lack of it, that took place at this school. I was interested only in becoming a famous portrait painter, and I wasn't very taken with the other things I was supposed to be doing. Etchings held no interest for me, and planning murals and posters grabbed me even less. I was rapidly losing interest. Going to art school had been my prime reason for coming to England in the first place, but the pressure to make some money to pay the rent was taking me in all sorts of different directions.

I'd got a regular job entertaining every Thursday night at the Down Under Club. It was a wonderfully noisy place full of Australians, New Zealanders and South Africans, and I felt right at home there, singing my songs and entertaining, while accompanying myself on the piano accordion.

Also, every now and again I got a booking at the Royal Court Theatre Club, which was run by the late Clement Freud. Later that year a booking at the Gargoyle Club, closer to the heart of Mayfair, started to take me away from art school altogether.

This club put their cabaret on at two in the morning, and I would be there every night for two weeks at a stretch. I used to go to bed early evening, setting the alarm to wake me just in time to dress and catch the last tube into the West End from Earl's Court, where I shared a single room in a boarding house.

After the show I'd try to walk all the way home to save money, but I was usually exhausted by the time I got halfway back. So I would keep looking over my shoulder for a taxi to take me the rest of the way.

As you can imagine, when it came time to set off for art school at eight the next morning, I was usually too tired. Instead I'd turn over, switch off the alarm, miss breakfast and skip the whole of that morning at school. Soon I started to think, What's the point of going in at all? I'm learning nothing that I'm interested in.

It was a gradual process, but in the end I just stopped going.

All this time I was in constant touch with my parents at home in Western Australia. The air letter was a great invention, and the cheap little pale-blue folded letters flew back and forth between us. They carried my news of all the excitement in London, and their news of Buster and all the other aspects of home life that made me feel so homesick. But *still* there was no mention of the wax disc I had sent them.

Some time during the summer of 1955 I started getting very upsetting news from them about my darling dog.

Buster had developed very bad arthritis and was having a hard job climbing the steps up to our house. Galloping around in his usual mad-cap way was becoming a thing of the past. It was very hard to imagine my vibrant little Buster creaking and groaning as he walked.

He was getting medicine from the vet, but it didn't cure anything. The medicine was just keeping the pain at bay. In the middle of my fourth year away from my home, I got an air letter telling me the worst news of all. Buster had died.

I cannot tell you how sad I felt. The main

feeling I had was one of guilt. Guilt at the fact that I hadn't returned to my little dog, and guilt at not being able to explain to him that I was still alive away on the other side of the world. I kept getting flashbacks of Buster. I saw him riding around on the back of my bike. I saw him leaping from the front seat to the back in my old car, and then back again. I saw him plunging into the river to doggy-paddle back and forth with me and my mates during our endless swimming sessions in the river.

It was a very homesick, sad time, for Buster had been such a huge part of my life.

Somehow, though, life carries on. I was able to remember the good times, which dear old Buster Fleabags had been very much a part of.

In a way Buster has never left me. My life has always been full of animal stories. I grew up surrounded by animals. I tried to understand them and was never afraid to touch them, which is why *Animal Hospital*, the television series I presented for so long, was, for me, a programme made in heaven.

I must have been involved with thousands of animals over the decades, since I used to charge round Bassendean on my bike, with Buster galloping along beside me, trying to launch himself up beside me. There were thousands of animals, but one stands out from all the others. One little ball of fluff with funny light brown patches above his eyes.

Chapter Twelve

Buster, I'm So Sorry

Towards the late 1950s I was getting more and more work in the entertainment field, and I felt that I could at last ask Alwen to be my wife. We had met again, having not seen each other since those early days at art school, and we eventually married in 1958.

Not long after that, I was approached by two talent scouts from my home town, asking if I would come back to Perth and run children's television when the first TV station started there. I jumped at the chance, and very soon Alwen and I were on a boat heading for Western Australia.

When we first got back we stayed with Mum and Dad at Bassendean. It was so strange being back there without Buster Fleabags bouncing around everywhere I went.

One day I plucked up the courage to ask about

the record I had sent them. 'Did you ever get it?' I asked Mum. 'You never mentioned it, and I just wondered if it ever got to you.'

There followed the most awful silence. There was a sudden coolness between us, which wasn't like my mother at all. The smiles fell off all our faces as Alwen and I stared at Mum, waiting for her answer. She stared back at us. How could my asking such a simple question cause my mother such pain?

Eventually Mum took a big breath and said, 'Yes, we got it. We were all so excited as we put it on the turntable, but the minute the record started playing and we heard your whistling coming from what sounded like way up at the top of the drive, dear little Buster went crazy.

'He was trying to get into the speakers where they stood on the floor. He was yelping with such excitement as he ripped the fabric from the speakers with his claws. He was so sure you were in there. He tore the speakers to shreds, yelping and howling at the top of his little voice.

'Your father jerked the needle off the record as fast as he could and I burst into tears. We couldn't bear it. That dear little dog stood there with his nose in the air, howling at the top of his little voice. He wouldn't stop. He must have howled on and off for days. It was awful, just awful. We never played the record again.'

This time it was my turn to lapse into a stunned silence and, as I write this now, I'm crying as I remember my mother in floods of tears, telling us what had happened. It was the first time in my whole life that I'd seen Mum cry. I'm so glad Dad wasn't there at the time, as I'm sure he would have been in tears too. I don't think I could have borne that.

I'm so very sorry to have put my little dog through that. I never thought. I just never thought. I was so busy showing off how clever I was and looking for praise.

Sorry, Buster. You deserved better.

After all, you were my dog, and I was your human.

Quick Reads

Books in the Quick Reads series

Quick Reads

Short, sharp shots of entertainment

As fast and furious as an action film. As thrilling as a theme park ride. Quick Reads are short sharp shots of entertainment — brilliantly written books by bestselling authors and celebrities. Whether you're an avid reader who wants a quick fix or haven't picked up a book since school, sit back, relax and let Quick Reads inspire you.

We would like to thank all our partners in the Quick Reads project for their help and support:

Arts Council England
The Department for Business, Innovation and Skills
NIACE
unionlearn
National Book Tokens
The Reading Agency
National Literacy Trust
Welsh Books Council
Basic Skills Cymru, Welsh Assembly Government
The Big Plus Scotland
DELNI
NALA

Quick Reads would also like to thank the Department for Business, Innovation and Skills; Arts Council England and World Book Day for their sponsorship and NIACE for their outreach work.

Quick Reads is a World Book Day initiative.
www.quickreads.org.uk   www.worldbookday.com

Quick Reads

Hello Mum
Bernardine Evaristo

Penguin

A short, sharp shot of rage

It's a hot summer afternoon. Tension is in the air. A gang of youths on bikes gathers outside a chip shop. A teenage boy is stabbed and left bleeding on the street.

The boy's mother doesn't understand how this could have happened to her son, but when he tells her his story she's in for some surprises.

Hello Mum is a powerful and moving novel about a frightening current issue.

Quick Reads

Last Night Another Soldier...
Andy McNab

Corgi Books

A short, sharp shot of danger

Afghanistan, 2009. A rifle section is halfway through their tour of duty in Helmand Province. Sixteen men have already been killed and forty-seven wounded.

The last three months have been hard and it shows. Their kit is in a bad way. They are in a bad way. Young men with tans, scruffy beards, peeling noses and lips burnt raw by the Afghan sun. Despite the hardships they are enjoying their time out here.

Last Night Another Soldier... is the story of four of these young men, partly told from the point of view of eighteen-year-old squaddie, David 'Briggsy' Briggs.

Quick Reads

Life's Too Short
True Stories About Life at Work
Foreword by Val McDermid

Bantam Books

A short, sharp shot of laughter and tears

What does it feel like to drive a lorry that's out of control? What really goes on in a school full of unruly children? Could you travel all over the world for work?

Whether we love it or hate it, work has a huge impact on our lives, and in recent times working life has totally changed. So what is life really like at work today?

From builder to baker to social care worker, these writers let us know. Some stories will make you laugh and some might make you cry. The one thing they all prove is that you can never be sure what your working day will bring.

Other resources

Free courses are available for anyone who wants to develop their skills. You can attend the courses in your local area. If you'd like to find out more, phone 0800 66 0800.

 Don't get by get on 0800 66 0800

A list of books for new readers can be found on www.firstchoicebooks.org.uk or at your local library.

 read
readingagency.org.uk

Publishers Barrington Stoke (www.barringtonstoke.co.uk) and New Island (www.newisland.ie) also provide books for new readers.

 Barrington Stoke    OPEN DOOR

The BBC runs an adult basic skills campaign. See www.bbc.co.uk/raw.

 BBC raw
skills for everyday life

www.quickreads.org.uk   www.worldbookday.com

PENGUIN BOOKS

MATRIX

'... ry leader, queer lover, 12th-century writer . . . the life of Marie de
... is triumphantly reimagined in an assertively modern novel about
f... e mbition and creativity . . . a highly distinctive novel of great vigour
... oldness. From mystical visions that may or may not be divine, to the
... arthy business of abbey pigs, diseases and account books,
Groff does it all with purpose and panache.'

Guardian

'... writing is muscular and precise, her themes wildly resonant.
... are dismissed and contained, subject to misogynist attacks and
... t gain power collectively – "alone, together". Shockingly, this
... age is as poignant today as it was, perhaps, 800 years ago.'

Sunday Times

'... robust and pleasingly strange slice of historical fiction.'

The Times

'Fascinating, beguiling, vivid.'

Marian Keyes

'... live with lust and glory . . . Groff paints a portrait of sisterhood
... shines out of the past and into the lives of women today.'

C Pam Zhang

'An electric reimagining . . . feminist, sensual, magisterial, de France's saga is one of hardship and triumph, an unforgettable character whose far-seeing vision and devotion to the nuns in her community enable them to transcend what threatens to erase and silence them.'
Oprah Magazine

'In this bildungsroman about the real-life 12th-century poet Marie de France, a teenage Marie is exiled to a blighted Benedictine nunnery, where she finds strength and power as a prioress.'
Vanity Fair

'*Matrix* explores the story of Marie de France, a young woman sent to languish in a struggling convent that she begins to transform through her own leadership. Both epic and intimate, this sweeping novel explores questions of female ambition, creativity and passion with electrifying prose and sparkling wit.'
Brit Bennett

'Just when it seems there are nothing but chronicles of decline and ruin comes Lauren Groff's *Matrix*, about a self-sufficient abbey of 12th-century nuns – a shining, all-female utopian community, although a utopia constructed in wily, complicated stages. The leader is Marie de France, a real but little-known figure whom Ms. Groff has extravagantly fictionalised . . . depicted with a degree of detail and specificity that make this historical fantasy feel far more real . . . For all its moral ambiguities, though, it is finally its spirit of celebration that gives this novel its many moments of beauty.'
Wall Street Journal

'This is a novel you feel in your muscles. It will give you delightful aches and shivers, make you revel in the pleasure of the moving, living body . . . Groff writes brilliantly about closed communities . . . and in *Matrix* she simultaneously captures the thrill of the working physique, the fearful enchantments of spiritual rapture, and the glories and entanglements of an all-female world.'
Vulture

'Animated with sensual detail on every page and filled with lush, gripping storytelling that cuts to the bone, *Matrix* resonates right into the present moment. I never thought I would find myself longing to be a medieval nun but Groff is a worker of wonders. This book is a ferocious joy.'
Madeline Miller

'Beautifully, unsettlingly rendered . . . Aside from the terrific storytelling, *Matrix* is compelling for offering a vision of a feminist nun – one might even say a radical separatist feminist – who is not "modernized" so much as she understands the opportunity available to her, seizes it, and finds immense meaning in her work.'
Vox

'A marvellous historical novel . . . Lauren Groff has woven a rich altar-cloth of a story: She imagines Marie as . . . a wonderfully compelling character and so are all the women around her at the convent. Groff has created a really convincing little corner of medieval England here; you can almost hear them all snoring in the dormitory at night or squelching around in the spring mud.'
NPR

'*Matrix* is another masterpiece from a writer whom few at this point can best. Groff spins the life of Marie de France – the author of a series of narrative romantic poems, and a figure about whom historians know very little – into a transfixing rumination on creativity, power, and endurance.'
Atlantic

LAUREN GROFF

MATRIX

PENGUIN BOOKS

PENGUIN BOOKS

UK | USA | Canada | Ireland | Australia
India | New Zealand | South Africa

Penguin Books is part of the Penguin Random House group of companies
whose addresses can be found at global.penguinrandomhouse.com

Penguin
Random House
UK

First published in the US by Riverhead Books in 2021
First published in the UK by Hutchinson Heinemann in 2021
Published in Penguin Books in 2022
001

Printed and bound in Great Britain by Clays Ltd, Elcograf S.p.A.

The authorised representative in the EEA is Penguin Random House Ireland,
Morrison Chambers, 32 Nassau Street, Dublin D02 YH68

A CIP catalogue record for this book is available from the British Library

ISBN: 978–1–529–15786–4

Book design by Lucia Bernard

www.greenpenguin.co.uk

MIX
Paper from
responsible sources
FSC® C018179

Penguin Random House is committed to a
sustainable future for our business, our readers
and our planet. This book is made from Forest
Stewardship Council® certified paper.

For all my sisters

ONE

1.

She rides out of the forest alone. Seventeen years old, in the cold March drizzle, Marie who comes from France.

It is 1158 and the world bears the weariness of late Lent. Soon it will be Easter, which arrives early this year. In the fields, the seeds uncurl in the dark cold soil, ready to punch into the freer air. She sees for the first time the abbey, pale and aloof on a rise in this damp valley, the clouds drawn up from the ocean and wrung against the hills in constant rainfall. Most of the year this place is emerald and sapphire, bursting under dampness, thick with sheep and chaffinches and newts, delicate mushrooms poking from the rich soil, but now in late winter, all is gray and full of shadows.

Her old warhorse glumly plods along and a merlin shivers in its wicker mew on the box mounted behind her.

The wind hushes. The trees cease stirring.

Marie feels that the whole countryside is watching her move through it.

She is tall, a giantess of a maiden, and her elbows and knees stick out, ungainly; the fine rain gathers until it runs in rivulets down her sealskin cloak and darkens her green headcloths to black. Her stark Angevin face holds no beauty, only canniness and passion yet unchecked. It is wet with rain, not tears. She has yet to cry for having been thrown to the dogs.

Two days earlier, Queen Eleanor had appeared in the doorway of Marie's chamber, all bosom and golden hair and sable fur lining the blue robe and jewels dripping from ears and wrists and shining chapelet and perfume strong enough to knock a soul to the ground. Her intention was always to disarm by stunning. Her ladies stood behind her, hiding their smiles. Among these traitors was Marie's own half sister, a bastardess sibling of the crown just like Marie, the sum of errant paternal lusts; but this simpering creature, having understood the uses of popularity in the court, had blanched and run from Marie's attempts to befriend her. She would one day become a princess of the Welsh.

Marie curtsied clumsily, and Eleanor glided into the room, her nostrils twitching.

The queen said that she had news, oh what delightful news, what relief, she had just now received the papal dispensation, the poor horse had exploded its heart it had galloped so fast to bring it here this morning. That, due to her, the queen's, own efforts over these months, this poor illegitimate Marie from nowhere in Le Maine had at last been made prioress of a royal abbey. Wasn't that wonderful. Now at last they knew what to do with this odd half sister to the crown. Now they had a use for Marie at last.

The queen's heavily lined eyes rested upon Marie for a moment, then moved to the high window that overlooked the gardens, where the shutters were thrust open so Marie could stand on her toes and watch people walking outside.

When Marie's mouth could move, she said, thickly, that she was grateful to the queen for the radiance of her attention, but oh no she could not be a nun, she was unworthy, and besides she had no godly vocation whatsoever in any way, at all.

And it was true, the religion she was raised in had always seemed vaguely foolish to her, if rich with mystery and ceremony, for why should babies be born into sin, why should she pray to the invisible forces, why would god be a trinity, why should she, who felt her greatness hot in her blood, be considered lesser because the first woman was molded from a rib and ate a fruit and thus lost lazy Eden? It was senseless. Her faith had twisted very early in her childhood; it would slowly grow ever more bent into its geometry until it was its own angular, majestic thing.

But at seventeen, in this spare chamber at the court in Westminster, she could be no equal to the elegant and story-loving queen, who, though small in body, absorbed all light, all thought from Marie's head, all breath from her lungs.

Eleanor simply looked at Marie and Marie had not felt so small since she'd last seen Le Maine, her six amazon aunts gone to death or marriage or convent, and her mother taking Marie's hand and pressing it to the egg growing between her breasts, smiling hugely but with tears in her eyes, saying oh darling forgive me, I'm dying; and that great strong body so swiftly reduced to skeleton, acrid breath, then no breath at all, and Marie pressing all her vitality down into the ribs, all her prayers, but the heart stayed still. Twelve-year-old Marie's bitter anguish at the high windy burial ground; and afterward the two years of loneliness because her mother insisted her death remain a secret, for the family wolves would strip the estate from Marie as soon as they heard, she being just a maiden bastardess formed of rape, not entitled to a thing; two lonely years of Marie wringing what coin she could from the land. Then the hooves on the far bridge and the flight up to Rouen then across the channel to her legitimate half-sibling's royal court at Westminster, where Marie appalled everyone with her ravenousness, her rawness, her gauche bigboned body; where most privileges accorded her royal blood she lost due to the faults of her person.

Eleanor laughed at Marie's refusal of her favor, mocked her. But but but. Did Marie truly think she would one day be married off? She, a rustic gallowsbird? Three heads too tall, with her great rough stomping about, with her terrible deep voice, her massive hands and her disputations and her sword practicing? What spouse would accept Marie, a creature absent of beauty or even the smallest of feminine arts? No, no, this was better, it had long ago been decided, back in the autumn, and her entire family agreed. Marie knew how to run a large estate, she could write in four languages, she could keep account books, she did all this so admirably after her mother died, even though still a tender little maiden, and what's more she did it so well that she fooled the whole world into thinking for two years that she was her own dead mother. Which was, of course, to say that the abbey where Marie would be installed as prioress was so poor they happened just now to be starving to death, alas. They had fallen out of Eleanor's pleasure some years earlier and had suffered grave poverty ever since. Also, there was a sickness still raging there. And the queen could not have the nuns of a royal abbey both starve to death and die of a horrible coughing sickness! That would reflect poorly on her.

Her cold eyes rimmed in black bored into Marie; Marie had no courage to look back. The queen told Marie to have faith, in time Marie would make a rather good nun. Anyone with eyes could see she had always been meant for holy virginity.

With this, the ladies were released into laughter. Marie wanted to squeeze their twittering beaks shut. Eleanor extended her hand, encrusted with rings. She said gently that Marie must learn to love her new life, that she must learn to make the best of it, for this was the desire of both god and the queen. She would go tomorrow with a royal escort and Eleanor's own blessing.

Marie, not knowing what else to do, took the small white hand in her great rough ones and kissed it. Such things wrestled inside the girl. She wanted to take the soft flesh in her mouth and bite it to blood; she wanted to strike the hand from the wrist with her dagger and guard it as a relic in her bodice for eternity.

The queen swept out again. Marie went dizzy to the bed, to her servant Cecily, who kissed her head, her lips, her neck. Cecily was as blunt and loyal as a dog. She seethed and murmured calumny, saying that the queen was a dirty licentious southerner, that she had only been made queen the first time because of a single raging French sow, the second time because of a choking plate of English eels, that anyone could bed her for the price of a song, indeed just sing a romance and she'll lift her skirts, if none of her children looked alike it was for a reason, that the devil sent malice into that royal head, oh Cecily had heard dark stories indeed.

And at last Marie roused from her shock and told the servant to hush, for the queen's perfume lingered, a watchful ghost, in the room.

Then Cecily began to weep her fresh face ugly, all snot and blotches, and delivered the second blow. She told Marie that she, herself, would not be going with Marie to the abbey. That though she loved her mistress, she was too young and had far too much life to be lived to be buried alive forever with a bunch of dead-eyed nuns. Cecily was made for marriage, look at these hips, they could bear ten hearty babes, plus her knees were weak and she was not made for kneeling all day long in prayer. Up and down, up and down all day, like marmots. Yes, tomorrow morning, Cecily and Marie would be separated.

And Marie—who had been born into this friendship with Cecily, the daughter of the cook on her family's estate in Le Maine, this rough person who had up until this moment been everything to Marie, mistress and sister and servant and pleasure and single loving soul in all of Angleterre—at last understood that she would be sent into her living death alone.

The servant wept, saying over and over, oh sweet Marie, oh her heart cleaved.

To which Marie, pulling herself away, said it must be the most unloyal form of cleaving.

Then she rose and stared out the open window at the garden in its cloak of fog, feeling the sun go down inside her. She put in her mouth the apricot pits from the fruit she'd stolen in the summer from the queen's private trees, because in the autumn and winter she liked to suck the bitterness out of them. Over the landscape within her the chill of dusk blew, and all in shadow went grotesque with strangeness.

And she felt ebbing out of her the dazzling love that had filled those years in Eleanor's court in Angleterre, that brushed even the difficulties and the loneliness in Marie with a fine and gleaming light. Her first day in the court in Westminster, she still had the salt of crossing on her lips when she sat at supper, overwhelmed; and at last the lutes and hautboys played and in the door was Eleanor, swollen with the end of pregnancy, belly and breasts, her right cheek enflamed, for a tooth had been pulled that day, and she moved with such tiny footsteps she seemed to glide like a swan, and she wore that same face that Marie had seen and loved in her dreams from the time she was small. The light in the room drew to a tiny pinprick illuminating only Eleanor. This was the moment that Marie was lost. That night she returned to Cecily in the bed already snoring, and woke the girl by moving urgently against her hand. Marie would have hunted for a grail, hidden her sex and ridden off to war and killed without sorrow, she would have borne cruelty with a bowed head, would have lived patiently among the lepers, she would have done any of these things if Eleanor had asked them of her. For it was out of Eleanor all good things flowed: music and laughter and courtly love; out of her beauty came beauty, for everyone knew beauty to be the external sign of god's favor.

Even now, after being thrown away like rubbish, Marie considers, ashamed, riding toward the glum damp abbey, that she still would.

For she is stunned at the poverty of this place in the drizzle and cold, the buildings clenched pale atop the hill. It is true that all England is poorer than France, the cities smaller and darker and fuller of filth, the people scrawny and chilblained, but even for England this is pathetic, the derelict outbuildings, the falling fences, the garden smoldering with burn piles of last year's weeds. Her horse plods along. The merlin cheeps, unhappy, plucking down from under its wings. Marie slowly nears the churchyard. All she had known of the place was that it had been founded by a royal sister made saint centuries before, whose finger-bone in death can now cure a boil; and that in the times of the Danish invasions the place had been sacked and looted, nuns raped, that in the marshlands all around there were still sometimes found skeletons with runes that had been tattooed so deep their tracery showed on the skulls. And when, at the inn where she had rested for the night, Marie had tentatively said the name of the abbey to the girl who had brought up her dinner, the girl had blanched and said something in English swift and incomprehensible, but the tone of her voice made it clear the people of the countryside found the abbey a dark and strange and piteous place, a place to inspire fear. And so Marie had dismissed her escort in town to arrive at this place of her living death alone.

Now under the yew she counts fourteen fresh black graves, shining beneath the drizzle. Later she will learn that buried there are the bodies of a dozen nuns and two child oblates taken only weeks before by a strange disease that made the flesh of the sufferers blue as they drowned in their own lungs; that some of the nuns are still sick, wheezing and giving rattling coughs in the night.

There is cut holly on the raw graves and the red berries are the only things that glow faintly in the mizzle, in the world at large, which has no more color in it.

All will be gray, she thinks, the rest of her life gray. Gray soul, gray sky, gray earth of March, grayish whitish abbey. Poor gray Marie. In the tall doors of the abbey now, two small gray nuns have emerged in their woolen habits.

As she nears, Marie sees that one of the nuns has a great soft ageless face, billowy, eyes gone white with the clouds in them. Marie has been told little of the abbey, but enough to know this woman is the abbess Emme, to whom an internal music has been given as solace for her blindness. She has heard the abbess is terrifically mad, if in a kindly way.

The other nun has the face of a medlarfruit, yellowish, sour, which the people of this strange wet country called openærs, or open arse, for the anus that god thought fit to press into it. This is Subprioress Goda. She had been selected in haste when the former prioress and subprioress died of the choking disease, as she was the last nun remaining who could write Latin in a hand legible. The queen's proposed dowry was enough to keep the nuns alive for some time, Goda had written Eleanor begrudgingly, they may as well take the bastardess Marie. The faults in Goda's letter were grave.

Marie stops her horse by the doorway and painfully slides off. She tries to move her legs, but they have ridden thirty hours over two days and are now boneless in her dread and terror. She slips in the muck of mud and horse shit and falls swift upon her face at the feet of the abbess. Emme looks down with her white eyes, vaguely seeing the form of her new prioress against the ground.

The abbess says with a voice more sung than spoken that the new prioress's humility speaks wonders for her. Thanks be to the Virgin, Star of the Sea, who has sent such a modest and self-effacing royal creature to guide and heal the abbey after its sorrows, the coughing sickness, the hunger. The abbess smiles airily into nothing.

It is Goda who lifts Marie to her feet, muttering what a great clumsy lunk this girl is, a giantess too, and how peculiar-looking, though these clothes are quite fine, or were, now that she has gone and ruined them but maybe Ælfhild can clean them new again, someone must of course sell them, the sleeves alone would bring in a week of flour. So speaking, she gooses the girl into the hall inside and the abbess follows. Goda has the affronted air of someone who lurks in corners to hear herself spoken ill of so that she can hold tight a grievance to suckle.

There is no glass in the windows here, only wooden shutters covered by waxed fabric letting in thin bands of light, and the chill of the outside is somehow deepened in the great long room with the tiny fire of sticks alight in the hearth. The floor is bare of sweet rushes; it shines, cold clean stone. Heads peer at her from all doorways, then withdraw.

Moths, Marie thinks. She is perhaps delirious.

Goda rakes the mud to the floor with her nails and removes Marie's filthy headcloths, pinching her on purpose with the pins. A servant brings a bowl of steaming water. The abbess kneels, and takes Marie's muddied useless slippers and the stockings off her frozen feet, and washes them.

Marie feels needles and the deep burn as her feet return to life. It is only now under the gentle hands of the blind abbess that the shock is fading. This colorless place may be the afterlife, yet under the abbess's hands Marie feels she is becoming human again.

In a low voice, she thanks the abbess for washing her feet, she does not deserve such kindness.

But Goda hisses that Marie is not special, that all visitors have their feet washed here, doesn't she know anything, it is in the Rule.

The abbess orders Goda to leave and bids her to tell the kitcheners to bring the supper up to her rooms. Goda goes, muttering.

The abbess tells Marie not to mind the subprioress, because Goda had had her ambitions, but they were dashed with Marie's advent. Goda is of course the daughter of the most noble English families, some Berkeley, some Swinton, some Meldred, and she cannot see how a mere bastard sister of a Norman upstart throne-thieving clan should supplant her in the hierarchy. But of course, Emme says, Eleanor demanded the place for Marie and what could Emme do faced with the will of the queen? Besides, Goda would fill the role terribly. She's more fit to lead the animals she cares for than she is to lead her sisters, with whom she quarrels and whom she torments with her tongue-lashings. The abbess pats Marie's feet dry with a soft once-white cloth.

She leads Marie barefoot against the cold stone up the dark stairs. The abbess's rooms are tiny, parchments and books haphazard where Goda has piled them, but there are expensive windows filled with transparent horn that casts a waxy light into the room and makes it glow. Already the merlin sits warming itself on its stand near the small birch fire, a pretty blue flame snacking on the white bark. On a table is set some food, hard dark rye bread with a thin sheen of butter, wine blessedly unwatered and brought in better times from Burgundy, a soup with four slices of turnip in each bowl. The abbess tells Marie that they are in a famine, the nuns starve, alas, but suffering purifies the soul and makes these holy meek women even more holy in the eyes of god. And at least tonight Marie will eat.

She considers Marie, looking beyond her head with her cloudy eyes, and asks what Marie knows of a nun's life in an abbey. Marie confesses she knows nothing at all. The food is tasteless, or she has eaten too quickly to taste it. She is still hungry, her stomach rumbles. The abbess hears the noise and smiles, and pushes her bread and butter over to Marie.

Well, the abbess says, surely Marie will learn quickly, the queen told of no deficit of intelligence in the child. She describes the rhythm of the days. Eight hours of prayer: Matins in the deep night, Lauds at dawn, followed by Prime, Terce, Sext, chapter, None, Vespers, collation, Compline, bed. Work and silence and contemplation throughout. All they bend their bodies to is prayer; the daily office is prayer, the hard work of the body is prayer also. The silence of the nuns is prayer, the readings they listen to prayer, their humility prayer. And prayer of course is love. Obedience, duty, subservience; all is manifestation of love, directed at the great creator.

The abbess smiles serenely, then begins to sing in a high and wavery voice.

But no, love is not abasement, love is exaltation, Marie thinks, affronted. She feels her small dinner settling poorly. The nun's life seems as bad as she thought it would be.

The abbess breaks off her song and says that Marie can keep her little merlin and the things that are in her trunk until she takes her vows, when all she has brought will be owned by the abbey. Marie does not know enough to understand this is a great kindness that no one else would be allowed.

A bell rings out in the wet nightfall. Compline. The abbess leaves Marie to rest in her chambers. Marie hears the voices of the nuns in the chapel singing the Nunc dimittis, and falls asleep. When she wakes, Emme is before her again, flushed with the glories of the divine office.

It is time for Marie's bath, she says gently.

Marie says thank you but that she needs no bath, that she bathed in November, and the abbess laughs and says that cleaning the body is also a form of prayer and at the abbey all the nuns bathe every month and the servants bathe every two months, for god is displeased by bodily odors.

Now out of the shadows in the corner of the room there detaches a deeper shadow, an old nun with long white chin whiskers and a face as though hacked from a log. The bath is ready, this nun says in a whiny furious voice. Her English accent is so heavy that her French sounds like she's chewing pebbles. It makes Marie wince.

The abbess starts and says plaintively that she hates it when people leap out of nowhere to surprise her. She tells Marie that this is the magistra, the mistress of novices. Her name is Sister Wevua. It is quite strange but though Marie has been hastily consecrated as a virgin at the cathedral in town and of course she comes to the abbey already prioress, she still is a novice until she has given the oath and taken the veil. Wevua is rather efficacious with the novices. Her methods are harsh, but under them, all novices learn so swiftly that they take their vows in astonishing short time.

The magistra nods. Dislike pours out of her toward both Marie and the abbess, a spiritual wind. She has a strong-weak walk like a heartbeat, because a horse stepped on her foot when she was a growing girl and crushed the bones and nerves there.

I saw the foot when she came to the abbey oh many decades ago and I had to wash it, it is a mangled horror, the abbess says, it is the stuff of nightmares.

Hurts to this day like the flames of hell, Wevua says with satisfaction.

And down they go, the three women, through the dark cloister with the cold wet stones on Marie's bare feet and out to the lavatorium still rich with the voices and the mud of the nuns who had come in from the fields to wash for divine office. In the great wooden basin to the farthest edge of the room, steam is rising ghostly into the chill damp air. When they near, a scent of herbs arises so powerfully that Marie must breathe through her mouth or else in her weariness the odor would make her swoon. The herbs are for the lice and fleas that the court is infested with, Wevua tells her, as if biting off her words with her front teeth. She will hang Marie's clothes in the garderobe where the nuns relieve themselves, the ammonia of the piss kills the beasties in the night.

Now the two nuns between them remove Marie's remaining clothing, the silk dress that had been cut narrow from Marie's mother's billowing own, the underthings. Marie covers herself with her lanky arms, burning with fury. Wevua bends to look closely at the girl's privies, then touches Marie with her cold hands there, saying that this new prioress is so large a person with hands so great and voice so deep and face so unwomanly, it needed to be seen that she is female, but now she is satisfied Marie is what she says she is and she pushes her shoulder to make her step into the bath.

Marie drops her arms and gazes at Wevua full in the face, and the old magistra takes a step back.

The abbess says mildly oh but the magistra did a needless violence to the girl. Then she gestures gently at the bathwater, saying that surely it will feel luxurious after the long chill ride Marie had borne. Marie steps in. The sear over her ankles, her calves, her knees, her thighs, her pudenda, her belly, up her chest, her armpits, her neck. The stench of the herbs goes up her nostrils and drives itself deep into her head.

Sister Wevua and the abbess cover their hands with sackcloth, lather them with wet soap, and rub gray worms of skin from Marie's body, in some places rubbing to blood. And in the hot water, in the warmth and the overwhelm, in her tiredness and anguish, Marie's body betrays her. She begins to weep into the water, though she vowed that she would never, she would bear all this loss with strength, no more court, no more Cecily, no more future, no more color, no more Eleanor to look at from a distance and feel her longing accompanying her like an invisible friend. She weeps through the braiding of her dun-colored hair into a wet whip, through the standing out of the good heat into the cold, the drying of her giant bony body with a length of cloth, the dressing. Linen shift with a great brown stain from breast to hem; it is clear a dead nun once owned this one. Wool smock that smells of lavender and someone else's body, which falls only to just under the knee. Wevua sounds angry when she tells the abbess it is far too short. The scapular too is far too short. And of course the shift under it all, which means those poor legs are bared to the evil weather of the end of winter, the sleet and angry wind.

The abbess sighs. She says that tomorrow, Ruth will cut the worst of the spare habits and sew the remainder to the bottoms of the smock and scapular. Marie will get three pairs of stockings to compensate for the cold weather. She will suffer, but suffering is the lot of humanity, and every moment of suffering brings the earthly body closer to the heavenly throne.

With her own hands, the abbess puts on Marie the white headcloths of the novices, coif and wimple and veil, while Wevua pulls on the three pairs of stockings roughly. She says in her screeling voice that none of the clogs will likely be big enough.

The abbess mutters something about the poor child, but then says well, what could she possibly do? The queen has not yet sent along Marie's dowry and they have so little to spare, she has no money for clogs to be made just now. To which Wevua says that Marie cannot be barefoot, even the servants at the abbey are not barefoot, it is an awful sin to make their new prioress go without. The abbess says that indeed, Marie will wear what she came in with, and Wevua says that she came in with idiot court slippers of kidskin, which are useless, imagine the prioress out in the sloppy spring fields overseeing the sowing, how frozen and damp her feet would be in moments, she would die of the cold infecting her upward from the mud, and then they'd have to reckon with an enormous dead royal bastardess sister in addition to everything else. Now the abbess's voice loses its song, it becomes cutting and she tells the magistra that then Wevua must add a prayer to her nightly devotional to provide a miracle of shoes, but until said miracle comes, Marie will bear her lot which is surely not the worst of the deprivations in the abbey right now. There is a very old hostility here between the women, Marie sees, a war of suffering between the mangled foot and the cloudy eyes. Decades thick, and visible, like the rings in a felled tree.

The abbess turns and through the dark she walks sure, while the other two take tentative steps, touching the wall. Into the night, through the cloister. The abbess goes back again up her stairwell, and calls down to Marie to sleep well, new prioress, for Marie will begin her good work sorting through the parchments and account books tomorrow.

Marie follows Wevua into the chapel, where one beeswax taper is left burning. The abbey in its distress has sold all its ornaments, and only a wood carving remains: skinny shanks and wounds and thorns and blood and rib-bones, that ancient story she knows by heart. Up the black night stairs to the dortoir, where a single lantern burns over the rows of twenty nuns already asleep in their narrow beds, wearing their full habits, for perhaps it is tonight that the Angels of the Resurrection will blow their horns and they must be prepared to fly into the arms of heaven. There is a sense that eyes are watching Marie but what faces she sees are smooth with sleep, feigned or real. There are whispers down the line, a rattling cough. Wind blows through the gaps in the window shutters, there are flakes in the dortoir's air that melt before they touch the ground. Marie lies down on the bed that Wevua gestures toward. She is too tall for these bedframes and has no comfort until she slides down to bend her knees and put her feet on the floor, which meets her heel flesh with its implacable cold.

Oh for her mother's large goodness, the rumbling laugh that made everything better, the verbena of her neck; but her mother has been dead these five years. Or for Cecily to warm her body, to speak rough sense, to share in Marie's hatred of this frigid and awful place so she does not have to bear it alone. What Cecily would think of this place, who, as a child in the dust and stink of the chicken coop where thick light poured sideways from the chinks, reached under the hens for an egg, her filthy kitchen smock as her vestment, and, wearing her sternest face, swinging a bucket of ash for her censer, intoned gibberish in the girls' play of Mass while cracking into Marie's open mouth the egg still warm from inside its mother, the body and the blood mixed as one, and Marie crossed herself and could barely swallow the overrich viscous warm egg down. Then Cecily's breath in Marie's face, she'd been chewing the peels of the carrots she'd been paring, and her hard small tongue licking the spilled yolk on Marie's chin. Second heresy, mouth on mouth. Her frank and knowing body; there was no privacy among the servants, where she learned such arts. The heat, the discovery within this stout dimpled girl with straw in her hair. The pulse of her body on top of Marie's.

Marie clutches her own hands, but they are cold and bony, they are not Cecily's.

Slowly, the dortoir warms with the breath and body heat of the nuns. The wind howls lonely outside. Marie stops shivering. She will never sleep again, she thinks; then she sleeps.

She dreams immediately and vividly. A memory, a dock steaming wet and a sea beyond, brilliant with reflected sun. An aching dry heat and the mouths of fish in nets silently screaming, a crowd, women bearing terra-cotta pots on their heads, smells of rot of blood of bodies of smoke of salt sea. Children swimming below through the dark thickets of legs. Everywhere, the white tunic and red cross of the crusaders. Hubbub of voices in ungraspable languages, distant flutes, groaning of wood, slap of waves. Under her haunches the feel of strong shoulders, a woman's hand steadying her child thighs, oh it is her mother. A circle forms of the mob. At the circle's bare center stands a naked woman shining oiled in the sun, so beautiful. Hair in loose black curls to her waist and puffs at the armpits and groin. She wears a silver chain around her neck, a slave. In her face there is contempt, she does not look at the gathering crowd, she looks above them at the distant heavens. There is shouting, a wheeling music starting up, a whip snapped in the air perilously close to the woman's soft belly. Insolent as a cat the naked woman slowly steps backward into a wooden box that rises to her knees. She bends and is hidden. Then the box's top is hammered shut upon her. Now a sword is held glinting up; with a loud roar, it is thrust into the box, and Marie's breath is hitched, there must be a red puddle growing; don't look, Marie looks, but there is no puddle at least not yet before another sword is brandished, thrust in, and another, another, swifter and swifter. What is frozen within the dreaming Marie thaws, and there is a struggle, a terror, someone must stop this, where is the authority to stop this, the box already bristles with hilts. Hush now, her mother's voice now in her ear, hush, be calm, it is only a trick. Swords are slowly withdrawn. Lid prized up. A long pause of gasping horror. And then at last the woman slowly rises out of the low place where she had lain. So beautiful, still shining, still so full of spite and hate. She is alive and her skin is unwounded, not a cut is on its smooth and perfect length, all of her blood remains inside her skin. The hat is passed around, it is filling with coins. Shudders ripple Marie from the bones outward, and her beloved mother's voice in her ear again, It's all right, my love, that poor woman slithered herself around like a little snake in there.

Marie wakes to Wevua a great dark cloud before her, and a pain in her knees because Wevua is kicking Marie's legs with the toe of her clogs, telling her to get up, lazybones, to get up great frail whingeing thing, that it is now Matins, up up up, blueblood lagabed rawboned unlovely shadow-hearted bastardess of a false prioress, up up up, the magistra spies no love for god within Marie's wicked heart and Wevua will seed it there by force or see the girl perish unshriven.

Marie rises in a panic and sees through the window the moon fat in the black sky and all the landscape swallowed in darkness. Ahead of her in the single lantern light the other nuns are disappearing down the night stairs, faceless in the dark. Marie, still in the vividness of her dream, hears their habits rustling dry and cold and can think only of the wings of carrionbirds descending in slow circles to their feast of death below.

2.

Marie descends the night stairs. She feels as though she has stepped from a blazing day into a dark room. She sees nothing around her but ghost fragments of the brightness of what she has lost.

Wevua shoves Marie down on the bench and sits beside her. Another novice is next to Marie, and with the back of her hand, she touches the back of Marie's to comfort her. Marie steals a look at this girl who has bulging eyes and protuberant front teeth; this she will later discover is Swan-neck, and the novice on her other side is little Ruth, whose eyes are always telling a small joke. Both will become Marie's deep friends.

The shadows at the edges of the chapel change shape threateningly in Marie's fatigue.

Matins, she discovers, is singing prayer; it is shivering in the cold of the night beside strangers. It seems to last forever. The taper flickers, the wind howls across the raw countryside. She feels a pain in her chest that is the pain of a fist clenching all the meat inside her. She nearly cries out from it. The numbness that had held her safe has left her. She smarts everywhere.

And for a moment, the chapel wavers in her eyes and it vanishes, the queen's court hangs before her as it had been, as though she were still solidly within it, and the great hall is warm, the servants are darting fireflies in the dim as they light the candles and as they go the shadows are chased out by the glowing, the mastiffs and alaunts and greyhounds trot in, and up to her nose rises the smell of good food carried on platters to the tables, and now the nobles enter singly and in groups in their bright fine clothing, the ladies' voices are low and happy and the lutes begin to play in the corner, two voices weaving together in sad song of chivalric love, and she hears the pattern in this new thrilling kind of loving, sees it unfurling like cloth in the air: marriage is no excuse for not loving, one who is not jealous does not love, no one can be bound by two loves, love is always growing or diminishing, easy attainment of love is contemptible but impossible attainment makes it precious. On the table is a roasted swan with its neck twisted back, mutton, heaps of soft white bread, a wheel of cheese, figgy pork pies, ale and wine at intervals. And the great surprise, a gift for delight, a cockatrice made of a boar's head greened in a parsley bake and a roasted peacock's body, tailfeathers sewn back on, and rags in its mouth soaked in camphor and aqua vitae set alight so the monster is breathing green fire. The noise, the brightness, the colors, the warmth.

And at the heart of the gathering at the head of the table, the great love of Marie's life sits shining so bright Marie cannot see the human form in all the brightness, she can only see the radiance.

The moment fades. And once again she is among the ghosts and shadows, the wind playing at the eaves of the building, and even the ancient walls of this abbey so poor they seem resigned to the sickness and hunger they clasp within them.

Roused again, the flock goes silently up the night stairs once more, to the beds gone cold. Swan-neck lets Wevua limp before her off to her bed, and holds Marie's hand to keep her back. She whispers in her ear that she is so glad Marie has come, Emme is useless, Goda only fit for animals, someone has to take charge, thanks be to the Virgin for delivering Marie.

Sleep again but too soon it is Lauds, half dreaming in the dark and rising song, then ablutions running out to the lavatorium to wash in the cold water drawn by the servants, to the garderobe to piss and shit, back to the chapel for Prime as day begins to slice through the shutters of the windows. In the refectory, they are given work, the weakest given the hardest things, for pain in this place is proof of godliness. Wevua takes the novices to scrub the chapel's floors with frigid water. Marie has never scrubbed a thing in her life. She wonders, hands aching, how Cecily did not hate her. Then first meal, a bite of black bread and some milk still warm from the cows. Terce; contemplation in the warming-room, the nuns each reading aloud from their books, but Marie is given nothing and she tells poems she's memorized in her head. Sext. Psalms, always psalms, sparked by the quavery voice of the cantrix.

Goda shuffles up, sour. Marie is wanted in the abbess's quarters, although why Goda does not know, she herself is perfectly capable of taking dictation. The subprioress wraths herself outside to collect the eggs.

The warmth of the abbess's little white room is such a relief that Marie sits abruptly on a stool. The abbess smiles vaguely and starts speaking, which Marie only belatedly understands is meant to be the dictation of a letter to Eleanor. She scrambles for parchment and a pen, but it doesn't matter, the abbess's letter is so strange and disconnected, so full of both obsequy and brimstone, that Marie writes nothing, listening for the gist, and then composes a short, coldly polite letter in Latin requesting the immediate delivery of Marie's dowry, for the nuns are starving to death. Only into the salutation does she imprint her love. The abbess smiles in satisfaction when Marie reads the letter back, and says with delighted surprise how precise Marie is at dictation, she repeated the abbess's letter to the very word.

First writing a letter to Eleanor, then the mess of the account books when Marie gathers enough courage to look into them, all together the work makes Marie nauseated. The families of villeins, the peasants attached to the abbey, have lined up at the eastern door to meet the new prioress. And the long day is not yet halfway done.

Marie wants to lie on the floor in this white warm room. To leave this prison of flesh in this miserable boggy stinking place, to rejoin her mother in death, to give up the ghost.

Instead, she works on, and Emme sleeps with a gentle wheeze in her nose and a fly beats its crisp body on the shutters.

But soon she can hear murmuring, even though speaking is forbidden during work hours, perhaps it is the women who are below in the silk-spinning room, she finds a hole in the floor, perhaps for ventilation, and she comes near, crouching, to listen.

Someone is saying now, Oh there was a broom flower tucked behind the helmet's visor and this is how the poor violated maiden's mother knew who had raped her daughter; and with this, Marie knows with a shock of cold that they are speaking of her own mother; of the circumstances of Marie's birth. Oh yes, the voice said, warming up, just a maiden of only thirteen, but tall and lovely and out in the fields innocent one warm day, making a poppy wreath and dreaming, when she heard a rattle of metal, and before she could run she was scooped up to the pommel by the hair, for you see the army was camped not far away, and the girl was so tempting just out there in the field all alone. And when the girl staggered back to the château, and told what she remembered, only the broom flower, her mother was so enraged she took the family sword and rode to camp and made a terrible uproar. A broom flower is the Planta Genêt, you see, Plantagenet. Descendants, by the way, of Mélusine, fairy queen who lived among the humans with her children until she was spied upon in the bath where her tail unfurled; then she flew through the window, abandoning humanity forever. And the issue of the Plantagenet violation after nine months was of course our new prioress Marie. Thus, you see, this is how our new prioress finds herself a bastardess half sister to the crown. By the horrid stain of rape. How strange it is to have royal blood, yet mixed with such ignominy!

Marie feels sick. If she had any self-love left she would flee, but she puts her ear angrily to the hole to hear what else they know of her.

Someone begins to whisper an Ave Maria.

Someone else is saying quickly now indeed, that the prioress comes from Le Maine, very near Normandie and Bretagne. A medium-sized estate, not bad, by a Roman road and a river, quite pretty there, the speaker herself is a distant cousin and she knows firsthand that Marie's is a famous family of viragoes, Marie's widow grandmother with her seven daughters and along comes Marie, making eight too-ferocious girls. And in fact, when the speaker was a maiden, the girls in her own family used to be told that they'd be strangled if they turned out like their unwomanly cousins, all wild, flying across the countryside scandalously galloping astride, with their swordfighting and daggerwork tutors and their knowledge of eight dialects and even some Arabic and Greek, all those dusty manuscripts, those loud opinionated unnatural women talking over each other, arguing, drawing blood, learning the battleaxe, so strange and so uncouth. But not the speaker. No no, she herself and her sisters, they are quite feminine, the voice says smugly.

And Marie yearns again for her river in Le Maine, muscular as a vast serpent. The green fields with little gold birds darting through them. The hugeness of her grandmother and aunts as Marie remembers them, when she was so small and the family was intact, all the constant stories and songs, the armarium full of books.

But someone with a sweet soft voice now cries out, oh she too had heard of this family, they were witches, yes, they turned to wolf-women on a blue moon and stole girl children from the servants and raised them as dog-girls with pointy muzzles and sharp teeth, who ran beside them as they hunted.

False, the previous voice says, shortly. Lies. In fact, the family was known to be pious. In fact, the four older girls and Marie herself as a very small child went on crusade with the Queen's Ladies' Army.

Our prioress is a crusader? the sweet soft voice says with wonder;

and Marie sees again the Ladies' Army pouring down a hillside in the Byzantine Empire, riding astride unwomanly, shouting, swords drawn, their hair loosed and flying behind them, all in the white and red tunics, ululating, fearsome. And the other nuns murmur, awed, for crusaders wore the holiness of their pilgrimage upon their bodies, upon their skin the sanctity of bloodshed. Marie thought of her aunt Euphémie, able to turn somersaults off the back of a horse, her aunt Honorine, of the twin white peregrines, her aunt Ursule with her golden boots and furious beauty, her strong laughing vibrant mother, all merely girls then, seizing what adventure and godly grace they could take through the crusade.

Then Marie's vision cracks open farther and she sees the plains of Thrace, Byzantium glowing on the horizon, the night that she, a tiny girl, rose when the breath of all the sleepers had settled into smoothness, strapped on her dagger that served her hand as a sword, and went shoeless out into the dangerous dark, running with all her speed past the fires, past the hands stretching a moment too late to catch her, coming to the tent with the eagle atop it. For when her mother and aunts had seen it, they had whispered of poisoning wine and slicing throats with daggers and garroting with their bow bands, and Marie had known obscurely that it had to do with her, for they looked at her while speaking, and that some kind of revenge was hers to take. At the tent she found a peg loose in the earth and prized it up with her dagger hilt then went under the lip of the fabric and in. A single lantern burned. The ground was thick with sleeping bodies and the dogs at the door lifted their heads and sniffed at her but held their barks in their throats. She went toward the bed with her dagger drawn. She saw two lumps there, the farther one emitting thick wet snores, and the closer one that upon long looking resolved into flesh, a breast above the fur coverlet, a long throat, an entanglement of shining hair, an eye rimmed in black and open and looking upon her. A woman. Powerful as a punch to the chest, the wonder Marie felt then, this first love. The woman asked in a whisper if Marie was a demon, then in a moment, seeing the dagger and the little face, she understood and said to herself that, no, it was just a hideous toad of a child. Marie neared. The woman sat up in her nakedness and, looking at Marie's face, said that ah, this was the famous bastard that she could see the likeness clear though how curious there was not a trace of the famous Plantagenet beauty. But she said, what a strange stalwart creature Marie was, such a pity born a girl. Then the woman put a silken robe upon her body, closing her flesh up, and reached toward Marie and took the dagger from the child's hand. She said drily she must be gone back to her marital tent anyway, her poor meek ecclesiastical bed. She took Marie's hand and led her past the sleepers and the guardian dogs who cowered away from the woman; she carried a thickness of power in the air around her body. Far enough out in the night not to be heard by any left awake in the tent the woman asked in a low voice, which of those terrible sisters was Marie's mother, the beautiful one in golden boots or the one with the birds or the one with the monkey's face or the one so fat she makes the ground shake when she walks. And Marie said that her mother was not fat but immensely strong, and the woman said that she understood and that the girl's heart was clearly loyal and brave and that she had come to avenge the wretched sin done to her mother. But such a foolish little mind. For she had come not to the tent of the one Marie sought, for said coward had refused the cross and was staying fat and lazy at home. No, no, this tent belonged to a friend who had argued against Marie's paltry interests when she was just a seed. A rapeseed, ha.

And the lady said, besides, didn't Marie know a real lady does not ever make her hands bloody but rather she gently influences others to do her worst work for her?

Then the woman cuffed Marie's head and told her to run along as fast as she could fly, for if the heathens caught her they would sell her and make her scrub floors and feed her the leavings of the dogs. She pushed Marie and the girl took three stumbling steps and when she looked back the woman was vanished into the night. Marie ran to her tent in wonderment and washed her filthy feet in the basin. There was no cloth to dry them. With wet feet she climbed again inside the furs near to the rolling heat of her mother, who felt the ice of the girl and clutched Marie to her in her sleep. Then half waking her mother asked where Marie had been. At last, fully waking, she sniffed and sat up and asked why in the world she smelled like the perfume of the queen.

And this would be Marie's first encounter with Eleanor the mighty, regent of France at that time, and later of England, mother of ten, eagle of eagles, power behind the powers. Until her death, Marie would live with this early vision of the queen barbed in her the way an ancient sheatfish carries embedded deep in its flesh the first hook nipped at in its youth.

It was love she felt in her, a love hard and sharp and fixed.

But Eleanor has been lost to the distant world of the court; she had sent Marie away forever. Of all the losses, mother, home, court, this is the one that just now proves unbearable. Marie is too sad to listen to any more gossip about herself.

She stands and goes to the shutters and opens them to the gray, wind-scoured landscape.

When she grows too cold, she closes them and turns and now senses that Emme is no longer sleeping. The abbess opens her cloudy eyes and says mildly, Forgive them their loose talk. They mean no harm. Marie says nothing.

Then the abbess lifts her arm with a great broad smile across her soft face, and brings it down just as the bells shout out, summoning them to divine office, as though she has brought the sound out of the skies with her plump pale hand.

3.

Later, Marie will remember those days just after arriving at the abbey as thick and black. When she would peer back into that time, it was like looking from a well-lit room through the window into night; nothing to see but her own face hovering like a moon.

So hungry, the nuns' faces are skulls skinned of flesh in the dark dortoir. There are soups in which meat is boiled and removed to save for future soups. Fingernails the cold blue of sky.

And then one Terce a week after arriving, as she pretends to sing in her dismal darkness, all at once she understands what she must do.

Eleanor's best currency is story; love that is given and received through song.

What has come to Marie is a Breton lai in rhyming lines, sudden and beautiful, in its entirety. Her hands begin to shake in her lap. She will write a collection of lais, translated to the fine musical French of the court. She will send her manuscript as a blazing arrow toward her love, and when it strikes, it will set that cruel heart afire. Eleanor will relent. Marie will be allowed back to the court, to the place where none ever starve, and there is always music and dogs and birds and life, where at dusk the gardens are full of lovers and flowers and intrigue, where Marie can practice her languages and hear in the halls the fiery tails of new ideas shooting through conversations. Not just the tripartite god of parent and child and ghost who is talked about here, not all this endless work and prayer and hunger.

Marie runs out of the chapel when the service ends and digs into her trunk and takes her money and bribes a servant to go off to town to fetch a bundle of tapers and parchment and ink and tablets of beeswax for the composition. She takes a feather from an outraged goose and whittles a pen. She moves, she breathes, she eats what little the nuns have to eat. In the night she waits for the noises of the dortoir to smooth into sleep, then rises barefoot and creeps to the night stairs and down.

The world is blue with night. The stars are sharp, accusing. Inside the barn it is warm out of the whipping wind and with the heat cast off by the animals' bodies, and she presses her face to her horse's neck until it is no longer numb. The old warhorse turns and snuffles at Marie's cheek with her damp soft nose. She takes out her things, careful not to awaken the servants sleeping in the loft above, and goes to where the rats click in the deepest dark and sits upon the last few sacks of oats heaped against the stone wall. Then she strikes a spark upon the hay and causes a tiny fire that she uses to light the candle, then steps upon the little fire in the hay until it is out. By this small stub of light with the eyes of rats shining green at her from the deeper dark, she writes.

As she moves through the days she imagines her lines of the night.

The life of the abbey is the dream. The set of poems she is writing is the world.

Into the poems she puts the tent she had known in Outremer, which still haunts her, a great and royal purple thing surmounted with an eagle of pure gold and a woman lying nude on sumptuous furs within. She puts in poor Sister Mamille, who is noseless, for a jealous hound had bitten it off the day she came to her marital house, a new bride; then she was given, still a virgin, to the abbey for the fear that any children of Mamille would be born without a nose. She puts in the words of the poor child oblate Adeliza, hit on the neck by a rotten windfall apple in the orchard thrown by the cruelest novice, Edith, Tels purchace le mal d'altrui dunt tuz li mals revert sur lui! May evil done to others rebound upon the evildoers. Marie modifies an ancient lai so it can be read doubly as itself and as the story of the queen's grandmother Dangereuse, a famous beauty who did what she pleased, who, though already a mother and wife, fell in love and ran off in a grand and unapologetic adultery. Marie puts in a remembered weasel running past with a red flower in its mouth when her mother dragged her back from the failed crusade in Outremer—was it a weasel or a vixen?—she chooses weasel. She puts in Mélusine, the fairy, whose strange blood beats in her own veins. She puts in the queen herself, her great beauty and perfect education, her body in which nature has lavished care to mold a perfect harmony, her gracious allure, her beautiful face, brilliant eyes, lush mouth, perfect nose, hair blond and shining, manner courteous, words sweet, a rosy tint to her cheek. No woman her equal in all the world.

And in the lai she secretly loves the most, she writes the very first vision she ever had. In the weeks before Marie's mother died and all Marie's other aunts were either dead or married off, her remaining aunt, Ursule, took to prayer in the little family chapel. At last she came to Marie's mother, weeping, saying that she would rather die than be married. I would not mind it so much if I could be the hunter, the knife going into the flesh, but I will not be the prey. I will not lie there and let the knife go in and out of me, Ursule said. And Marie's mother swallowed her smile and said gently not to worry, that she had already arranged the dowry with Fontevraud Abbey, where they would take Ursule as a novice.

Two nights before she left, Ursule took Marie on one last hunt. They rose in the chill April night and went on foot to a pool of water in the woods, where the animals came down to drink in the darkness. There Marie and Ursule sat at the foot of the trees, letting their thoughts dissolve to make themselves more like the roots of the trees they sat upon and erase some of what was human in them. For long hours they sat without thinking, when, in the earliest stirrings of the long dawn, the fog lifting in peels from the surface of the warming water, Marie saw at the farthest edge of the pool the shape of a deer. And it was a doe, because a fawn was nuzzling at its belly, but it was unworldly, because it wore a rack of antlers upon its head and its body was made of the purest white. Seeing this creature as if fog gathered and made flesh, Marie held her breath and went entirely still. If her aunt had seen the doe, it would already be dead, blood unspooling in ribbons into the water.

Then the white doe lifted her head and looked at Marie across the pond; looked her entire self into the girl. She spoke something there into the wordlessness at the center of Marie. Time stilled. The forest watched. Then the doe turned and with a single bound disappeared into the shrubbery with the fawn leaping behind. Ursule went off the next day to Fontevraud, and Marie carried that doe with her, this awe and mystery, until at last she put it on the page.

She writes for days, copies the lais to fineness. She writes in a fever and sleeps little and her skin grows translucent and what small fat she once stored under her skin is gone; she is all sticks and knots in her hunger to return to the barn to make her work in the guttering light of her candle stub. With a small portion of her mind, during the day, she works through the account books and begins to understand the creaking and neglected machinery of the abbey, but hardly cares what she learns.

Poor Sister Eulalia, whose acne bursts into horrible pus whenever she bends over, who often has to change her wimple halfway through the day it becomes so greasy, says, watching Marie, that the new prioress is now become only two great eyes, burning bright.

Swan-neck says that Marie's skin burns also, she throws off enough heat to warm both girls on their shared bench in chapel.

Ruth says she thinks that Marie will die soon, for Ruth was born into a family of fortunetellers and she can see the handprint of death shining on Marie's face.

Marie writes a prologue to her collection. Those to whom god has given understanding and eloquence must not be silent or hide their gift, but must return the gift so that it flowers under the admiration of others. In the prologue she does not direct the manuscript toward its true target, but rather off a little to the side, to the far lesser spouse, if the far greater power. Perhaps if the lais fail to move the queen, the frenzy of her jealousy at this dedication will call Marie back to the court.

And when her little pile of parchment is finished and as beautiful as she can make it, she looks up to find that it is the day before the Feast of the Annunciation, Lady Day, that weeks have come and gone since her arrival at the abbey. She takes some more of her coin from the trunk and skips Sext without permission to ride into town, the world greening all around her. She will buy enough soft white flour for breads and honey for cakes, a heifer to slaughter for the feast, for otherwise the next day would be a sorry affair of nuts and dried berries and a stillborn calf that Goda had carried on her shoulders from the distraught bellowing heifer to the kitchen. Roasted and with an apple in its mouth, it won't strike anyone as so sad, the subprioress had snapped to the kitchener, whose face had shown horror. Marie rides with the manuscript held tight to her chest in a celebratory mood. In town, she wraps her book with its letter in the finest leather coverings she can buy, and pays a fortune to have it galloped the leagues back to the Westminster court that very day, to be placed within the royal hands that will, she is sure, deliver her, if not that day then very soon. She laughs because the pennies she pays to send the gift bear the likeness of its stated recipient, though not the true one.

And then she waits, nearly panting. She imagines Eleanor bending her head over the manuscript, reading, at last fully seeing Marie, fully knowing her. Marie feels she will die of her love. Or, perhaps, of the glory sure to come to her. For Eleanor will be like a cut glass through which Marie's light flows; the queen will have the manuscript copied and given to those she loves, and each new person who reads Marie's poems will be filled with the girl's own brilliance.

Through the queen's intercession, through her returned love, Marie thinks drunkenly, she will live on forever.

She watches the sun come up warm on the day of the new year, Lady Day, this day of first creation, the day when the angel descended and whispered the word in Mary's ear and filled her with divinity.

She is too agitated to do any work with the abbess and so she takes the *Amores* down from the armarium and reads as the abbess dictates into the nothing a stern letter to a creditor. But the book is not speaking to her today, Perfer et obdura, dolor hic tibi proderit olim, it is speaking to some other woman with no hope in her heart.

And so she stands in the middle of the abbess's dictation and takes up her little merlin upon her shoulder, and ignoring the abbess's voice raised in admonition, she goes out to the stables and saddles her horse and trots down the hill to the winter-rye fields and once there she sets her falcon free; and she gallops through the fields and forest the length of the road to town, watching for her deliverance. But when no messengers come up the road and she can see the town through the trees, she pulls her horse up and walks it back, listening behind herself for the sound of hoofbeats. But there is nothing all the way back, also. The nuns working in the garden rise up like a family of pine martens to watch her drawing near, because it is outrageous to head off for a pleasure ride when there is always work to be done. Wevua will surely fall on Marie with savage vengeance.

The fine bright sky clouds over and a heavy rain begins to fall. She whistles and whistles for her merlin but the bird does not return. When the rain is so harsh she can no longer whistle, she leads the mare inside the stable and curries her and picks the mud from her hooves with a sharpened stick. The bell rings None; in the chapel, her habit runs with water that pools under the bench and she shudders with the chill. After, Wevua slashes her hands with a switch for running off, for being so careless as to get herself soaked, until they are swollen and bleeding and unusable. But Marie, thinking how soon she will be rid of this place, hardly feels the pain.

And shivering in her wet habit and with smarting hands she goes into the refectory, from which good delicious smells of the feast of Mary are emanating, and though they are supposed to be eating in silence, the sisters whisper with joy until the abbess stands with a rare anger in her soft face and says, Enough. Silence. And then they eat the soft breads and meats and cakes and roasted turnips quietly, eating and eating until they are full and then beyond full, and poor child oblate Adeliza has to run out to vomit, then runs in again frantic that she will not have time to fill her stomach again. But there is enough food and just barely enough time. The alms to the beggars at the wicket that day are enormous.

The rain stops, but the ground is soaked and cold, the mud thick on the road.

Vespers.

Compline. Her ear aches from listening. But still no messenger.

After Compline a villeiness who works in the kitchen is waiting in the cloister outside the chapel. When Marie comes out, she thrusts into her hand a filthy cloth through which Marie can feel the light body of her bird.

At first she feels a terrible pain to have lost her merlin, that good small fierce friend of hers. Then a strange happiness bolts through her, because in her poems there is a story in which lovers exchange a message through a dead nightingale wrapped in an embroidered cloth, and perhaps this is the message she has been longing for.

Yes, she thinks, she would sacrifice even her bird for it.

She opens the cloth and sees what she had expected, the torn bloodied body of her bird, which a greater falcon has killed; the merlin had been made slow and dull with the long winter inside. But though she searches, she finds no message in the villeiness's dirty cloth.

The servant says something in a pious voice. Goda steps forward and translates into French. The villeiness had said she was walking back to her home and saw from the skies a great haggard, a wild ladyhawk, shooting down as though an arrow from the silver early moon and catching the merlin in its talons as it flew, it squeezed so tightly the little bird's blood scattered like wheat upon the ground and the servant followed the blood drops and found the prioress domina's falcon in the path and knew that the great prioress domina would want to know what had happened to it, for, though it is unnatural to keep the fierce devil birds of the forests as pets, the gentlefolk have strange desires and there is no profit in judging them, for all godly folk of the church know that the flow of judgment like the flow of water must go not up but down, alas. The villeiness smiles the gaps in her teeth at Marie.

Marie says in a very low voice to please, subprioress, tell the woman thank you and she will find her tomorrow to give her a penny.

But with this the woman seems to object, and Goda speaks to her harshly and the woman snatches the cloth from Marie and drops the dead bird back in her hands, and disappears muttering into the darkness.

Goda says with a jutted jaw that the woman had wanted two pennies and then Goda had said she was greedy and would get none at all.

The other nuns have already moved off to the dortoir. Only the blind abbess stands with Marie. She reaches up and touches the prioress's face, and feels the wetness there.

The abbess says that ah, so Marie has discovered what happens when one neglects one's duty and is disobedient.

Marie says yes, though it is with hatred that her voice is muted.

The abbess says she was going to send the prioress to the misericord for her punishment. Five lashes and between Prime and Terce kneeling on unhulled barley. But she thinks now that Marie has suffered enough. Plus they can't spare the barley. Poor little bird. The abbess had grown to be fond of her little noises in the night.

Marie says yes.

Wevua slides out of the doorway. She says that Marie's sisters have already begun to sleep and yet her own bed is empty and if she does not want to be lashed she will go in.

Marie says yes. Dumbly she follows Wevua inside. She lies down. She holds her cold aching hands in her sleeves to warm them. She listens all night, twice tricking herself that the yew's branches clacking in the wind are the hooves of a galloping horse. But they are not. And no one comes. And no one will come. And there would be no one at all fetching her home.

In redoubled sorrow, with the nuns around her starving despite the single feast, with the grayness and misery of this life, she thinks then very seriously of letting herself die.

She sits at Lauds unhearing.

Acedia, she knows, is a sin. Despair.

Hatred is worse; and Marie's hatred would rip her limb from limb, if she lets her attention stray from it.

She thinks of running away from the abbey; of running into the woods alone and catching beasts to eat with her hands and drinking from the freshets, becoming a wildwoman or a lady brigand or a hermit in a hollowed trunk of a tree. But even on this island there are few wild places left, no place that did not at last end up too close to a village with other humans in it. No, she is caught in a great net made by her sex and the excessive height of her body, she would be easily known, she is imprisoned by her lack of English, she has been made stuck by those years of loneliness she had already lived in secret after her mother died, when she impersonated her mother in all business, because the wolves of her mother's family would never let a bastardess girl child inherit such wealth. Marie is caged into her fate by the isolation of those two years, only mitigated by busy Cecily; Marie would never want to live through that desert of her soul again. She is not built to thrive without others.

Into Marie's mind flies the pet nightingale the queen had raised by her own hand from a tiny egg found in the gardens. In that court so thick with bodies that even some of the nobility sleep shoulder to shoulder in the great hall, the bird was given its own chamber. All day the bird would fly from window to perch and open its mouth and sing, and the queen and her ladies delighted in the song. But Marie had known well the nightingale—le rossignol, le laüstic—and she had often heard the wilder type of this breed of bird through her window during the long hot summer nights of her happy childhood as the river slid past the château with its hush. She found the captive bird's song unbearable. It sang no inspired flights or strange tunes lifted from the hearts of other birds, it sang the same few songs the same few ways. Its imagination had been limited by the closeness of the walls of the room, the smallest tooth of sky seen through the window, the stifling inside air, the worms fed it one by one out of the hand of the queen.

When she had been feeling especially suffocated by the expectations of the court, Marie had often wanted to take the bird in her hands and snap its neck.

And the ladies whose eyes grew misty in listening to the sad creature—these ladies in their endless circulation between court and chamber and chapel, with never a thought of galloping through fields, nor fighting nor hunting nor disputing nor reading the great dead philosophers nor swimming naked in a river whose current could grab their feet and throw them a mile, nothing but sewing and sighing over stories of courtly love, adultery, and secret suffering—these bony lady necks Marie could also imagine snapping in her huge hands.

As the light from the window dawns against the white plaster of the western wall of the chapel, she feels a fire at the ends of her fingers. And this fire brings her back into the blunt truth of her body. Her body is pressed against the wooden bench. Her hips are against the hipbones of Wevua and Swan-neck. Her nose smells their skin, her tongue tastes her own sleep on her teeth. Beyond the voice of the cantrix, she can hear a common wood thrush singing in the hawthorn outside, a bush that just yesterday had dressed itself in a shivering lace of white flowers.

It seems to her now that she can see this second bird's song visibly in the air, how it moves upward out of the little beak so wild, but because it is sung into the wider day, the song soon dissipates on the wind.

She brings her attention in close, because the nuns all around her are singing. The abbess's milky eyes are shut in fervor, her voice rises silvery and sure above the rest.

And this song too Marie can see in waves made visible.

The song rises from the mouths of the nuns in puffs of white breath, it expands as it flies, it touches the tall white ceiling and collects there until it grows so heavy that it begins to pour down the walls and the pillars and the windows in a cascade; it trickles back across the stone floor to where the nuns' clogs press, and up through their wooden heels and it reaches their tender living skin and passes into the blood and purifies itself as it rolls through their bodies, up through the stinking entrails and the breath exhaled from the lungs. And the song that rises into them and leaves their mouths is prayer intensified, redoubled in its strength every time it pours through them anew.

It is because this prayer is enclosed within the chapel, she sees, not despite the enclosure, that it becomes potent enough to be heard.

Perhaps the song of a bird in a chamber is more precious than the wild bird's because the chamber itself makes it so.

Perhaps the free air that gives the wild bird its better song in fact limits the reach of its prayer.

So small, this understanding. So remarkably tiny. Still, it might be enough to live for.

Fine then, she thinks with bitterness. She will stay in this wretched place and make the best of the life given her. She will do all that she can do to exalt herself on this worldly plane. She will make those who cast her out sorry for what they've done. One day they will see the majesty she holds within herself and feel awe.

Her love for Eleanor she buries deep within her, even though it is still alive, and it will flare up in her life and have to be banked again and again; it will morph to hatred then flare into love, then be snuffed into grief that leaves her empty.

Marie looks around and sees the knobs of the women's spines delicately pressing through the thick wool of their habits.

She looks down at the unfleshed bones of her own hands, and wrenches herself out of the last of her stupor of despair.

In the thin cold light of the cloister, she turns as the nuns come out and does not let them go on to their work. She is prioress after all, she is superior. Wevua tries to order her to silence, but Marie fixes on her a look so sharp, even Wevua goes silent.

In recessing, she had made a plan, she tells them, separates them into groups. She will take this place in hand, she says to them grimly.

First, she brings the silk-spinning nuns to the pond and shows them how to fish for trout with hempen line and worms dug out of the manure piles, which is so easy she did it as a child of four, and she tells them she is ashamed of them for squealing with disgust. She makes the field nuns collect the tender new nettle leaves and search out mushrooms, but certainly not the ones that bruise when pressed, she says, unless they want to have waking nightmares full of devils and strange flaring stars in colors bright. That evening they will have fish and soup, at least.

Next she flies, her fellow novices Ruth and Swan-neck in her wake, to the cellatrix, and demands entry to the cellar, where she discovers a side of bacon and keg of good ale set aside for the secret hunger of the cellatrix and her minions.

Bacon? Marie says. But I have read the Rule, there is a prohibition against eating four-legged animals.

Goda snorts derisively in the door and says, Impossible to feed so many on bread alone. Only the bodies of my animals have kept us alive during the starving times.

Marie thinks, truly, she does not believe she could live here in this bitter sodden place without at least the consolation of bacon. Fine, then; she will allow it.

But now the cellatrix is saying with her mighty arms crossed, in an angrily defensive voice, that it is not unheard of to serve meat at an abbey, other abbeys serve four-legged animals every day but Friday, she was only doing what the other cellatrices do.

Ah. Do other cellatrices keep food to themselves despite their sisters starving? Marie asks, and Ruth would later recount that Marie's face was terrible, granite, inhuman in this moment; that the cellatrix, a stout and loud woman prone to slapping the servants and lesser nuns, cowered in fear. Marie does not shout, though she demotes the cellatrix to work in the fields, though the field nuns are mostly drawn from the English, and certainly not the French of bluest blood.

She promotes to the cellatrix position noseless Sister Mamille, who has not felt hunger since her nose was bitten off and who has a mind that slides only along lines of justice and fairness. She would prove a most excellent and thoughtful cellatrix even to the last days of Marie's own abbacy.

Only a short while afterward, Marie bestirs herself to dig from her trunk the coin by which she sends Goda, who is perhaps horrible but honest, into town to buy enough flour and pigs and geese to feed the abbey until the gardens can be used; and while she is there, Goda must buy Marie some giant clogs for she is tired of feeling the bite of cold stone through her soles. She hands the subprioress a stick on which she has drawn the span of her feet.

Goda takes the stick and the coins, then looks at them, shaking with anger. She spits when she speaks. If Marie had this money all along, why did she not spend it earlier, why did she not spare the nuns their weeks of suffering.

Marie says to herself oh for god's sake because she thought she was going to have to fund many more years of her life at court and not among these reject simpleminded nothings of nuns at this pigsty of an abbey; but she calms her face until there is no insult there and says that her mind had been full of other things, which is also not untrue.

She goes up to the abbess's chambers, and sits in the light through the horn shutters, which makes her feel as though she's the wick of a lit candle. What she must do next comes into her sight whole and clear and very large.

Marie spends the afternoon with the account books, tracing how Emme, in trying to curry favor among the local gentry, had allowed so many of the abbey's lands to be defaulted on. The abbess hums in the corner, smiling. When Marie asks with fury in her voice why the abbess let the renters escape without paying for so long, Emme says only that, herself being blind and at the time subject to unscrupulous inferiors all around, she had considered and had believed that if she sued the renters for their sums, the gifts made to the abbey would dry up, for all the gentry were related, as Marie herself knows, and a strike against one would be seen as a strike against all.

Better to lose rents than friends, the abbess says, as if this were a piece of actual wisdom.

Marie asks if the venerable abbess was truly saying that she had chosen the gifts of a few pounds of pepper and a few wagons of wood over the means by which the nuns in the abbess's care would eat and thrive.

But the abbess, having said what she wished, considers to herself that she can explain herself best in song, and begins to sing in her high and silvery voice.

Marie stuffs what she can of her outer pair of stockings in her ears and bends her head to work.

That afternoon, from among all of the renters who had chosen to default upon their rent to the abbey, claiming the abbey's land as their own, Marie selects the most egregious, the family who lives as though they are gentry upon the land that is not theirs, that is the starving nuns'.

In the night, a voice in her whispers that she cannot do this, she is but an uncouth girl belonging nowhere, beloved by no one, merely seventeen, not even a real nun yet, and her habit is shamefully patched in different-colored wool, and her face holds no beauty, and her arms are merely women's arms. How dare she.

Well, she says in return, if she truly cannot, the worst that would happen is she would die, and that would not be so very sad, now, would it be. But the child oblate Adeliza's face stays before her, pinched and blue and piteous, and the rage begins to boil in Marie. She must at least try.

And so she rises and her army of nuns follows her, for by now they have all heard that she is a crusader who knows the holy righteousness of the sword. They arrive at the farm in the very early morning. Marie wears her most royal mien and looks terrible upon her warhorse. She knocks on the door. But the door is opened by a yawning underservant who sees the strange and far too tall nun standing there, and slams it upon her.

Marie, very calm, jumps upon her horse, wheels about, and bids sister Ruth knock again. When the family's slattern opens the door to shout at her for rousing the household, Marie thunders past the girl and rides her horse into the hall where the family and servants are sprawled about still sleeping; and with the abbess's staff that she took with her, she lays all about her until, in terror and confusion, bruised and bleeding, the household flees out of the kitchens and into the forest. Then from the nearer trees where she has had all the servants and laborers of the abbey wait with pans and shovels in case a hand-to-hand war would be needed, Marie summons a destitute widow who has long been faithful to the abbey and who has six mostly grown children, each hardy enough to fight. She installs them as the rightful inhabitants of the estate. At last, she piles into the nuns' and servants' hands what she takes from the disgraced family's things, room by room, until every hand is heavily laden: all the silver the family had stored, all of their plate and paintings, even the half-moldy manuscripts and a herbarium found in the study, for the abbey had sold off nearly all its precious things to feed hungry mouths and there were few books for the nuns to meditate upon. She also takes all the milch cows save one she allows the widow, as well as all the goats and chickens.

In high dudgeon, Prioress Marie herself rides that day out to the rest of the delinquent renters with her gold-embroidered sleeves poking from under her habit, with her Plantagenet face, seconded by Goda on the donkey because the subprioress often has to translate to French and back again. By then, each of the delinquent renters has heard of Marie's routing of the prideful family. Each understands that, with the advent of the young prioress, a grim new day has befallen them.

And on the day they are summoned to appear to repay what was owed, the disgraced renters come and Marie shows no mercy to those who weep poverty or too many children; and at last they too relent and reach into their pockets and pay the abbey's portion, some grumbling but most half proud to have a woman so tough and bold and warlike and royal to answer to now. For it is a deep and human truth that most souls upon the earth are not at ease unless they find themselves safe in the hands of a force far greater than themselves.

TWO

This first spring that she has come to the abbey, Marie plants the apricot pits she had stolen from the queen's garden, to get them away from herself, for they are a souvenir of all she has lost. They will struggle to grow, sprouting weak thin leaves. She will feel as though her own life is bound up in the trees. She doesn't yet know if she wants them to shrivel or thrive.

The pressure of the hierarchy upon the nuns is daily, crushing. Marie learns to recognize certain steps of her diocesan superiors in the hall, for they wear boots, not the clogs of the abbey's women, and when she hears them she leaps up and goes silently out the back ways and leaves vague Emme, who after all is still abbess, to deal with the demands, the rules, the shaking down for money, the endless requests of gifts of the nuns' time, effort, prayers, all of which Emme affably agrees to, then conveniently forgets to tell Marie.

Well, Marie decides, she must train her superiors in the community like dogs or falcons, with rewards, and slowly, so they don't know they're being trained.

She is reprimanded for making herself scarce. She apologizes in writing, for she is less uncouth in writing, more like the self she yearns to become. She includes a list of the things she'd had to attend to that day: the pruning of the apple trees, the bad taste of wild onion in the milk, an aged nun who cannot stop her nose from bleeding, a little villein girl bit by a dog, both now frothing at the mouth, an estate in arrears, and a servant caught eating the laundry chalk. I so wish my time could be spent in little chats over good wine and cakes instead, she writes in the words of humility, carefully revealing a flash of anger.

Still, her superiors with their stinking breath, their cheeks pimpled from shaving with dull ecclesiastical razors, their self-important smiles, their potbellies, keep trying to find her. She keeps stealing away, throwing Emme in their path.

Soon they learn to remove their persons back to the city, to write letters to which Marie responds with intricate courtesy and concessions, but slowly expanding silences. She flips their demands into favors she's doing them.

Her mastery will be gradual but, by the time she becomes abbess many years later, complete.

After Easter is the hungriest time, between the last of the winter stores and before the bounty of the garden. A family of peasants, tired of starving, steals winter rye from the abbey's fields a half day's ride away and bakes the rye into bread. But there is a disease in the grain, or perhaps it is cursed by the devil, and after eating it, some dance uncontrollably and sing naked in the streets, others scream with terrifying visions, others go stiff and barely breathe.

Nothing can drive out the disease: not praying, not bathing them in holy water, not tying them to their beds, not leaping out from the night to frighten them, not holding them by the ankle in the cold river, not beating them around the head with a yew branch, not burying them crown to toe in warm manure, not hanging them upside down from a high tree and spinning them until they vomit, not drilling a tiny hole through their skulls to let the bad humors out of the brains. The rumor spreads that the abbey's lands are stalked by the devil, that those who eat of the abbey's land are taking the devil into their bodies.

Ah, Abbess Emme says, hearing past the music to the predicament, and mutters that it's a short leap from the abbey's grain going unsellable to the sisters themselves being agents of the devil. Nuns already are suspect, unnatural, sisters to witches.

She bids the horses be readied. She and Marie will ride out to exorcise the fields.

A fine morning; haze where the tops of the grasses touch the air. Marie watches the way the windswept landscape empties into a great dark forest pressing tight to the abbey's closest fields. Then above the treetops there looms a giant man-made arch, as soon glimpsed as lost. When Marie makes a low noise in wonder, the abbess says, Yes, Romans. Something to carry water, I think. She hums her song again and Marie marvels at the kind of people so magnificent they can create something to last a thousand years beyond their lives. Humanity must be disintegrating to dust, the people of today paltry in comparison with what they had been a millennium before. The Romans, the Greeks, such giants compared with the Normans, or far worse, the paltry brittle-boned English. In a thousand more years humans will be as thoughtless as the cud-chewing kine of the fields. She longs to be among the greats of the generations before. Marie might have discovered others like herself in that era. She would not have felt so alone.

They arrive at the blighted fields near dusk. Marie and the abbess dismount and sing a shortened Vespers as the villagers draw close. They go into the house where the family lies in panting rigidity. One girl's eyelids are peeled back, her eyeballs jutting from her skinny face as though she's staring at a demon dancing on the sooty ceiling. The abbess blesses each afflicted person, then has Marie lead her into the fields. Emme orders torches held unlit circling the diseased rye, and shovels and rakes carried by each body capable of using them.

Then a marvelous transformation overcomes the abbess; she sharpens. She grows beyond the boundaries of her thin body. She stands in the very last shock of daylight through the trees so that her pale face glows visible to those even a furlong away. She raises her arms. Her voice grows deep and loud and she intones a prayer in Latin that Marie has never before heard or read. When the abbess shouts Amen and nods, Marie touches her torch to those on either side of her, and each person runs to light the next torch, and on the fire goes in the deepening darkness until the field is encircled in points of light. At last the abbess gives a cry and brings her arms down, and all lower the torches to the fields. The greasy rye goes up quickly; the rabbits and nesting birds unloose. A screeching vole darts past Marie, and she runs it down and kills it with her clog because its little body is licked with flames. At last the fire, which the shovels keep from blowing into unblighted fields, burns itself to embers and the abbess and prioress kneel and pray through the night. Everyone else steals off in the darkness to sleep.

The two nuns stay in the smoldering fields praying until the smoke clears with dawn. Marie is chilled to shuddering, her body aches everywhere, she hates such unnecessary suffering with a powerful hatred. To take her mind off the pain in the night, she prayed for each of her sister nuns one by one, each nun's flaws blazing bright. Slowly, she decides that instead of the abbess's practice of assigning work according to what the nuns do least well, as a lesson in humility, Marie will assign work due to strength. No more sickly nuns coughing in the fields or weakly hanging up the wet washed sheets, no more Goda ministering to disputations, no more milking done by weeping terrified Sister Lucy, whose sister was killed by a heifer kick to the head. So many hours have been forever lost through feebleness and reluctance. There is nothing wrong, she thinks, in taking pride in the work of one's body. She has never been convinced by any argument for abasement. Surely god, who has done all good work, wants work to be done well.

At last, a rim of sun appears, and Marie helps the abbess off her knees and half carries the older woman to the cottage where the horses had been kept.

The abbess gives final instructions: only wheat will be planted in that field for three years, a great wooden cross shall be erected on its north side to keep the devil off. The woman of the household takes the abbess's cold hands in her own and chafes them until Emme has stopped her shivering.

They have given the food they brought from the abbey to the starving people of the village, and ride off hungry. When they are long out of earshot, Marie asks the abbess where she learned to exorcise fields. No book she knows holds such a ceremony in it.

The abbess is exhausted and pale. She smiles and says, Oh of course I made it up. Ritual creates its own catharsis, Marie. Mystical acts create mystical beliefs. And then, lulled by the rocking of her fat little horse, the abbess falls asleep.

In this, Marie catches a gleam of the true purpose of the night. Women in this world are vulnerable; only reputation can keep them from being crushed. This abbess who found herself unmoved by her own nuns' starvation was alarmed to action by the threat of dark gossip.

And Marie sees the outline of Eleanor now, the way that she has built walls around walls around herself, walls of wealth and blood and marriages, friends and spies and advisers, and the outermost is her reputation, which she spends a great deal of money to maintain. A woman's power exists only as far as she is allowed; wise Eleanor understands that she must find her freedom only within such unbreachable form. Marie has a swift vision of herself as a tiny figure, climbing the walls; oh someday she will find her way over the queen's rampart, someday she will be inside, out of the wind.

Eleanor will be a model, then, Marie thinks, for her own purpose on the earth, at this abbey she hates so much. She will build around herself walls of wealth and friends and good clear reputation, she will make her frail sisters safe within. Marie will mold herself in the queen's form, she thinks. The abbess snores, the horse farts, the day draws on, and Marie's mind leaps and runs, making her plans.

Marie takes the veil on the Feast of the Ascension, after a night of fretful sleep during which she dreams of the great river of her youth freezing suddenly under a hot summer sun and shining its dazzling light back into her eyes, blinding her. She rises to the morning that is to end her brief novitiate and feels flighty, hot, unsettled. She is far too nervous to hear the Mass, to see and sense the joy in the faces of the nuns as they smile heat in her direction, it is too much, she drops her eyes, she will see nothing but what is in her hands, her own folded habit in one, the unlit taper in the other, she follows Ruth and Swan-neck as they remove themselves with great solemnity to put the habits on, they return to the altar with the candle now lit, oh she is desperate, she prays it will not blow out, at last the blessing with *Accipe virgo Christi velamen virginitatis* and the sprinkle of holy water, and the strange weight of the black veil placed upon her head. Color of death, she thinks, of night, of despair. Still, she opens her hand to the gift of a ring.

There is a three days' silence for the brides, and then there is a wonderful feast. Marie and her two newest consorors sit blushing at the center of the celebration.

She has passed from the temporal to the everlasting; she has committed herself to this scraggly awful place, to these women she hardly knows. There is in fact a change in her, something subtle, but every time she tries to touch it, to turn it around and consider it, she is left holding nothing.

But at night, in the dortoir, doubt steals into her, the bitterest blackest feeling that she has made a wretched mistake by submitting to her own living death. She lets her tears drip from the corners of her eyes to her temples, to be absorbed by the cloth that still smells of the sheep that grew it and the hands that spun and wove it.

Now, it seems Marie is always struggling, that she cannot catch up. The longer she is at the abbey, the faster time spins.

No space for breathing; Marie's first years' struggle is simply to keep her nuns alive. All day she rides out to the nobles, the renters, the fields. Rats have gotten into the groats, the heifers grow goiters and their flesh shrinks against their withers, half the apple harvest is lost with a late freeze that snaps the blossoms off the trees, there is a bitter aftertaste to the cheese, someone is seeking her, always seeking her, there is no aloneness except upon the back of the horse. She sleeps little. When she wakes, her mind is already galloping. She stops returning to her bed after Matins; these hours, she writes her letters to cultivate her garden of friends in the greater world. She gives favors, for every family has an extra daughter or niece, a girl who revolts at marriage, every household would be glad for abbey honey or soap or ale and prayers for their beloved dead.

Sister Ælfhild dies of scrofula, her poor neck swelling until it chokes her.

Marie has seen other bodies. There was her mother's, and during the crusade, there was her aunt Euphémie's, who had been too thirsty to have patience, and she dipped and drank infected water at a simmer, not a boil, and for three days shat herself out until on the fourth day she lay on her cot with skirts hiked above her waist and a fly crawling across her eye, for she was dead. And then after the women had given up the crusade—there would be no Jerusalem in their lives—and they were waiting for the boat back to France, her aunt Honorine, of the peregrines far above her station, absently reached down to scratch a bite on her leg and nobody knew the extent of the mistake until they went to a bathhouse and undressed and the attendant, screaming in her language, drove them out. Honorine's leg had gone yellow and black and red with pus and rot and for three days in the hot disgusting inn, this aunt who had been so silent in life raged and blasphemed and they had to put a horse bit in her mouth to silence her. At the moment the breath kicked in her chest, her birds flapped their great wings and screamed a scream like two women keening. Then Honorine too was dead.

Still, Marie is shaken seeing Ælfhild, who has huge black lumps upon her neck, and she has to steel her stomach and hold her breath to wash the woman's body.

As though Ælfhild were a harbinger, it is that very afternoon that Marie is sent a short letter from the court with the announcement, in an anonymous hand, saying that Empress Matilda is gravely ill.

You know Matilda? Emme says, incredulous. She has always been my favorite queen, you know. A warrioress. The stories! She once fled all night on a frozen river to avoid being captured. Oh I loved those stories, I loved the rebellious queen. She hums with happiness.

Know her, no, Marie says. I don't know her. She is the wife of my. The one who. In a sense she is my stepmother, but. Well, never mind. I came to her once after I was thrown off my mother's lands.

And she tells the abbess that when her maternal family had come to roust her from her mother's estate, which she couldn't be allowed to keep, being bastard, she had fled with all the family treasure she could take in her trunk, with her bird, her horse, her Cecily, her aching orphan heart. Through the countryside they went at night, and it was glorious.

Too soon, they came to Rouen. Hunched, suspicious, leering city. The entrails of some large animal glistened purple in the street, guarded by an enormous cur showing its teeth. The palace of the Empress Matilda in the royal park of Quevilly. Frightfully small, overly neat.

Inside, the wall hangings were moth-chewed, the furniture thick and dark.

The empress rustled in at last after long waiting: a dried-up husk of a woman with tiny features squeezed into the center of her face. In the days when Eleanor had hopped from the bed of France to the bed of England, it was this empress—Eleanor's new mother-in-law, Marie's almost nothing of a stepmother—who instructed the queen in the subtler statecraft needed. Marie felt astonishment that such a tiny trembling woman could have led armies, courted allies, been crowned in both Rome and London, withstood sieges, crossed frozen rivers on foot to keep herself from conceding to defeat. A hard wind could have somersaulted her like a leaf. A sneeze could have.

Empress was what Marie would call her, the old lady said without asking Marie to sit. Not stepmother, never stepmother. She was in no way a relation of Marie's and yet here the girl was, bastardess, made of rape. Well, the empress did not hold bastardy against a person, some of the best people were bastards, most of her own siblings, in fact. The best of her siblings, in fact. She did, however, begrudge the money spent, which she did not want to spend and did not ask to spend and had to spend for she was the only one with any money at all at the time of the, well. The violation. At first when Marie's mother wrote asking for aid for when she was dead and gone, the empress thought she would keep Marie with her, but now that Marie was here, she was quite glad she would not. Such a great rustic with leaves in her hair and a stink that frankly affronted. Come closer so she could look, the empress said. No she must stand in the light, turn toward the empress. Oh bless her, sweet mother of god, Marie would not do at all would she, not at all, so tall, it was frankly obscene. Three heads taller than any woman should be, crown brushing the beams, bony as a heron. Flap those wings and take to the skies. No, it was right Marie was going over to Angleterre, which, to be absolutely clear, if not for the empress would be a country entirely lost to the wild pigs and the Celts and the devil, the empress was the one to have saved that awful place. No, no, in her old age she could never have kept Marie or taught her to be a lady, exposed as she had always been to those famous unwomanly aunts. Those horrors. How fortunate that the empress's daughter-in-law, Eleanor, oh she would civilize Marie and quick-quick, she could not abide a rube, she would slap lily-root powder on that face and line those eyes and put that awful body in decent dresses, Marie did swim in these awful old dresses, she looked simply ridiculous. What a waste of fine blood, what a waste of the blood shared by the empress's own children. No Marie had nothing of her siblings save for the jaw perhaps and the height and the nose and the forehead and the hair and perhaps those eyes. Never, Marie would never make an advantageous marriage, it was hopeless. To imagine Marie in jewels! A scarecrow dressed up, impossible, ha ha ha ha ha. Oh, she said, she must order wine to recover and a great deal of it, this child looked as though she could eat three cows snout to tail and still have room for a goose. The empress shouted at the door to bring food and more of it than one thought four hearty souls could eat.

Irritatedly, she asked why Marie was standing. Marie sat. A long silence of waiting and the log crackled in the fireplace.

At last the empress said into the silence that perhaps she had been hasty and she had given it more thought and who knew, why should an old empress say what was possible and impossible in this world, perhaps Marie would dazzle some fool, no telling what strange tastes existed in the world. Oh she could tell some tales of pairings she had seen, that Clotilde with a hog's face and hump on her back become a sudden duchess. Duchess for a humpbacked hog-face! And so on. Perhaps Marie would marry and bear a great brood of nobles. Marie did have in her veins the blood of the fairy Mélusine, after all, as did her siblings, and they all had a magic to them that was visible, something under the surface shining. Like moonstone. Marie too shone with it, the empress now saw that wicked underglow. And the more the old lady's eyes were accustomed to Marie's face, although she was of course entirely devoid of beauty, in fact she was truly quite-quite ugly, really rather remarkably ugly, she could see that those eyes of Marie's were not at all ugly. They were full of fire. And that was not nothing, the inner fire. Oh what a pity for Marie that she was born a woman, though not a pity for her own children, of course. No, no. She was quite glad for her own children's sake.

The table was set, the servant withdrew, they ate. With her mouth full the empress said suddenly that she forgot Marie was a recent orphan. Well, the empress was an orphan too. It was most lonely, to be an orphan. Marie's mother had little to admire in her but she was persistent, she at last made the family agree to take Marie.

Marie said quietly that her mother was the best of women.

The empress hissed in displeasure and bits of chewed bread sprayed at Marie. She said quickly that Marie's mother was indeed not at all the best of women, oh no, there were far, far better. But she was fine, at least, fine for a ruined woman. Fetching in her maidenhood, even. So fetching she seduced one who couldn't belong to her. Yes, well, perhaps not seduced, although it is true that a woman's blood is often hotter, everyone knows this. Eve's sin was that of passion. No, Marie's mother's fault was that she was fetching and a fool, for she didn't run fast enough. The empress was fetching too, there were songs about her beauty, but at least she wasn't a fool, she knew how to run fast. She ran very fast and no one caught her and therefore she was not violated, not even once. Despite Marie's ugliness, the empress hoped the girl knew that it could happen to her, sometimes it was not beauty but rather power that stirred the blood. The empress said she hoped Marie was more like herself than her mother. She hoped Marie knew to run fast-fast.

The empress waited. Marie said, very slowly, that she did indeed run quite fast.

Marie could not possibly run as fast as the empress, the old lady said, eyes bright; and Marie had the dizzying sensation that the ancient empress wanted to be challenged to a footrace. Out in the torchlit streets of Rouen, skirts gathered up, the dirt road dark drawn swift beneath. Marie would have been beheaded for winning.

Marie said that no, it was true, she was surely not as fast as the empress.

The empress smiled. She was glad Marie had some diplomacy in her, a nice thing to discover. Oh, well, fine, she would help Marie, she was surprised to find she did not dislike the girl though to be frank she fully expected to hate the very face of her. But no matter she would provide an armed escort across to the court of Angleterre. This was what she could do for the girl. Though she had already done quite enough.

Marie said thank you but her servant and she could make their way across the channel alone; after all, they had found their way to Rouen alone.

The empress laughed girlishly, and Marie saw now that she had lost her central teeth upper and lower and her molars were black at the hearts with decay. Foolish girl, the empress said, now it was known everywhere that she had been the guest of the empress, that she was blood relation to the crown of Angleterre. Though she was nothing at all to look at, still she was worth some kind of ransom; that or a forcible marriage as conduit to bring some family closer to the throne. What a child Marie still was, to not understand this.

Marie breathed in and out, and thanked the empress humbly for her protection.

The empress said, standing, that, well, to kin of kin, perhaps some kindness was owed. She laughed at her own quip then said suddenly that now she must toddle off to sleep. She gave Marie a slap of affection on the cheek with her dry small hand.

Then with a rustle of silk and a smell of moth-herbs, the empress was gone. This is the last Marie saw of this woman great by birth, greater by marriage, greatest in offspring, or so her stone in the Rouen cathedral will read after she goes to her eternal reward.

Marie puts away the letter.

No, she tells the abbess now, Empress Matilda cannot be gravely ill; she cannot die. She will live on perennially in Marie's mind, only desiccating in her vanity and bitterness year by year until at last she vanishes, the size of a flea, leaping and biting, into the folds of her voluminous skirts.

But all along the abbess has not been listening. What I wouldn't give for a gooseberry tart, she says, smiling like a child, and Marie sighs and rings the bell for the abbess's kitchener, who runs up, already grumbling.

The pressure of her diocesan superiors on Marie intensifies. They demand a conference, so Marie sends them Abbess Emme, who sings until, bewildered, they bundle her off.

An abbey servant steals a wagon and is apprehended three leagues away. Marie fights to prevent the hanging, arguing the punishment down to only an eye scooped from the socket and a patch worn over the woman's fair soft face, which Marie has always liked the looks of, had wanted to stroke with her hand.

News of Eleanor comes in drips, through what gossip those seeking alms bring, through lines in letters from her friends and spies: now the queen is in Aquitaine, now she is whipping up the royal blood to set siege to Toulouse, which she considers hers, now she is furious for the siege has failed.

Marie knows such events of the world, seen in the distance like a dark cloud in a clear sky, will one day come and bring rain and thunder even upon her nuns so removed from the world.

Then a dry spring, parsnips and turnips coming up weak and wrinkled. This will be a hungry winter, she thinks, kicking at one withered plant, and wants to weep, for there is no way Eleanor will recognize Marie's competence and require her advice, when year after year the nuns have hungry times, when she must sell her nuns' prayers simply to have enough to eat. There is no way that she can become known all through Europe as a great leader when struggle is all she does all day long, all year long. The daily kills her greatness.

As if god hears her, the reading at the meal that very day is Proverbs about how with pride there is disgrace, but wisdom for the humble.

Marie laughs to herself, stricken to the core.

The third spring of Marie's tenure, Sister Pomme, the gardener nun, puts the apricot seedlings in wicker cages and gives them manure, and they leap to Marie's height quickly.

The fifth year of her life at the abbey, they are twenty-six nuns, and more will arrive, dowries having become far better, Marie slowly, painfully becoming known for her competence, her strange long face and virago bearing reassuring the nobility that their daughters are well placed with her. They would hesitate if they knew she is only twenty-one, but her height and austerity and years of worry make her look far older. Sometimes when rising too fast from her bed or desk she is dizzied with sleeplessness. If she does sleep, she dreams of money because there is never enough, it melts from her hands.

This is the year that Marie stops the silk work. In its stead, she creates a scriptorium. The four newest novices can all read and write. Sister Gytha, who sees fairies zipping about on birdwings and her own mother's face in the moon, cannot write or read but can make stunning little illustrations and paint them in vivid colors. Marie clears out a room with windows and has standing desks made, then quietly bruits about the nuns' copying services being at a quarter the price of the monasteries' same work, for women are not supposed to be scriptrices, they are not thought able or wise enough. In a single year, copying brings in more than ten years of silk spinning and weaving ever had, and the alms at Christmas even include twelve good wool tunics for the freezing poor.

But her seventh year at the abbey, as though to erase Marie's small gains, there comes a summer of miasma and the child oblates die one after another, these last least daughters of the nobility, pitifully dowried, unloved slovenly mewling sickly, perishing of an evil look or cold draft from a window.

Then one day, in a peat-smelling hovel where Marie is invited to eat, she sees a freckled, long-lashed child of six years old keeping her six younger siblings in line. Wulfhild, daughter of Wulfhild, a long line of Wulfhilds as far as memory stretches back into the Saxon shadows and who knows the paternity, the mother shrugs, they bear her family name, which is Thrasher. How are seven children possible when Wulfhild herself is no more than six years old? Marie asks the girl while the mother, red hair frizzed wild, scoops pease pottage into an unclean bowl for Marie. Wulfhild says softly that her mother had litters like a bitch, two sets of triplets, only Wulfhild the lonely eldest. And this she tries in a mix of English and Latin, because Marie's English is still bad; this small girl had somehow picked up enough Latin through the church to converse.

Marie looks for a long while at this child with the long thick eyelashes, and in her head there blooms an army of child oblates all of whom are endowed with intelligence or vast strength or family knowledge; girls who have absorbed from the family businesses glassblowing, cobbling, coopering, carpentering, who can calculate without beeswax tablets, who can learn languages, who will grow to be powerful nuns or female merchants caring for the abbey's needs or marry higher than their stations and become among Marie's host of spies she has dreamed of planting in the rooms of quiet power throughout Europe.

She asks the girl in Latin how she would like to come to the abbey; but Wulfhild's face goes dark and she says she would not like that at all. Marie says that Wulfhild would never be hungry again and she would sleep in her own bed and not in a pile of children, but the girl again says no stoutly, and Marie smiles at the adamant of her will.

Marie makes preparations, finding three other girls, a blacksmith daughter of thirteen, a cobbler daughter of twelve, a nine-year-old so astonishingly tall and strong she can lift a cask of beer by herself. Marie rides herself to fetch Wulfhild, whose mother weeps at the thought of losing her, but agrees that a life at the abbey is higher than any she could give her daughter. The girl trembles on the pommel of Marie's warhorse all the way back through the night to the abbey but is stalwart and does not cry. Apple cakes begin to be stolen from the kitchen; a dog's rear leg tied to its stomach so it hops around crying, other small mischief sparked up, until Marie pulls Wulfhild into her lap and says she knows the child is making a nuisance of herself and asks if a devil has gotten into her or what.

Then Wulfhild says that she feels bleak inside because she has enough to eat and she knows her family does not. The girl does not look sorry, she looks fierce.

Marie says that she would send along to Wulfhild's family a ham and a tun of flour every Christmas and a tun of apples in the fall, would that do?

And the child's shoulders loosen and she rests against Marie's chest for some time in silence, and at last she says gravely it will do. For now.

Marie tells herself sternly she must not love Wulfhild more than she loves the others; but she smiles when she sees the girl, she cannot help it.

Time compresses, springs forward. Now they are thirty-three nuns and four oblates; and on Fridays, Marie has pilchards and salmon served, for the abbey can at last afford it. She has cajoled the nobles into donating the land surrounding the abbey, she is persistent and vaguely threatening until they give in and show their bellies, playing dead.

In her letters, Marie reads that Eleanor has broken from her marriage to live on her own lands in Aquitaine. The abbess's spies say that the queen is fomenting rebellion against the English crown in her own children's breasts. The queen's children are restive, riding about making alliances and promises. Marie is sent the song sung on the streets of Paris and London about the queen: a great eagle throwing her eaglets out of the nest too soon for them to fly.

The apricot tree fruits at last; the kitchener is scandalized that Marie plucks up a fruit and eats it raw and not baked in a pie. She says oh no no Prioress, we are women we are not *animals*, and Marie thinks of her good courageous horse, now quite old, how quiet and loyal and loving and patient the beast is; and at the same time she watches the idiot kitchen wench reach with a bare hand into the boiling parsnips, withdraw her hand, look at it dumbly as it steams and goes pink with a terrible burn.

Before the girl begins to wail and Marie crosses the room to plunge the burnt hand into the washing water, Marie thinks that true we are not animals; but it would be foolish to think we're better than animals. Animals are closer to god, of course; this is because animals have no need of god.

News trickles in that Eleanor is kidnapped in flight for the sin of rising up against England, kept first in the Château de Chinon, then dragged across the channel, and kept captured in a series of castles and houses in this very damp mizzling country the queen so despises.

The first flare in Marie's heart is joy: Marie is the free one now, she is the mistress of her own lands, she oversees estates and servants. Now it is Eleanor who has found herself in a cage.

Then the moment passes and she sees how impossible keeping Eleanor would be; surely they could have only taken a phantom of Eleanor, not the real woman. She remembers a play of Euripides, how the true Helen of Troy was not in the besieged city during the long war, having been replaced there by a goddess-conjured figment; the true Helen was living in the sunlight and flowers of Egypt, far from bloodshed and the stink of death.

She writes to the queen but has no reply, as her letters chase the queen who is dragged here and there at her captors' whim. At last, she hears that the queen is in a château thirty lieues to the north of the abbey and she creates an urgency in the abbey's lands there. She carries comforts for Eleanor: sweet-smelling herbs and the last length of abbey silk, soap, wine, a clever prayerbook that fits in the palm of a hand, unruined by Gytha's having painted the first parents blue and the serpent red. Marie rehearses how she will treat the queen with such gentleness in order to illustrate her own freedom. How she will use the best of her manners to show how very little she still forgives the queen for rejecting Marie's gift of lais, which was, of course, the gift of her own soul.

As she sometimes does when she rides out to the abbey's estates, she leans forward against the horn of her pommel, and lets the motion of the horse's gait build against her until she gasps and something in her breaks.

She is always calmer afterward.

But when she arrives, her heart is thudding as if she were a girl of fifteen not a great lady of thirty-two, striding purposefully forward, all her authority haughty on her face, she is met with bewilderment: But dear lady prioress, she is told, the queen was rushed from the castle only hours before and they were not told where she was sent.

Marie returns to the abbey rueful, crushed.

Sister Ruth, who has an eerie gift to understand things left unsaid, and who knows something of Marie's terrible love, catches the horse's bridle in the yard and sees Marie's face. When the prioress descends, Ruth says angrily, Even if you saw her, she would not deliver you from this place. You are stuck here with us.

And Marie opens her mouth to protest, but feels the truth of what Ruth said landing somewhere in her gut.

The wise inherit honor, but fools get only shame, Marie says at last with a hot face.

A Welsh sister comes, Nest, a young widow so sad she could only take refuge in a nunnery. She has a lovely face with great large lips and a mole near her left nostril that seems to draw her beauty out, although her skinny shoulders are hitched so high with nerves that they press against her jaw. Her Welsh is somewhat incomprehensible and at first she moves alone through her days, but when the sacrista develops a goiter that presses out from her throat like a fat butterfly, Nest goes into the fields and returns with a little blue-green weed that she boils in the kitchen until it's a thick syrup. After a month of administration, the goiter sinks back into the long smooth throat of the sacrista and her eyes stop bulging.

Marie calls the novice to her. At first the nervy woman is quiet when Marie tries French, then her poor English, and the few words of faulty Welsh, but when she shifts into Latin, knowing Nest can sing the divine office, an intelligence blazes behind Nest's eyes and she leans forward and speaks quickly, her high and bony shoulders trembling. Until Terce, the women speak of herbs and poultices and the balancing of humours, until Marie is comfortable that Nest's knowledge of medicine outstrips Marie's own. As they descend for prayer, Marie tells Nest that she has just now made for her the position of infirmatrix, she surrenders the responsibility of bodily healing of all the abbey's people to Nest. It is a burden for a prioress, to be in charge of pus and broken bones and rotted teeth and death-rattles, the vomit the flux the frenzy, on top of the never-ending business of the lands and the squabbles among the sisters. Plus, when Goda was put in charge of healing, she only ever purged the worms out of everyone.

Nest accepts. Within weeks, she has a large apothecary garden planted beside the infirmary.

Marie sometimes catches Nest watching her slyly from the corner of her eye but has no time to discover why; she struggles still passionately against the land that is always giving her too little in drought and disease, or too much in flooding or extended winter, against the new diocesan who seems to believe this abbey of virgins to be a source of personal wealth. She must draw up herself a dummy account ledger to show the abbey's great debt, which is false, for, she considers, to counter corruption, a similar corruption is only logical and right.

Small fires are used to battle a whole forest afire, she says aloud, and Goda says sharply, I do not know what passes through your mind, you are indeed a strange one, prioress.

And just as the plague of greed is driven off, a plague of locusts eats the wheat; Marie weeps for the lost bread but presents a calm face to her sisters, for she is learning to control her emotions to give her sisters peace in the world.

Sister Wevua begins to slide through time in her mind, and has to live in the infirmary now.

The child oblate Wulfhild has sprung up to the height of Marie's chin, tall for a growing maiden, she can do math in her head as fast as Marie, writes fluently in three languages.

Sister Agatha dies of tripping in the field during harvest and knocking her temple upon a stone.

And Elgiva crosses the cloister thinking of the novice Torqueri eyeing the kitten at its dish in the creamery; how she bent her own kittenish face close to the surface of the fresh milk and dipped the point of her pink tongue in; how Elgiva, straining the milk across the table, had to close her eyes because it was as if she could feel the tongue running lightly up and down on the inside of her entire skin. When she opened her eyes, she saw Torqueri still bent there, laughing; and that Lilas too had stilled her motions and was watching, flushed and mouth open, from over the butter.

———

They are forty nuns now. Marie is thirty-five. She has been eighteen years a prioress.

This is impossible, she thinks; she has been here in this damp stinking mud-befouled corner of Angleterre longer than she has been alive anywhere else. And yet how much more vivid for her remains the château in Le Maine with her wild, fighting aunts and the constant music and storytelling and the dogs panting from a day on the hunt dragging their tired bellies to the fire where the ticks rained off their hides; or the court with its lovers stealing into the embrace of trees in the allée, the grottoes, the laden table, all the beautiful ladies in their silken dresses shining like jewels in the brackish fog breathed up from the river.

She sees the abbey as though with a stranger's eyes: the stones scrubbed now, more white than gray, the fences neat, the fields rich. This is not the place she had come to, miserable and heartbroken, so long ago.

At the fair she overhears women talking about the livestock and they say in their strange English that this spring's lambkins are as happy and fat as abbey nuns.

Marie laughs in astonishment; it is true, in eighteen years the nuns have gone from pitiful skeletons to gamboling like spring lambs.

She is moved right there in the street to thank the Virgin, not only with the words of her mouth but with the words of her heart, and is surprised to find them in earnest.

How strange, she thinks. Belief has grown upon her. Perhaps, she thinks, it is something like a mold.

Wulfhild is eighteen. She comes to Marie saying that she cannot take the veil, she wants to marry.

Marie carefully checks her anger. Is there love?

There is, Wulfhild says, a blush starting in her cheeks and streaking down her throat.

Marie asks if there is money.

None whatsoever, she would be poor as dirt. Wulfhild laughs.

All those languages learned to fluency, all that reading for nothing, all those numbers so elegantly mastered. And though there is pain inside Marie's chest, she has learned by now to control herself.

Then Wulfhild will be the abbey's bailiffess, Marie says. It would give the prioress a chance to rid herself at last of the snakes around here who are using their power to steal from the abbey. And the salary would be a handsome one for Wulfhild and could pay for servants, a nice house in town.

Wulfhild says in alarm that she has never heard of a woman bailiff. And who would accept her authority?

Marie says that she herself would ride with Wulfhild for the first month, and after that month, everyone will accept her authority.

And it is the gentlest month Marie has yet had at the abbey, the hot still August days with the struck-iron shimmer of insect noise and Wulfhild growing into her role. Marie's pride blooms maternal when Wulfhild proves herself a lady among the gentlefolk; her pride doubles when, out in the fields, Wulfhild switches in a breath to the grossest, most scathing English to roust the lazy from their naps in the shade.

Honest Wulfhild. Her scrupulous accounts show how profoundly the abbey had been robbed by those previously entrusted with its business, even under the threat of Marie.

One night, Marie steals out to smell the apricots ripening. She takes a raw fruit in her hand to feel its weight, to marvel at the large and healthy tree that god compressed into a seed. But this fruit comes off its stem easily and its flesh has a little give to it like the firm thigh of a girl, and in the dark Marie rubs the soft down of the fruit upon her cheek and feels a thrill up the length of her skin. She thinks of her lost servant Cecily, her comfort, her mouth, her hands. It has been nearly two decades since Marie's body has been touched in love, since the white waves have risen up from the very center of her and swept her spirit briefly out of her body. The perfume of the fruit's flesh, the soft give under her teeth. But on the pit Marie cracks the front top molar on the right side of her mouth all the way to the throbbing nerve.

For the rest of the night she lies in contrition upon her face on the cold stone of the chapel until the bell for Lauds rings and there is a rustle on the night stairs and the nuns began to descend. She can barely sing. Even the abbess, whose mind is lost in her neumes, sees with clouded sight the fatness of her prioress's right cheek and asks if she has been bitten by a spider. Although Marie had meant to ride off to visit three noble families that day, she cannot with a face so swollen. At release from Prime, Marie searches for the infirmatrix, until she finds her weeding her herbs, whispering encouragement to each small plant in her native Welsh.

Lovely Nest looks up and a shy pleasure comes over her face. Marie feels a stirring in the long-neglected center of her, beneath her ribs.

Nest asks Marie if it is that time again, because she has eased Marie's twisting pain of the womb with her mother's recipe for dwale: bile of a gilt in heat, lettuce, henbane, hemlock, bryony, and belladonna in a solution of vinegar.

Marie says no, toothache, although Nest's dwale would take the sting off.

Nest tells Marie to come inside and she stands and brushes the dirt off her hands, and leads Marie past the three nuns set out on their chairs to warm their bones in the sunshine.

Sister Estrid looks at Marie with terrible hope, saying Maman? Mindless Duvelina smiles beautifully at a mote dancing in the sunlight. Wevua, who would forever see Marie as a novice, mutters, Here comes that whingeing weeping godless brat of a prioress.

The beds are empty in the infirmary, with the old nuns all sitting outside. The back room, hung with last year's herbs, smells rich with horehound, beebalm, honeycomb, rosemary, the herbs that infiltrate Nest's habit. There are no windows and the only light comes from the door and the embers where Nest is simmering herbs in a kettle. Nest lights a little clay lamp, and Marie feels the heat of the fire on her lips and tongue as the infirmatrix tilts the lamp into Marie's mouth and peers in. Nest says that the prioress must be suffering; she has to have the tooth out. It is rotted. A shame, Marie having kept all her teeth so late in life. A marvel of good health.

Marie blushes, and tastes the dirt of the garden on Nest's fingers when the infirmatrix ties the thin strong catgut around the dead tooth.

Nest says she will pull on three, and Marie braces herself and closes her eyes and Nest says one, then on two there is a sharp pain, and Marie opens her eyes again to see Nest holding the string with a bloody black and white stump at the end of it.

Marie says that she thinks thou shalt not lie is a commandment, not a suggestion.

Nest says that an infirmatrix's deeper commandment is that thou shalt not cause more pain than thou must. She gently takes Marie's face in her hands and looks in her mouth again. In a jug she has steeped betony in aqua vitae and bids Marie rinse her mouth thrice with it, and spit into a basin until there is no more blood. Then she takes a little brush and paints the sore gum with honey and makes Marie sit with mouth gaping until the honey dries.

The third time Nest looks into Marie's mouth, Marie closes her lips upon Nest's fingers. Honey, earth, herbs. She kisses Nest on the soft skin between the eyebrows. Nest does not draw away. Marie takes the infirmatrix's head in her hands. Nest flushes and kisses Marie on the mouth. She stands and closes the door and when she returns in the dark, she has already removed her wimple and veil and coif. She takes Marie's hand and puts it on her shorn head, removing Marie's headcloths with practiced fingers. Nest pulls Marie to standing, unties Marie's belt, removes her scapular, and tells her to lie down. The infirmatrix's hands lift the hem of her shift and then Marie feels the shock of smooth skin upon the flesh of her inner thighs and understands when she feels Nest's breath that it is not a hand there but Nest's far softer cheek. She feels her eyelashes brushing her skin. Her skin shivers the length of itself. And then Nest's mouth is there, her hands are there, and Marie is brought violently to the swift central current of a river where she is released, she spins, she goes under. When she comes up again, she shakes and presses the heels of her hands to her eyes. Sparks fly in the dark.

Marie lets the infirmatrix dress her. Nest pulls Marie's hands away from her face and says sternly, no no, oh prioress, there is no shame in this bodily release, that it is an expression of the humors, not unlike bloodletting, it is utterly natural, it has nothing to do with copulation. She will still meet her god a virgin. It's simply that some of the nuns require such expression of the humors more than others. Some as often as once every two days, some once a year. Nest has often wondered that Marie might be one who required it rather frequently. There is sometimes, well, a wild look in Marie's eye. She tells Marie to come back to the infirmary when she feels the need.

Marie is speechless in gratitude. If such things are medicinal, they are no sin. She had felt filth on her soul since the days of Cecily. In an afternoon, Nest has washed her of it.

Then she remembers where she is and says sadly, but alas there can be no special friendships among nuns. They are against the Rule.

And Nest swallows her smile and says that, as she said, there are others who come to her for relief from these humors. Such treatment is not as special as Marie may believe; it is quite common, in fact.

The idea that there are others like her makes Marie laugh. She goes into the daylight with her tongue darting into the raw new hole in her mouth.

And she sees then what she missed going in, the simmer of sun through the wind-shook branches, the hummingbird with its invisible wings darting among the flowers, the scoured hickory-bark skin of the faces of the old women with their eyes closed and chins tilted to the sun. Nest's kindness to the fleshly body has brought about an inner shifting. Nothing is all stark and clear any longer, nothing stands in opposition. Good and evil live together; dark and light. Contradictions can be true at once. The world holds a great and pulsing terror at its center. The world is ecstatic in its very deeps.

Marie is thirty-eight.

There has been trouble among the villeinesses, and come summer, three of the unmarried women are swelling at the belly like rosehips. They are not nuns, true, they are not sworn to virginity, but Marie feels shame that she cannot control these bodies under her care, what the larger world would think of the abbey if they knew. Great scandal. She would be removed as prioress. Thank goodness she has trained her superiors well with her flattery and competency, they are never here at the abbey any longer to oversee. She speaks to Goda, who explains to her some finer points of procreation by use of animal metaphors, the moment exactly at which children ripen to adults. At last, she has the whole community, over fifty nuns and eighty-some others, gather beyond the garden.

It is the harrowing time, she tells them in her deepest loudest voice. From this day, the abbey lands enclosed here by the surrounding forest will be a place only of women. Everyone else must be gone.

All servants remaining shall be women, she says.

Beggars of all sexes will be given alms not here but at the almonry Marie is establishing in town, she says.

All visitors will remain at the hostelry next to the almonry, she says.

She takes a deep breath and delivers the last blow. At the age of twelve, none of the children of the villeinesses can stay if they are not girls; and should the villeinesses not want to be separated from their families, Marie can have them all moved to abbey lands outside the central estate to work there.

It is no sin to be born not female, she says to the downturned heads before her. It is no fault of any newborn babe to be the unfortunate sex it is. But sin is introduced at the time in life, around eleven or twelve years old, when the bodily serpent wakes and yearns to spread its venom. This is the true story of our first parents; this is the understanding of Eve.

There is great weeping and, privately among some of the nuns, re-joicing. Only four villeinesses trundle off to farther abbey estates with their broods. And for those who choose to stay, and let their children go, Marie finds four places in good pious households in town for their banished children.

Queen Eleanor sends a cousin to the abbey, a girl of twenty named Tilde, whose thin pale face belies a clever mind and a humble devout soul. Marie can see the girl's true vocation written on her face, and feels a flare of envy. Tilde spends her days happily in the scriptorium, often has ink smeared on her chin. Marie watches her. The girl would make a fine prioress someday, she thinks. There is judgment there, gentleness, fervency.

And one day Wulfhild, having dropped off the rents with Marie, stops in the scriptorium to kiss Gytha on the cheek, to slide a packet of candied fennelseed into the mad nun's pocket. Gytha smiles bluely. Later, when in weariness Wulfhild takes off her leather tunic at her house at night, out falls a tiny painting of a fantastical beast on a cut-up old letter, a green tiger with a human smile or a porcupine playing the lute, which her daughters will one day pin to their collection on the wall. Some nights, going in to kiss her girls in their sleep, she will stop and look and feel before these many beasts of Gytha's something akin to what she felt as a child when the nuns sang their most beautiful, most awesome psalms, a slow internal pouring of ecstasy. Awe. If only she had time to examine this feeling, Wulfhild thinks ruefully; but she does not have time, she never has time, her children call, the business of the abbey calls, the hungers and fatigues of her body call. She will come closer to god when she is old, in a garden among the flowers and the birds, she tells herself; yes, someday she will sit in silence until she knows god, she thinks, lying down in her bed to sleep. Just not now.

Work. Prayer, which is the element of the abbey as much as the damp, the wind. The fields, the sows, the orchard.

And Eleanor, still a captive. The queen, forced into a cage, remains an open sore in Marie. She does not reply to Marie's letters, still. Maddening.

A loud and arrogant novice arrives; she has black brows so huge they crawl across her face like caterpillars. She doesn't bother to learn hand signs and shouts for what she wants at refectory: Lettuces! Fish! A warm day after weeks of rain and the novices take baskets and run to the forests to go mushrooming. An argument when they find a circle of little pointy mushrooms with upturned caps; these are poisonous, the other novices try to say, but the new novice says no, she picked them all the time at home, they're delicious, her voice goes loud, louder, she is bellowing, she scoops up a handful of the mushrooms and crams them in her mouth. The other novices turn away. They pick baskets and baskets in silence. When they hear the bells of Vespers, they find the girl is missing. At last, they discover her curled dead between two great mossy stumps, face an angry bruise, her tongue huge between her lips, another pale mushroom.

Marie is forty-five. There are ninety-six nuns, twelve child oblates, all skilled. The abbey is rich.

And at last, one blustering afternoon, blind singing useless kind Abbess Emme takes to her deathbed, where she will linger, more music than body.

Marie is forty-seven. From Rome, from Paris, from London, her spies have written swift panicked letters: Jerusalem has fallen again to the infidel.

Marie weeps. She is angry that she had never beheld the city when she was a child crusader. Unseen, longed for, dreamt of, it has grown in her year after year until it is the ideal of cities, place of perfection, a city no mortal city could ever resemble. Cedars, fig trees, lilies, gazelles. And now with Jerusalem's fall, there is ripped a rent in the earthly kingdom of her god. Through such rents great evil does creep. She does not sleep at night, fearing a dark cloud she feels approaching. It is all the more terrifying for remaining cast in shadows; none of her vision can bring what is coming into the light. It is also true that she is sleepless because the curse of Eve has been removing itself from her body in flames that cook Marie from the inside out.

Flames from deep inside, licking outward. Horrid. She rises in restlessness, she runs.

The pond at the abbey is dark, matte. The night is moonless.

The feel of the abbey on its hill at the back hunched and half watching in its sleep. Heat still rising from the soil, the frogs thumping their drums, some chirping bug in its millions, some single nightbird with its few notes.

Her body is inhabited, electric with heat, her skin has a roiling fire stuffed into it, the heat is unbearable, she is now running toward the low light off the water. Night in its heaps of darkness spins by. Off with the clogs and the stockings wet from night dew, and the mud cools her toes, the water is at her ankles, dragging hard at the hems, at knees at shame at belly so cool at chest and the arms, the wet wool pulling her body down. The frogs hush in the disturbance. Only her head is aflame, water lapping through the cloth at the chin. A body like a dog's in the dark water. A vision of the great dumb alaunt of childhood on an August afternoon with only her reddish nose above the surface. In remembering that long-dead dog, Marie's laugh deep and low skids across the surface and resounds on the far side.

The heat is passing from Marie's limbs and the coolness enters, a relief. Unbearable, these flashes, enough to drive a mind mad.

And with pain, because the clothes are heavy, a return to the shore.

But a figure is standing there. A hand seizes Marie's heart. Dread: lashes on the back, a hungry stomach, a chute in the dignity of the prioress. So be it. She would not waste a prayer to the Virgin to stop it. Her steps are heavy wading up. The pale face in the dark habit comes clear, Sister Elgiva, freckled round cheeks, long pale eyelashes, old Saxon family.

Elgiva asks with a laugh in her voice if the prioress felt like a night swim. How strange the French remains in the mouths of these English, thirty years at the abbey and an ear raised on the continent could never grow used to it.

But Marie says that, no, it was mortification of the flesh. But now, mortification of the pride to know the sister had been watching.

Sister Elgiva extends a hand, helps pull the heavy body to shore. So short she is, well, they all are in comparison to Marie, her crown comes only to Marie's clavicle. She reaches up to help off with the wimple, the veil, the coif.

Elgiva says that she heard the prioress running outside and guessed where Marie was going. Her own mother lost the curse of Eve early, also. Once, they found her outside in a storm, stuffing snow into her bodice.

So good the breath of the night blowing through Marie's cropped hair, cool slide of air upon the scalp. Elgiva bends and takes the hem of the scapular and lifts it heavily over. The hem of the habit now. So free. Now a shock, because the sister bends for the hem of the linen shift but bodies are not naked here, bodies are bared only for the monthly bath, the night has eyes. But a languor has set in post-pond, the heat flash removed from Marie's body is always like a deboning. What is the harm to let Elgiva help her. And so she lets her own bare skin be exposed, the sister's eyes on skin like the brushes of fingers, the length of dry linen in her hands, in the night chafing on her. When Elgiva wraps the clean fabric around Marie, her veil brushes the bare skin of her chest.

But a surprise; and deeper, it is not truly a surprise. Elgiva's lips are warm, her breath good, she has chewed mint on her way here in the dark, her skin is soft.

No, Marie thinks, stern with herself, already knowing the answer is yes. She is weak.

Elgiva's own wimple and veil and coif are off now, the belt the scapular the habit, she laughs, she would not wait for the linen shift to fully be removed, she takes Marie's hand so giant in her small callused hands and puts it at the center of her, a delicious damp give under Marie's fingers, a sinking like touching the moss in the forest, rich and giving, the small sounds she is making under the pressure of Marie's mouth. On their knees in the damp warm dirt. Elgiva smells down there like barley and chives and the sea salt and riverine mud. A small music of her breathing so close, and the frogs have forgotten the water's disturbance and returned to their songs. Marie's own fingers so expert. Perhaps Elgiva is another of the secret ones hidden at the abbey, there are a number here like them, after Nest awakened her, Marie has seen them stealing kisses in the shadows at the edges of the blackberry patch, waiting beside the garderobe in the night for another body to steal out under cover of dark. Slide into English in Marie's mind, French no good for the animal body, hand mouth tooth breast lip thigh skin cunt, words that hold the hot blood of feeling. Under Marie's mouth the humming in the girl's white throat, the rising, the coursing in her, it is a tide, the wave itself, and soon a second whiteness gathers in the back of Marie's head, the bursting outward. Her body slowly retakes her senses one by one, frogsong, sweet mud underneath, the taste of Elgiva's mouth, numb skin ticking back into feeling.

And when Elgiva has caught her breath she says that she had thought so. She had heard the prioress also visits Infirmatrix Nest.

For a moment, Marie cannot breathe to imagine her nuns talking about her like so. A release of humors, like bloodletting, the infirmatrix has always said. Nest with her kind pretty plush very skilled mouth. There is no mention of female sodomy in any of the books, and the great angry moralists would have mentioned it if it were a sin, surely. Marie has searched; she has found only echoing silence.

Linen wrapped around again, wet fabric gathered up, quick steps across the dark ground. The scent of Elgiva she carries on her fingers, don't wash, no one will know. No stars no moon tonight, this is good. There is the sense the bells for Matins are gathering their silence into themselves, readying themselves for ringing.

Elgiva hesitates, then whispers she is often alone in the creamery when all the others are at their chores.

Marie says that she has suddenly become interested in butter-making. A laugh. The hawthorn in the dark clothed all over in its shivering white flower. Final swift kiss. Then Elgiva goes into the chapel. Marie watches how in the darkness the other nun lays herself at the altar to Mary, face flat upon the stone floor, arms in a cross, to pray and await the night office.

She feels, watching, a sadness within, perhaps it is pity; there will be no taking what the pretty freckled nun has offered, Marie has lied to her. Love attained too easily, she knows from courtly romances, is not love. Love that flows from high to low, prioress to dairy nun, is counter to the laws of goodness. For Marie's rigid heart, there can be no entanglements but those she has entered into long ago with Eleanor, impossible and distant. For the sating of her body's hungers, these carnal and lesser appetites, there had once been Cecily and now there can only be Nest's medicinal hands.

Inside swiftly to the kitchen then the cellar. No linen shift, the other is being laundered. The wet cloth spread on the drying rack and on the shelves the bottommost habit to the left, the only one great enough and long enough to clothe all Marie's expanse of body. Hated thing, with its patches and its supplemental hem of thirty years ago. And scapular, stockings, headcloths, quick-quick. The bells are already ringing. There are the footsteps of half-sleeping nuns descending the night stairs.

Final pinning while running out of the kitchen. And across the cloister with its pillars standing naked as maidens in the darkness, oh hush mind, such wicked thoughts as these are unmeet, it is time for prayer. And the late entry the genuflection the seat beside the abbess's empty one. In the single candlelight on the other side of the abbess's chair, Subprioress Goda's face turns, her nose sniffs, is it possible she can smell the pleasure upon Marie, the mud of the pond, what she carries on her fingers? Tiny smile. Perhaps. Goda works among the heifers and pigs. She knows the animal body.

Deus in adiutorium meum intende. Matins.

The downturned faces of the nuns, singing, hidden by the small light. Sleepy voices raised in the Venite, with antiphon.

And, what wonder. What miracle is this.

Because the deep heat is stirring again, unquelled; the devouring fire of the curse of Eve as it leaves this body beginning to pulse from the inside out to the skin. But this time as it circles, unbearable, within, the new habit already soaked with sweat, there is something strange that begins to happen: the sear of this flash rises out of Marie's body and pours outward and descends upon each of the other nuns one by one in a luminous rush. And as the heat falls, it falls in new colors: within the child oblates in the front benches it strikes a tiny pale lick and in the novices so young a barely deeper red flame and it grows the richness of gold as it flows lapping outward to the older nuns, and blue and green within the nuns who are within their own times of losing the curse of Eve—the time of panic, the thoughts of throwing themselves out of windows for relief from the hot humors of the body—and it even pours gold and red to those bent and toothless nuns who had decades ago passed to the calm beyond the end of fertility. Upon the nuns' heads one by one the heat descends; and when it rises again out of each, it builds a great sympathetic shining that gathers strength and speed as it goes along, a swirling of red white and hot blue flame. The heat spreading from the body of one to the other is shared as all things in this abbey of women are shared. Marie can see it passing body to body. She can see that even the abbess in her deathbed in the rooms above the refectory is made a tallow candle that shines against the dark.

And all souls as they sing shine radiant into the world.

THREE

1.

Marie stands in the twilit fields.

These too are winter rye.

It is 1188 and Abbess Emme is newly dead of her long illness. Marie has been made abbess in Emme's loss. A box full of white clay balls for the election, a solitary black ball among them, and Goda turning her face into her sleeve at the announcement. For days the subprioress was rough with the milking, made the animals groan, until the bucket was taken gently from her and she was led into the vineyard to walk the long rows of vines back and forth, singing an entire slow Magnificat with each row. By the final row, she had stopped weeping and returned to herself again, if shrunken, if whispering her sorrows into the beasts' warm ears in the mornings. Kind confessors, they blinked and forgave, no penance.

Then the great pomp of Marie's consecration as abbess. The unbelievable expense, for so many had to be feasted, so as to show the abbey's wealth and power, first in the town outside the cathedral and then again privately in the abbey for her women, her nuns and the servants. Marie sighed in her heart, considering the sum, all the kid goats and swans and pounds of spice and tuns of wine necessary. Luckily, she'd had the span of Emme's illness to save up.

But the diocesan superiors, seeing the outlay, wore unhappy faces that turned furious with their wine drunk to excess; there were mutterings of combing the abbey for hidden wealth and redistributing it. Her first act as abbess and Marie had erred gravely. She presided over the festivities smiling, but a clammy wind entered her.

When Ruth, who had been a novice with her, kissed Marie after it was all over and the night had fallen softly on them, she said, Marie, my friend, today you had a radiance to you. A heavenly glow.

I'm sorry, Ruthie. From now on you must call me Mother, Marie said, and both laughed.

By the time Marie was elected abbess, the heat of the end of her menses had withdrawn from her. Now she is no longer touched by the curse of Eve. When the blood stopped, the knives that had twisted in her since she was fourteen were at last removed from her womb.

She is given instead a long, cold clarity.

She can see for a great distance now. She can see for eons.

She will write of the first great, ground-trembling vision later in a private book, hidden from her nuns. She will describe vividly what happens.

It is shortly before Vespers. The twilight hangs over the hills, the sun dies in loops of gold and shadow. Behind her the abbey is small and white in the last blaze. The swallows flick in arcs above.

By the wagons, the villeinesses sing a song of lust so old that the words do not sound to Marie like English; and though they should not listen to such worldly filth, her dozens of strong working nuns listen half smiling with their bodies bent, their black habits falling like shadows in the fields, their scythes hissing the song's rhythm.

Marie shivers.

And in the space of an exhale, all the world goes quiet.

And then, in all its immensity, it turns the force of its attention upon Marie.

Lightning sparks at the tips of her fingers. Swifter than breath it moves through her hands, the flesh of her arms, her inner organs, her sex, her skin, and it settles jagged and blazing in her throat. Wondrous colors bloom in the sky above the forests. With a thunder that shakes the ground beneath Marie's feet, there is a split in the sky that opens. In the split Marie sees a woman made of the greatness of all the cities in the world together, a woman clothed in radiance.

And upon the woman's head she wears a crown of stars; and this is how Marie knows her to be the Virgin Mary, whose face is hidden by the blaze of twelve suns.

The Virgin holds a wine-red rose tight in bud. From her vastness she drops her rose upon the forest at her feet, and the rose blooms out of its bud and just as swiftly it blows. The petals circle in the wind and the soft petals each tear down the great trees of the forest in a pattern. And

Marie can feel the pattern in her fingers as though she is tracing it with her hand, and knows it to be a labyrinth; and at the heart of the labyrinth she sees a yellow broom flower holding upon its slender stalk a shining full moon.

Then with a hand the Virgin clears the veil of brightness from her face and Marie is allowed to look full upon the Blessed Mother; and she wears the face of her own mother, so young, and shining with love. Marie falls to her knees.

At last the Virgin hoods herself again in radiance and she steps backward through the wound reft in the sky.

The sky heals into its natural dark blue behind her.

Radiance bleeds from the day. Marie returns to herself kneeling upon the dirt in a ring of her daughters.

A voice yells that the abbess is old, she has had a spell; but another says angrily that the abbess is but forty-seven and strong, foolish child, do her eyes not work, can she not see the abbess has had a holy visitation?

Marie opens her eyes and smiles upon her daughters and they go silent in the force and radiance lent to her by the Virgin. She can feel in her own skin their wonder.

She says that she is well. She says that oh indeed, she is very very well.

The bell for Vespers rings across the distance. Marie sends her nuns home, and the villeinesses trundle back with the wagons and the freemartins to the granary, and Marie picks up the skirts of her habit from her legs and runs swift and strong through the fields despite her great size. She goes through the orchards and to the apartments of the abbess and up the stairs and though her own kitchener tries to ask her a question about her evening meal she does not stop. She goes to her study and writes out her vision in full.

Only when she has re-created in ink upon parchment what she saw does she fully understand it, she writes in her little book.

Visions are not complete until they have been set down and stepped away from, turned this way and that in the hand.

In the larger world, she sees, the beasts of the apocalypse are roaming, leaving their dark trail smoking and charred on the earth. The fall of Jerusalem, she understands, will make the whole Christian world fall. Christians will be slaughtered and raped and made slaves. Jews throughout the Christian lands will be blamed and caught in their houses and burnt at the stake and murdered without pity; women and children will be buried alive. Famines and conquests and earthquakes and fires and dead bodies littering the plains. A cloud of invisible evil has fallen upon the heads all around, it is darkening the air even where they stand. It is Marie's duty as Mother to her daughters to banish even the sight of the cloud from this place.

And in the vision given as a shining gift to her, the Virgin has told Marie how to remove her daughters from worldly influence.

For Marie herself as abbess is the broom flower growing up through the abbey and it is her strength alone that holds it aloft.

It is her daughters' faith that shines brightly as a moon, the light of the darkening sky.

And with the rose the Virgin made a labyrinth in the forests encircling the abbey, to show Marie that she must do the like.

She must build a labyrinth.

The abbey had always been an easy quarter day's walk from town. But if a labyrinth with a secret passage were built around it, a road that was so complex it would dismay all but the most determined visitors, she could hold her daughters aloof from the corrupting world.

There would be no authority but Marie's authority in this place.

And they could stay on this piece of earth where the place has always stood but her daughters would be removed, enclosed, safe. They would be self-sufficient, entire unto themselves. An island of women.

2.

In the night, Marie calls for her four most competent daughters.

The new prioress Tilde, twitchy and scrupulous, with the sweet, startled face of a dormouse. Oh how the girl loves god, hungers for god, believes in the goodness of all things with a kind of rigorous simplicity. Such knowing simplicity in this complex world takes great intelligence, Marie finds. She envies the girl, admires her.

And young eager Sister Asta, whose mind is clear and mechanical, seeing deep into the workings of things, who walks at a perilous forward tilt on her toes as if impatient to already be there, whose table manners are so atrocious it is counted a penance to sit opposite her at refectory.

And Sister Ruth, who had been a novice with Marie and whose judgment is large and fine.

Finally, Wulfhild, the lady-bailiff of the abbey, summoned out of her sleep from her house in town, where she has four daughters of her own, bright, strong little maidens, and a very fine house.

It is deep in the night when all are assembled in Marie's chambers. Marie's kitchener brings up cheese and bread and pies of fruit and good sweet wine carried over from Burgundy. With the arrival of the food, the women mind less missing their sleep.

Then Marie stands, huge, by the fire. Ruth thinks with wonder that she glows with a light that is not of fire. She tells them slowly of her vision in the fields that day, and of her plan.

Prioress Tilde bows her head in awe, there is no resistance; she is frightened of Marie, how swiftly her mind leaps and turns, and now she sees the light borrowed from the Virgin as it shines out of her superior.

In Sister Asta, the challenge of such a huge undertaking is thrilling, a puzzle to be attacked, and her small pointy face grows red with excitement, and she calculates swiftly and says that it can be done in two years, perhaps, if all hands inessential to the abbey's urgent needs are used and if they buy ten freemartins or draft horses to drag the felled branches to the burning piles.

In Sister Ruth, a great stillness of doubt takes place. She feels chilled and shivers. But then she thinks in the face of her unease of Marie as she had been a few months after she arrived as a novice: skinny rangy huge thing, silent with her sadness; how in the thirty years since that day of reckoning, the abbey has grown in its prosperity and comfort from twenty starving nuns until now there are nearly a hundred nuns and dozens of servants, and nearly as many villeinesses in their cottages with their children. And all these memories, all the weight of what the nuns owe Marie, her thirty years of control of the abbey and genius in the way she conducted the affairs of the abbey, pour through Sister Ruth. At last she thinks of the practical impossibility of the labyrinth, how nearly stupid it would seem if it were proposed by anyone else but the Virgin Mary through her firm enormous receptacle of Abbess Marie; and she at last arrives at the understanding that Marie's will is stronger than any practical impossibilities, and it will be done even if Ruth voices her objections.

She lowers her head and prays and raises it and says yes, though in a voice thick with worry when the vote is called.

Only Wulfhild resists the abbess. Twelve years now the abbey's bailiffess, in her strange leather tunic and skirt, shining with the tallow she rubs on to make them impervious to the weather. She is a dark-haired, sunbrowned woman who gives the impression of boiling turmoil held in check by willpower alone, smaller than Marie but like Marie holding a kind of natural authority in her shoulders thrown back. When she frowns, the real beauty of her high cheekbones and long lashes becomes a sudden grimness. It is this Wulfhild, with a strong spine to her, who now stands and tells the abbess no.

This, she says, is an insane plan. It is destined for failure.

Marie blinks slowly and the other women in the room hold their breath. The abbess repeats no, without emotion.

Wulfhild says that they have just recently saved enough for the abbess house, she herself has already had the workers begin the quarrying in the pits where all the abbey stone is cut, it is senseless to stop now. It will take ten more years to save enough all over again.

Marie asks very quietly if Wulfhild does not love her.

Wulfhild says she loves her so much that she dares to tell Marie when she is making a mistake and that not all even in this room can boast of such honesty when Marie puts on her murderess face, which she is wearing right now. But the abbess doesn't scare her, Wulfhild.

It is clear by the rapid pulse twitching in Wulfhild's neck that the abbess does in fact scare Wulfhild.

The silence stretches on and it is horrid.

In a voice so soft that all the women lean forward to hear, Marie says that when Wulfhild speaks, she speaks in the voice of Marie's own authority, which she has only lent to the bailiffess. But Marie herself speaks with the authority of the Virgin Mary who has bestowed upon her a great vision that very day.

Surely, she says, Wulfhild would not dare to contradict the Virgin Mary.

And so Wulfhild's resistance is overrun. She sighs. She adjusts. With burning eyes she bends over the table where Asta has already in excitement begun sketching her plans.

Outside the infirmary, the three ancient nuns are set out in the sun. One afflicted, one brainless, one who slides through time.

Estrid had died in her sleep, and has been replaced with Amphelisa, who stepped over a pair of copulating snakes and was cursed with a stroke in punishment; half of her body is set in stone and she struggles to speak.

Duvelina, who has the purest blood of any nun, of the greatest family in France, was born with a handful of words in her, a sly smile, a face as though she is squinting into a constant high wind.

And Wevua, who is becoming even more savage for being un-moored in time.

Prioress Tilde, run off her feet, has given them peas to shell, for now that the forests are full of the sound of breaking trees, the shouts of nuns, every hand must work, there is no leisure even for the aged and ill.

Wevua complains that since they started building the labyrinth, the dortoir stinks of sweat. Impossible to breathe enough to sleep. And nothing is clean anymore. The linens are atrocious. The refectory floor full of mud.

Amphelisa says with her slurry tongue that it is very hard with so few left to work here at the abbey. Poor Tilde.

They stop shelling for a moment to watch Prioress Tilde's head-cloths flitting in the windows. The prioress was left with only twelve servants and nuns to do the work of the whole abbey, she weeps as she churns butter, she weeps as she runs to pull the bread from the ovens, she has succumbed in despair to letting the weeds take over the garden.

Duvelina bows her head. Because of her simplicity, she is perhaps the most perfectly faithful nun of all, the one with goodness shot through her, cloudless. She begins to shell peas remarkably fast, her hands blur, she is quite excellent at shelling peas.

Amphelisa says the word *child*, meaning how awful that the child oblate died yesterday, standing in the path of a falling oak. Just that morning was the funeral. Amphelisa still can smell the sap of lilies her good hand picked to lay on the body in its shroud.

Wevua snorts. She tells the others that all child oblates who are sent here die. What can one expect. Starvation everywhere. So much death. And that stupid servant eating a root that looked like a carrot but was

LAUREN GROFF

not and frothing to death. Wevua's poor beautiful sisters going blue
choking on their lungs, what horror. She herself dug their graves. The
cold February rain. Her hands bloody. Wevua opens her hands and
looks at her palms. She looks affronted to find her hands suddenly
quite old.

With this gesture, Amphelisa knows Wevua has gone back to the
starving time before Marie took the abbey in hand, a few years before
she herself came to the abbey a novice of sixteen. She asks Wevua's
opinion of the new prioress Marie, curious to know how Marie had
been, so long ago.

Wevua scoffs and says that the new prioress Marie is a nothing.
Weak. Still a child in her massive body. Barely knows even the prayers
all Christian children know. It's shocking. Raised a heathen. True she
took the cross as a child crusader but gave up her vows in frailty to
come home without ever seeing Jerusalem. Failed crusader; worse even
than those who went to Outremer only to enrich themselves. Wevua
hears the girl Marie speak aloud in her dreams sometimes. At court
she had a great love, it appears. The girl still murmurs for her love.
Some nights Wevua wakes to find Marie's bed empty, who knows
where she goes. Wevua predicts she will die soon of a broken heart.
Good, she says. To let an unbeliever like her be a prioress of a community of holy virgins is a scandal, a sin.

Half of Amphelisa's mouth raises in a smile. Time has proved just
how Wevua is wrong.

Wevua says reluctantly that still, the girl does learn quickly. Sing an
antiphon once through and she has it by heart. But Wevua strongly
believes Marie should never take the veil for, it is clear, she does not
love god.

And Amphelisa laughs aloud at the thought of the abbess being anything less than radiant with holiness. Then she reminds herself in her head that they are all sinners, and none are perfect, even Mother Marie.

Prioress Tilde flies down the garden path, panting, crying out from a distance to ask if all the peas have been shelled yet, then nearly screaming when she sees the basket still half full. She pleads for her sisters to work faster and runs away.

Duvelina's nose almost touches the peas in her lap, she shells so hard.

The three nuns are silent while they finish; and they see Tilde darting to the chapel where she herself rings the bells for None. Wevua stands, takes the basket of peas for evening refectory under one arm and Amphelisa on the other, and carries both to the chapel. Her mind is slippery in time but her body is still strong, despite her crushed foot. Duvelina hums shuffling behind. At the door, Wevua leaves Amphelisa but carries the peas inside. Amphelisa waits, leaning on the warm stone. Wevua comes out and puts the basket of peas down on the ground and picks Amphelisa up and carries her in to her bench.

There are so few nuns left behind to sing None; the rest are in the chapel of the forest, all that sawdust and smoke and birdsong and sweat. There is Prioress Tilde, the three ancient nuns, Goda who is caring for the animals singlehandedly. Infirmatrix Nest returns to fetch some blister salve and bandages to the forest and she sits down impatiently to wait through the divine office. The light falls gently through the windows on the mostly empty wooden benches.

Prioress Tilde leads the service in the absence of the cantrix.

Nest sings, but she thinks of the forest. She can hear distant chopping; the crack of falling trees; the others, nuns and servants and villeinesses, have gone back so quickly to their work. She longs to be with them in the sun and wind. A strange magic has befallen their bodies. Every day since the abbess announced the project, the weather has been fine and not too hot, days lengthening so the women's increasing strength and endurance can be tested with longer hours of work. They return with callused hands, sunburnt cheeks, a swagger of exhaustion and pride in their legs, bodies that are sleeping even as they fall into their beds after Compline. All this time Nest has attended only minor wounds and a single fatality, the little oblate of eight years playing in the brush who didn't heed the calls to get out of the way of the falling oak. The smaller girls are in charge of the freemartins and draft horses and it is a delight to see how the beasts move to their little voices, to find that most of the girls can work as hard as the nuns of the veil. How swiftly the women have all been working, filled with radiance and conviction. The blinds and hidden paths that hide the shortcut from abbey to town have been made, its final secret tunnel has been dug, only a small stretch from behind the blind up into the barn behind the almonry and hostelry; Nest herself swung the pickax to reveal the exiting light. And through the forest, the streams are buried under roads, the baskets of dirt are carried, the straining creatures are pulling logs and trunks from the earth, the saplings that have been transplanted are somehow doubling their size in a month, the bushes are filling out the empty places as fully as though they had been planted at the formation of the world. And where there are spaces to be filled where bushes won't suffice, the clever blinds are constructed, completing the illusion of the road running endlessly in isolation, even though it is separated from other roads by a strip of trees and bush. On the surface of the road slowly unfurling itself, a forearm's fill of pebbles from the quarry underlies an equal thickness of dirt. Then a machine built by Asta and the carpenter and blacksmith nuns comes along, a stunning marvel of a contraption: ten of the strongest workers stand inside a giant wheel and walk together to press the dirt hard and flat.

What Asta could do if she were of a warlike mind: machines of awful death, things to flip fire and venom over a distance, crushing machines, machines of ardent substance ready to explode; the strange nun is so excited by ideas she forgets to consider consequence. Astonishing how much road can be carved in a single day out of the ancient forest. The first lobe of the labyrinth is already finished, the second lobe has been begun. And all the women who are out working together feel blessed in golden light, in the haze of the fires, in the fresh air, in their bodies' joyous sweat and effort. Even the abbess works and Marie's prodigious strength takes Nest's breath away; the abbess is not unlike a freemartin, that strange genre of virago ox not one thing or the other but both at the same time. Well: Marie has always been strong. Nest can feel just the power of Marie's flesh as though it is even now moving under her hand. Odd to imagine that there are some born to fine blood who are stronger in the body than the laborers in the field. This gives Nest pause; does this mean that there are those of commoner blood, then, who should lead? She laughs into her sleeve with the idea. Wevua across the choir blasts her a look of rage.

Versicle. Prayer. Blessing. Nest takes her basket of salve and bandages and nearly runs back to the forest to bind the hands of the afflicted and return them to their work.

Prioress Tilde watches her go, devastated. She says in a lost voice that the infirmatrix could have brought food along with her in the barrow so Tilde herself doesn't have to take it out to the working women.

And Goda, who is not a soft woman by any means, pats the prioress's shoulder and tells her to hush, now, to sit for a minute in rest, that Goda herself will take the food out to them. She tells Tilde sternly that she must learn to be more steady, that she must give tasks to others, so she does not die of overwork. Tilde should take her, the subprioress, as example, for Goda could drive the heifers out to the fields every day but her time is better used in seeing to the sickness of the animals, why, just this morning, she put salve on the pig with the extruded anus, and so gave the other sows a little peace from the first's constant screaming. Yes, Goda says with satisfaction, Tilde must find her own prolapsed pigs and order others to do the heifer driving, this is perhaps what they call a metaphor, but when she turns to smile at the girl, Tilde has already darted off again.

In the forest, Marie, thinking of the queen so newly released from her captivity, how Eleanor might appear after these long decades, for even the queen must age, looks up to see Nest striding over the packed new road, her cheeks flushed with walking, how pretty she is with her smile, the little flaw of the birthmark by her nose making her beauty coalesce.

Marie is hungry these days, hungry for everything, for food, for the work of the body, for this cold good air in her lungs; and this hunger rises up with such force in her at the sight of Nest that Marie has to close her eyes and hold her breath until it passes.

The nuns work until the wind pales with snow and the ground is too hard to dig, and then they enter the long dark hours of winter contemplation, yearning for the trees and open air, their bodies restless with suppressed movement and their dreams in the night full of labyrinths. They have accomplished more than Asta dared to calculate, two whole lobes of forest turned maze, from the town to the northeast to the hills to the northwest from which the wolves slink in the springtime to carry away the lambs. They finish their work in the bakery, brewery, dairy early so they can go to the woodlot to chop and stack wood, how good it feels to sweat again, for their muscles to strain in work. Their sunburns pale in the interior dim. The healthy glow of their cheeks is extinguished. Prioress Tilde watches the servants set the abbey to rights in mere days, all the floors and woodwork scrubbed and shining with polish, all the broken things mended. The manuscripts in the scriptorium that had been set aside in the outdoor work are finished with alacrity, long hours over the breviaries and psalters and missals finished and bound until there are no more commissions left.

Insane Sister Gytha, who is illiterate, because letters dance and shapeshift before her eyes, but who paints the manuscript's illustrations with wild imagination—perfect devils in blue, martyrs dying in great gouts of blood—has no more manuscripts to illustrate, and to keep her thoughts from flying off like dandelion spores, she begins whispering to all who can hear of orgies in the woods.

Blood pacts, unbaptized babes made into stew, virgins' blood drunk like wine, she speaks of.

Gytha stops the abbess after Prime one frozen morning and says in her swift breathless whisper that she watched last night as the trees bent and danced to the horns and drums of the witches who had gathered there in the night, full black for it was absent of moonshine, to enact their hideous and twisting rituals of midnight around the fires built not of wood but of the stacked dried flesh of babes. And that Gytha was telling the trees that they in their feigned innocence do not fool her, for she knows full well that trees are the instruments of the devil. She pants. Her teeth are lined in blue from where she sucks on the lapis lazuli brush to make it a finer point.

Marie says carefully that perhaps what Gytha saw the night before had been in fact a snowstorm full of wind and sleet that set the trees rocking, a wind that howled with the many voices of beasts. Marie can see the truth buried beneath in what others call Gytha's madness.

And that very morning, Marie sets the insane nun to work again painting a great Mary Magdalene with reddish hair loosed around her body upon the chapel walls. Apostola Apostolorum, Marie's favorite saint; she who, Marie thought, was the truer rock of the church. The saint's face slowly appears. It is Abbess Marie's long bony unlovely face in her halo of gilt. Something profoundly equine there. Gytha sings to herself as she works. Marie feels her actual fleshly face burn in dismay; there are no spyglasses here, no tin polished to a shine, and within the greatness of her power she has forgotten even the memory of her own profound lack of beauty until Gytha painted it on plaster.

The others make things. Reams of linens and woolens woven, baskets mended, leather worked. A new kind of gruit ale experimented with in the brewhouse that crouches over the frozen stream.

And out beyond the garden walls, where the nuns of the craft have made their work shelters, Asta, bouncing on her toes in excitement, and the blacksmith and carpenter nuns build machines for better, faster working in the spring. They are assisted by the other nuns of the craft: the cobbler, the glassmaker, the potter. They create a saw, operated by two freemartins or mares walking in a circle, that can take down in minutes a tree the greatness of three nuns linked by the hands. They make a sled that slides trees to the burning piles with only a single yoked beast. They build handcarts with great iron wheels that can move easily over rough ground.

The celebrations of Advent, Christmas, and Epiphany like lights shining in the dark.

And the cold darkness ebbs. Before the ground has fully thawed or green showed itself on the land, in the gray before Lent, they return in gladness to the work given them by the Blessed Virgin.

Marie's hands are bleeding. She has just watched an ash tree sigh in resignation, then give a terrible crack and fall in a slow and graceful crash through the weak March light.

A flood of squirrels flows across the ground, birds spray across the gash in the canopy.

And this is when the second vision of the Virgin descends upon her.

Later, after she turns and flies over the frozen ground and through the fields of winter rye and up at last through the orchard and to the abbey gone so still with the stillness of so few souls in it, and up her stairs to her cold anteroom, standing at the desk, Abbess Marie writes and eventually will copy this in Latin into her private Book of Visions:

The second gift bequeathed to me by the grace of Our Lady, the Star of the Sea, Seat of Wisdom, Mirror of Justice.

I was standing with axe in hand watching a tree fall in the woods when I felt my head heated by a deep throbbing, and then the snake of lightning whipped through my limbs.

A light grew in the forest behind me. It shone upon my daughters and the children seated upon the pulling beasts; and all that had just been in motion were stopped in their work and held there as though by a mysterious hand; and the dirt thrown off the shovel and the sawdust flying were held in its flight. I turned. And then I fell to my knees, for standing in the place where the road was to be made in the forest were two women whose holiness shone so brightly their radiance made me hide my face from them.

The one wore a gown of the green paleness of first spring, when the leaves burst in their richness from the boughs and the flowers first open in bloom and the wind blows sweetly and chill over the land; and jewels of emerald and sapphire and pearl adorned her head and her sleeves, and from her breast there bled a wound large and open and shining in gold, and this was the wound of her maternal sorrow.

For this was the Mother of God, Mary, the Blessed Virgin, who bestowed this vision upon me.

And this was the second time she deigned to reveal her face to me.

Holding her hand was a woman of equal radiance, cloaked in the red of blood, with diamonds and silver upon her neck and wrists, and upon her brow was shining in rubies the wound made by the staff of the angel who had chased her from the first garden; for this was Eve, the first mother of all humankind. And she held in her other hand a rib made of crystal, for she herself had been molded from a rib, and so proved herself a refinement of the first mortal made of mere clay. For is not gold pulled from the rock less perfect than the gold melted from the rock by handiwork and annealed to a shine that echoes that of the sun?

The women gazed upon me in silence and with faces full of love. And when I could at last dare to fix my gaze upon them and did not dare to drag my eyes away, they raised their clasped hands and kissed. Let her kiss her with the kiss of her mouth.

Thus they showed me that the war so often vaunted between them was a falsity created by the serpent to sow division and strife and unhappiness in the world.

For, I saw, it was from Eve's taste of the forbidden fruit that knowledge came, and with knowledge the ability to understand the perfection of the fruit of Mary's womb and the gift given to the world.

And without the flaw of Eve there could be no purity of Mary.

And without the womb of Eve, which is the House of Death, there could be no womb of Mary, which is the House of Life.

Without the first matrix, there could be no salvatrix, the greatest matrix of all.

And when I saw this all clear, the two women stood as one and rose up from where they stood in the dead brush of the winter forest and together they rose up in a slow and shining band of light to the heavens.

And all that was left was the thickness of the morning behind them and a smell of myrrh lingering in my nose and the sweetness of first birdsong, for though my daughters had been stilled in their work, the winter birds had seen all, and when the women were gone, they were stirred from their silent wonderment into wild exultation.

And while writing down this second vision, I have come to see the warning in it. I understand that it means the queen is coming here on one of her sudden chevauchées; and that we, my abbey of nuns, must make our united self steadfast in preparation.

Marie calls Sister Ruth to her. Marie's old friend has not been able to conceal her fears about the labyrinth work, she has sniped at Marie constantly, and to relieve them both, Marie sent her to the town, to become guest magistra and almoness at the abbey's buildings next to the cathedral, with a small staff of six servants. The buildings had been given to the abbey when Marie had just become prioress, at the time they were merely rat-infested warehouses for grain, a bad dowry a novice brought with her; Marie alone had seen the potential in the buildings and stopped Abbess Emme from having them sold. It took Marie five years to raise the money to finish them, more to build them out, but when the buildings were ready, they kept all visitors and those seeking alms out of the abbey's lands and enclosure, they no longer needed to take the morning-long walk through the forest and fields to the abbey upon the hill.

No more grasping hands at the wicket. No more trout poached from the pond, or does from the forest. No more threats to the nuns' enclosure.

Ruth comes in flushed with the cold, plumper than she has been, for she is responsible for giving a good board to the noble and illustrious visitors, the devout on the way to their pilgrimages. She has decided only the finest things are suitable; the abbey's white bread but the rye not, the abbey's ale but the wine not. Roasted meats every day. The aged cheese and not the fresh. Marie indulges her; since the famine time when they were young, Ruth has found her greatest pleasure in food.

The queen will be coming, Marie tells Ruth, squeezing her hands. Certainly by Carnelevarium, as Eleanor has always been an elegant gourmande and has never loved a Lent. Thank the Virgin that Easter is not early this year. She'll have a retinue for Ruth to put up, sizable, too. Dozens. It will be an immense burden on the hostelry, Marie is sorry to say.

Ruth grows pink and sighs and says that she will prepare.

Marie says that the queen will order Ruth to show her the secret way through the labyrinth to the abbey, but she must be firm and smart, and must not do so.

Ruth asks, rather testily, how in the world does a mere mortal tell the queen she cannot do something.

Marie says that one doesn't. That one washes the queen's feet very slowly and, after one dries them, one plies her with delicacies and good hot wine, having long before, as soon as one hears news of the heralds entering town, sent off one's fastest horse to fetch the abbess.

Ruth says after some thought that unfortunately theirs is a royal abbey. Marie, being made abbess, became a baroness to the crown. So why in the world can the queen herself not see the women's private way in? She is the regent, after all. Marie, though abbess, is but a subject.

The queen of Angleterre, Marie says drily, is a mighty personality, but she never could keep a secret. And even if she could keep a secret she is too fearful of being made captive again, for good reason, that she would never agree to come alone, and one cannot trust in the eyes of the retinue.

Now, though Marie's body yearns to be out among her nuns, swinging an axe, she spends her days writing her letters, and sending Wulfhild off all over the country with messages.

And when the news comes that the queen has been seen in the countryside nearing the city, that she travels swiftly and without a harbinger, Marie gallops toward the town through the hidden paths and tunnels and is already seated sweating by the fire in the almoness's reception room when the queen sweeps in, irritated at the interruption of her plans. The abbess holds her face in a mask. She rises to her full height and bulk and grandeur and begins her obsequies slowly, so that

Eleanor can stop her and bid her to sit. But the queen does not stop her; Marie feels the other woman's sharp eyes sweeping over her.

In the dimness of the doorway, Eleanor looked young, but now as she steps near the fire she shows the fine wrinkles under her powder and the hump of her back that has begun to grow. Her perfume so strong it is the avant garde of her attack.

And the world silences in Marie's ears; all she can hear is her thumping heart. She casts about inside herself, at a loss. If beauty has been stripped from the most beautiful, grace from the most gracious, does that mean god's favor has been stripped away, as well?

Without preamble Eleanor says, well it has been decades and hasn't Marie become a great mountain of a woman. She tells her to sit, if sitting doesn't break her chair, that is. No longer a gallowsbird, is Marie? She, who had once been frightfully bony. My oh my.

Marie smiles.

The queen looks at her. She says in a musing voice that no, perhaps these decades Marie has become a sphinx.

Marie says that they do eat well now at the abbey, that this place is not the starving place it had been when she arrived as a girl that Eleanor herself threw away, those weeks when Marie watched little baby oblates go blue and waste away of their hunger. They do eat well and plentifully, though of course none of the nuns are fat. Nearly all of the nuns have tremendous muscles. Perhaps the queen is simply just unused to female strength. Or perhaps it has been so long since Eleanor's Ladies' Army that she has forgotten? Perhaps any woman who is not so frail she would shatter with a shout would seem fat, at least to one so refined and courtly as the queen?

It is as though the queen cannot hear her; she says in a musing voice that it's not as though Marie was ever small, is it, her bones had simply been unfleshed all those years ago. Now she carries her own armor under her habit, yes, she would say Marie has become a great old monocerous. Hide of iron, single vicious horn, or so she hears. Monocerous. Yes, this is exact.

Marie breathes through her nose, and says that she hopes the queen accepts Marie's condolences that she has so recently been made a widow. A bloody ulcer, such a painful thing. Marie found it curious that nobody wrote to tell her, that she had to discover the news as though she were not blood kin. Although of course Marie is only a half sibling and a bastard. Surely the queen had been too busy to write Marie, her sister.

Half sister. And only by marriage, Eleanor says sternly. Yes, in fact, she is always busy. But that it also has felt wrong to accept the condolences when she was not in the least sorry for her loss. There had been real love there, Marie knows this, she saw it herself when she was a girl at court. Great love, even, once. Well, to be frank, the duties of the bedchamber of Angleterre were never the least onerous. And the queen laughs her breathless quick laugh.

But then Eleanor says that but of course if you put an eagle in a cage for more than a decade, she will try to peck your eyes out when you open the gate.

Marie says that well, things have worked out and the queen has been released from her long captivity, and now her best eaglet perches on the throne of Angleterre. Those years of prison are redeemed. Though they did say some of the queen's captors had been quite cruel during her captivity. They took her gyrfalcons from her. They kept her so starved of warmth she had chilblains on her beautiful face. Marie often thought of the queen in her captivity, especially since there were times she was so nearby and the abbey with its comforts could have soothed her torment. In fact, the queen might have been far better here as a nun than as a caged queen.

Eleanor blinks many times swiftly and Marie laughs inside; swift blinking has always been a window into the woman's mind. Then the queen says it is odd that Marie had thought of her often, that she must confess she hardly thought of Marie at all. Or if she did it was of a Marie when she knew her, fresh to court and so strange, all elbows and head knocking the doorway and big deep voice trying to engage in disputations, stinking and uncouth and but all the world fleeing before her stomping footsteps. What a poor specimen Marie was then. Before the girl had arrived, the plan had been to marry Marie off, but then in she flapped with her queerness, her panting eagerness. Her unlovely face. And one could not marry off such a creature at all.

The queen adds that should she retire to an abbey it will be the great Fontevraud, not this paltry muddy place on this hated island.

The food has come. Marie gestures for the queen to sit. Things have grown too heated, and to cool the atmosphere, Marie says in conciliation that she has had made for Eleanor a copy of her Fables. The abbey's illustrator is mad and sees devils in the grasses and evil exhaled out of hot onion soup, but her work is very fine indeed. Marie wrote the stories during a blue streak while Abbess Emme was in her decline and she stayed up in the nights in vigil over the old woman as she suffered. She had tried for a new kind of style in the Fables, distant from the style of her lais, she is no longer writing of terrible biting love, after these more than thirty years she feels only love for her sisters in her heart, and her style must change to reflect this truth, of course, as well.

In any event, she goes on, there's a story in the book about a crane and a wolf. Does the queen know the story? No? A wolf, chewing a bone, gets it caught in its throat. In pain, the beast calls all the animals of the kingdom together to demand that one pull the bone from its throat. Only the crane has a long enough neck. Of course, the crane is understandably reluctant to put its head between all those sharp teeth. At last, the wolf tells the crane that if it were to reach its head into the wolf's mouth, it would get a wondrous treasure. So the brave crane reaches in and plucks out the bone. The wolf, released from pain, tells the bird that it now will get its treasure. And that the treasure is its life. The crane must be happy not to be eaten.

The queen laughs and says, Delightful.

They eat in silence for some time until the queen, satisfied with her portion of white pheasant meat, sits back, takes up her wine, and begins. She tells Marie that all the world is astonished by the rumors of her labyrinth.

Marie says happily that it is indeed a feat of engineering. What women can do when given a task! Their abilities seem limitless.

Ah; but the abbess mistakes the tone of the queen's words. There are nobles saying that they'd like to bring an army to strip the nuns off this place; to teach them a lesson. There are wild rumors of magic. It is not to Marie's benefit in this situation that she descends from the fairy Mélusine. Some speak of wealth unimaginable that the nuns are hiding here. The queen has had to soothe the most belligerent. She has found herself having to threaten, to cajole. It is exhausting.

Marie sets down her wine. She says she knows all this, that she too has her spies and she knows who is saying what. How foolish, all this warlike talk about a community of pious virgins devoted to poverty.

Ungodly, to say the least. What the abbey does not spend on living, it gives as alms. They are poor as poor can be.

But is this true, the queen wonders aloud; she did notice in riding through that the poor of this town are wonderfully dressed. Better than the merchant classes of other places. And that Marie has put glass in the greater windows, neat clear circles embedded in lead, so that the overall impression is that of a sectioned beehive where now the light simply pours in. What awful expense. Perhaps the queen should increase her taxes on the abbey. Perhaps she could squeeze more levies for war mustering from this place.

Marie says that glass is cheap because one of the sisters is a glassmaker and that the poor here will have to wear the same shoes and tunics for many years to come. Their great project of a labyrinth has impoverished the abbey again. And she picks up the accounting books that she has prepared for this visit, and shows the queen the numbers, which seem very grave indeed.

Another charge against Marie that the queen has heard, she says, is that the abbess keeps her relics selfishly in the chapel and does not share the miracles they enact upon others who may need them.

Marie thinks of the assorted teeth and bones of the saints, the fragments of the True Cross. There are so many fragments of the True Cross in Angleterre alone that a whole Golgotha of True Crosses could be constructed on a moor somewhere. It is also true that so few of the abbey's relics shine with the light of authenticity; so much of the value is in the settings; the ornamented boxes, the phylacteries holding the phalanges and molars. Ah, well; this too will be no great loss. She says thoughtfully that on All Saints' Day perhaps the sisters of the abbey shall have a procession to translate the relics to the cathedral, as a gift of the abbey's to the devout of the surrounding lands.

Eleanor remarks that this is generous, but that All Saints' Day is a long time from now.

Marie's mask slips and she smiles, saying that they will need time to bruit these good plans around, the great beneficence they are bestowing out of generosity and mercy upon the laypeople of the countryside.

Eleanor sighs. She drinks quietly for a time. She too relaxes and says that she truly wishes that Marie would give up this little folly of hers. This labyrinth is being seen as an act of aggression. Women act counter to all the laws of submission when they remove themselves from availability. This is what enflames Marie's enemies.

Marie says with admiration that that was well put, gracious Regent. But not an order, perhaps.

Eleanor looks at her; relents, looks away. Perhaps not. Perhaps a warning. But even warned she sees that Marie remains unafraid. That the abbess will continue on.

Well, yes. As abbess of this royal abbey where the queen chose to plant her so many decades ago, Marie says, she discovers herself to be a baroness to the crown with all the rights attendant upon the barony; including the expectation of course to be protected by the powers of the crown. And so far she has been an excellent baroness, prompt about paying the taxes and providing the necessary fees for war when asked. Her loyalty is unquestionable. And, like all landed nobles, she finds that she is allowed the freedom to fortify her land from intruders.

Eleanor says slowly that all this is true. She puts the talk of the nobles away; it was only an opening sally. Now she bends to her true attack. Her spies also say that all of Rome is speaking of interdiction. They say Marie neglects the hierarchy and considers herself an equal to her diocesan. They say she does not let their messengers come to the lands, but that she meets all dignitaries of the church here in the town. She has enemies even in the church. And as Marie knows, anathema would be devastating for a community of the godly. No Mass, no confession. No singing of the divine office.

With this, Marie feels a bolt of lightning in her gut because the queen is right, without singing the abbey would be a cold damp impossible place.

The queen says, And some of Marie's daughters would die of grief and they would die unshriven.

Marie says that she too has heard these rumors. That the talk from Rome is more troublesome, that is certain. But she feels quite sure they won't be sent outside the pale. She has begun fighting Rome's way.

Eleanor laughs at this. She asks with what, with prayer? Please. Prayer is lovely. She herself prays every day. But for such a threat, Marie will need more powerful weapons than prayer. Perhaps she doesn't know this, having been removed from the world these many years, but to engage in war with the world, one needs the world's weapons.

There is such a long silence that Eleanor turns her gaze fully at Marie, who is looking calmly back; and the queen says with a thin smile that of course she has already been proven correct to have sent Marie here, she will not apologize for doing what god bade her do.

Marie lets the silence grow until the queen makes a gesture of impatience, and then the abbess relents and says at last that yes of course they are using prayer, prayer is the finest product of any abbey. They have such a great surplus of it that her nuns are granted generous benefices for their prayers.

But, Marie says, they are also fighting with gold. Rather a good deal of it, she is sorry to say. She is commissioning songs and stories to be sung in the streets. She is flooding the streets of London and Paris and Rome with songs and rumors of the sisters' piety and the abbey's strength and Marie's own holiness, and their great miracle of the labyrinth. She laughs. Money and stories. Information and sympathy. There can be no real defense against such a war. Eleanor herself was the one who taught Marie this.

Eleanor holds her cup tightly then finishes her wine, considering. Softly, she says, well now, hasn't Marie become a clever girl.

Marie says to herself, very sternly, Down, because she has not been a girl for decades and because her heart has lifted and soared with the praise. For she had once transferred her soul to parchment and the queen had ignored it. She remembers her pain from so long ago now, dwells upon it, so that the old rose of hatred, of love, buds in her and blooms again.

That night, Marie cannot sleep with the queen so near, just through the wall of the hostelry; she rises for Matins in the cathedral and stays until the hour of Lauds, praying. She loves her nuns' voices, but the polyphony of this choir of the cathedral chapter fills her with shivers; this kind of music seems to her closer to the songs of angels.

The queen comes with her handmaidens into the choir for Prime; and in the time she prays and stands, the glass windows fill with light and her retinue has been made ready. Her horse awaits her when she emerges into the pale chill. Townspeople stop, incredulous, to see the great notorious Eleanor. She has been a legend from more than a half century of tales told at the fire in the dark winter and songs circling the country, but now, a miracle, out of abstract story she has been made flesh. She stands on the cathedral step and her breath is white in the cold like the breath of all the living. The queen's first handmaiden whispers to her and the queen turns to Marie. She smiles.

She says that she lied when she said that she hadn't thought of Marie all those years. She has a spy installed in the abbey who gave regular reports. She has been impressed with Marie.

Marie's mind slows in surprise, and she spins through all her nuns in her mind, but cannot discover the weakness, or who would have access to messengers. She is unable yet to speak.

The queen laughs to see Marie stunned. Oh don't worry, the spy is one of Marie's stalwarts. The abbess remains mostly beloved by her nuns. Rare among holy women. Such a fractious lot, the weaker sex. All other convents are shrill with strife.

Marie tucks away the queen's *mostly* to turn over later.

The queen says that Marie will find she has left two gifts. She mounts her horse as easily as a girl. She tells Marie to make use of them both, and a slippery joy threads through Marie; she controls her face and tells the queen thank you, that she would pray the queen travels with god.

The retinue moves off, the queen impressive in her sable cloak that catches light and sparks with it chestnut and blue and black, the thick gold circlet on her head concentrating all the sun in the street. All is mud and stone and smoke, pigs rooting in the filth; the queen alone is made of higher stuff. Marie's hands in her sleeves tremble.

In the hostelry, an air of relief; an emptiness of bodies. There is much to clean. The servant girls in the sun of the window show each other their ankles speckled in red bites; the retinue brought fleas. Ruth comes forward nearly dancing. She pulls Marie by the hand to the presents. One of the gifts left for Marie is an abbatial staff; the note says it was made especially for her when the queen heard of her election; Abbess Emme's was carved ash wood with filigreed silver and a crook of horn, and it was fine enough, but Marie's hand needed something weightier. The new staff is solid copper, finely engraved with the entirety of the Garden of Eden in places highlighted in gold filigree, the hook made of the snake with the apple in its mouth, its eyes set with emeralds. Ruth tried, she laughs, but she cannot lift it. It is meant only for the strength of Marie. Marie feels its heft in her hand, up her whole arm, in her gut. It feels like the power she has struggled and scrabbled in the dirt all these years to amass.

The other gift is small, wrapped in a scrap of blue silk. When Marie opens it, she finds a personal seal matrix of herself, a giant with a head in halo, a book in one hand and a broom flower in the other, nuns gathered around standing the height of her waist.

Scribe mihi, the queen has embroidered on the silk. An order, not a suggestion. To seal a letter with the abbey's matrix requires either the prioress or subprioress to read and agree; what the queen is giving Marie with her own personal seal is a delicious and forbidden privacy.

For an abbey is collective; privacy is against the Rule, aloneness a luxury, time to think with all the necessary work and meditation and prayer too short to ever come to much. Even reading among the nuns is reading aloud; there is no private dialogue to challenge the internal voice and press it forward. Marie does not wonder why so few of her nuns have the capacity to think for themselves; she saw from the first moment she arrived that this was planted deep in the design of the monastic life. As abbess, she sees how dangerous a free-thinking nun could be. If there were another Marie in her flock, it would be a disaster. She feels a sharpness of guilt from time to time; yet she keeps her nuns in their holy darkness with their work and their prayer. She justifies it by telling herself this is how she keeps her daughters in innocence. Hers is a second Eden.

Marie protects only her own internal landscape; her spirit is the only one allowed to stretch to the farthest horizon, she gives only herself the hawk's height in the clouds to see the tiny movements below.

Already Marie is writing her first letter to the queen in her head. How long will you hide your face from me, she sings in her mind.

She rides alone to where her nuns are working in the forest. She feels scrubbed raw inside. A long cold anger that she had kept alive in her heart for so many years that she had nearly forgotten it was there has seeped away.

And into the emptiness where it had been there begin to tumble other, far more mysterious, things.

At night, the heavens spin into their summer constellations.

The nuns take pauses in the greater work to sow the wheat, to plant the gardens. Rains come in the night and the wet earth bursts to green.

In the abbey sleepy without its souls, a mother vixen with heavy teats trots out of the cellar dragging a whole dried sturgeon. Prioress Tilde opens the door and steps back for it to go, making a gift of the theft for the beast's bravery.

In June, a miracle; Amphelisa, whose half body had frozen after she stepped over copulating snakes, awakens having regained the use of her frozen face and hand, and only limps with a single unwilling leg now. She credits the intercession of Saint Lucy, of whom in desperation she'd molded a wax votive with her good hand and let it melt on a hot stone while praying. Now full of energy, she has taken the garden out of frantic Prioress Tilde's domain, and the vegetables grow fat; the lovage and fennel and skirret under her care grow madly; the coleworts are the size of three-month babies. Because she sings to them, the bees of the apiary sting her only infrequently when she smokes them to check on their honey. Wevua and Duvelina are her assistants, hauling brush to fire and weaving wattle, because if their bodies are tired enough, their minds, one simple, one sliding, are at peace.

Now the nuns are finishing the final lobe of the labyrinth, near the marshlands to the southeast. Asta had redrawn the final stretch to come straight toward the abbey from the farthest reaches of the forest, so that the weary traveler already come so far would see through the trees the spire of the chapel on its hill for the last slow and seemingly endless climb through forest, and would feel great despair in ever arriving. Her small sharp face beams, she bounces on her toes, jabbing her fingers at the map when she tells Marie of her innovations, false bends, earth-shaping to give the traveler greatest fatigue, so many tricks of mind employed, so much play in this strange formation of the land. Marie kisses Asta on the forehead. Her nuns are marvels.

Marie has reluctantly returned to her study and devotes herself to the parchments long ignored. Rent in arrears, promised bequests upon a great noblewoman's death yet undelivered though she has been dead a full year, mold discovered in the malted grain so the sacks of it have to be fed to the pigs, a shame. She keeps the window open to focus her mind upon her tasks. The labyrinth will be finished off by planting blackberries, sloes, plums, brambles, heatherberries, elderberries, raspberries, quickbeamberries, wild currants, and haws all the way around the edges of the fields for added protection in the case of accidental breaching; but also for the sweetness and bounty of the fruit.

She allows each nun a piece of trout the width of her psalter and a cake of filbert and honey in feasting. And though they eat while listening to the voice of Sister Agnes, whom they call Agnes Dei because she fairly bleats, they are rosy and happy.

And that evening when there is still light to travel by, the abbess goes off at a fast canter with a torch blazing through the secret passages where her villeinesses will pass to and from with their wagons full of supplies and letters. Those who come to the abbey to say Mass and take confession must be driven blindfolded through this secret passage, now. She had thought there would be a fight when she demanded this concession, but Marie apparently strikes fear in the hearts of those attached to the cathedral. In the morning, Marie will not ride the shortcut but rather the entirety of the labyrinth, the many leagues of it, to see it as though an interloper. She loves this estrangement from her own knowledge, shivers in the thrill of it.

It is full night when she comes up from the last tunnel into the great barn behind the hostelry. She does not bother the servants for more than a bowl of the pottage served to all the visitors and some cider, and she sleeps in the room where the queen had been. Though it has been months, it seems to Marie that the woman's strange perfume hangs in the air there still, a hint of her soul left behind.

She cannot sleep, and is outside in the cold before dawn. She has left a note for Ruth; she would be fasting during this day of prayer to the

Virgin. She saddles her horse, a destrier mare found cheap on one of her journeys to the fair in Salisbury, where the beast was being sold for food because her owner had starved her, beaten her, let wounds fester on her haunches and belly, a sorry creature with her windgalls and spavins and staggers, and such a mad desperate sorrow in her eye that she arrested the abbess when she passed. Later they would discover evidence she had been bred many times to bear her great strong foals that would themselves be fed to war. Marie thought the beast might die on the road, but she walked slowly the many lieues and at last was put in Goda's clucking horrified care. Within a few months, the horse's skin shone and she was capable of bearing three stout nuns with ease, or a single giant abbess. The mad light in her eye had become a near-human understanding. Having known suffering, redemption, resurrection, the horse, Marie believed, had become a kind of equine saint.

Out in the woods between the cathedral and the almonry, the new public path begins as a feint, they have made it unpromising, muddy and a squeeze, the width of a bridle track. Through it she sets the horse at a fast walk. The hours pass. The sun rises in gold, the day warms. As she rides, she is struck again and again to wonder; how lost a stranger who has not dreamed up the plans herself would become, and how soon the stranger would give up and turn back to the town. The road hardly looks as new as it is; the trees have grown thickly around it. At the first bend, even her own sense of direction begins to snarl. But the day is pleasant enough and she relaxes, she knows she will sleep in her own bed in the abbey tonight. She sees the few bare spots where the forest has been disturbed by the work, but the other roads are well hidden, and when the trees and shrubs are grown at last to full height and thickness, in two or five years, she thinks with satisfaction, the labyrinth will be unbreachable.

But midmorning comes and she is still in the first lobe and wind blows cold through her scapular and hood. She passes the time by telling herself stories as the horse walks on.

In time the horse's rhythm rocks her to sleep; and when she wakes she sees by the slant of sun through the split canopy that it must be at least the time for Terce. She finds she has lost where she is. Her stomach rumbles in hunger. She feels a creeping unease that night will set in soon with its wolves and its dark and its hostile mysteries to find her winding along the endless path still hours from her nuns. She urges the mare to a canter.

The horse senses Marie's fear and her ears stiffen and point forward.

But with the increasing pace, the anxiety in Marie also increases, this is bad, the road is darkening, the sun has snuffed itself behind a cloud, the trees themselves are staring at her with sinister shadows, the branches above are meaty arms paused in downward swing, something is moving in the shrubs like dark and hidden beasts slithering forward swift on their bellies to keep pace with Marie.

She senses the presence of the devil, the great evil is here, now, with her, she remembers the stories, the pack of glossy black dogs and the enormous spider leaping from the trees to sink a hellish death of venom into the earthly body, the burning eyes, the goat's horns.

And she sees for a moment her vast sin, for which she will be punished, because she has pressed it into the labyrinth, this once-pure gift of the Virgin: her hunger for her name to rebound in fame through time.

The horse hurtles forward over the road and it is as though a door opens inside her, and out of it pours a real prayer, from the deep and quiet parts of her, in her own language, in simplicity.

Thank you, she prays. Forgive me.

Then the horse rounds a bend, and with a great welling of relief she discovers the hills purple above the tree line. She knows where she is again. She slows the pace. She laughs at her fear, which is still sending shocks of cold into her hands and feet.

She believes she has been released from her sins.

What she does not see behind her is the disturbance her nuns have left in the forest, the families of squirrels, of dormice, of voles, of badgers, of stoats who have been chased in confusion from their homes, the trees felled that held green woodpeckers, the pine martens, the mistle thrushes and the long-tailed tits, the woodcocks and capercaillies chased from their nests, the willow warbler vanished in panic from these lands for the time being; it will take a half century to lure these tiny birds back. She sees only the human stamp upon the place. She considers it good.

At last, by sunset, she has come into the fields where the abbey's pale stone shines upon its hill, the moon cupped cold in the blue above.

Her daughters at this hour will be silent at their evening meal, gesturing for salt, carrots, milk, pottage. She imagines their heads in their dark veils bowed over their food. She imagines the cold sun slanting in through the window and lighting up the faces of a row, pearls on a string.

She reins in her horse, who dances with impatience to be so close to the stables and grain and water and rest, and bows her head and says a prayer of gratitude to the Virgin.

This trip, this day, she knows, is the completion of the first great vision given to her; the Amen to the prayer.

The wind blows and ruffles the dead grasses, throws the brown hands of oak leaves to the ground to tumble. The fields are cropped close to the soil like a nun's scalp. There is white in the air, it is too warm for the snow to stick, but the flakes dance and rise with the movement of the wind. It is Marie's happiness worn by the outward world.

She has not moved the abbey an inch, yet still she has built a great sea of road between the serpent and her daughters.

Of her own mind and hands she has shifted the world. She has made something new.

This feeling is the thrill of creation. It jolts through her, dangerous and alive.

Marie feels it growing in her. She gorges on it. And despite her vow, her prayer in her fleeing terror from the devil, she understands that she is hungry for more.

3.

For decades, Marie had seen revolt simmering behind certain smiles in the town, in the slowness with which certain hands released payment or gifts to the abbey. Now, just as the queen had warned, the resentment is coming to a boil. A shepherdess napping in a bosk overhears a conversation and tells her sister, a servant at the abbey; an unloved stepmother of three fiery youths, who consider her less than furniture, listens to her stepchildren making plans and writes a note to Marie; a maid in a tavern in town is so terrified by the open drunken boasting about the bloody lesson that the nuns will be taught that she takes up her skirts in her hands and runs to Ruth, who sends a messenger that very hour to Marie.

When Marie traces the plot she sees there are perhaps two dozen conspirators. Well, it's not so bad, there could be more. To make friends, one must make enemies, but her fearsome reputation still throws shadows in the larger world. She thinks of Eleanor, young, leading armies. She feels her own warrior blood stirring. She calls her council: Asta yelps with excitement, Ruth weeps, Wulfhild is pale and grim and thorough, but the surprise is Tilde, who has the clearest ideas and whose face flushes in readiness. Marie has not yet seen this side of her little dormouse. She is glad for it.

Ruth protests late in the talks that no, they cannot, all this is a sin. They are nuns. They cannot kill. They should be thinking of turning the other cheek, no?

Well, Marie says, certainly they must defend themselves. Remember the frailty of the ancient nuns when the Danes' boats came berserking up the rivers, what happened to the poor pious creatures, the sackings, the breaking of relics, the rapes.

With this last word, a cold wind enters the room.

And it is true, Marie continues, perhaps holy women cannot kill, but they can entrap. They can use greed and lust and sloth to drive evil sinners to their own ends.

And, Marie says, what is paramount is that they cannot let the labyrinth be breached. They cannot allow the story to be told in the larger world that it is even slightly pregnable, or else the whole point of all that work and ingenuity, that great flood of money, loses its—well, Marie says after a pause, it loses its effectiveness.

Wulfhild laughs and says that their dear abbess almost said magic.

If one looks hard at even the most powerful magic, one can see nimble human hands, Marie says. Alas, the nuns will not have time to train or to learn how to fight or to use swords. And female bodies are not as strong in muscle; though it must be said there is no greater strength than the power in their wombs to create life. No, no. If they are to keep the abbey safe, they must fight with the least possible fighting.

The bleary council splits to their separate duties in the morning. The field nuns are pulled off the reaping, the novices are set to work, the villeinesses sing because they do love a brawl. Asta's team of two dozen dig and build and bend the earth itself at the points they agree are the weakest, where with a few scythes and axes to clear the saplings and brush, almost anyone could push from outer roads to inner ones.

Marie sets her network in the area to high sensitivity. The schoolgirls she taught, now ladies, read letters not meant for them, for they are loyal to Marie; the renters who have blossomed under her law get their neighbors drunk and pump them; the servants she has placed in good houses listen at doors. Only days later, four separate spies send word that the attackers are massing that night. The villeinesses and servants mill about, excitedly; she is using all of them. There is a wild giddiness in the lavatorium as the forty selected nuns wash and bind their habits up to keep them from tripping. The rest will be left at the abbey to pray and try to sleep.

How foolish, Marie thinks, cinching the thick leather belt her mother wore to the second crusade. How foolish to choose to attack the abbey on a night with a full moon, windless, full of frogsong; how lazy the rebels have been to have chosen not a more interesting weak point or even two, but instead they found only the one nearest the town. Her women are always underestimated. She straps on her sword, holds her heavy abbess's staff in her left hand. She rides out.

On the top of the abbey hill, Marie has set the nuns who can ride astride on the ten horses. Six had been huntresses in their earlier lives and can use the bows and arrows they hold; those who can ride but can't shoot hold scythes. This would be the last line of defense, should it be needed. Marie looks behind her as she rides into the forest and sees that with the moon shining at their backs, the nuns on horses are huge and black in silhouette and their shadows paint the hill in terrifying shapes.

Now into the labyrinth, through the cleverly hidden paths on the inner roads to the sixth road out, which will be the point of engagement. Her women are there already, silent, waiting.

Marie comes to a stop. She prays. There comes into her a certainty that she will die tonight. There is a swift vision of an arrow in her throat, a choking for air, the red flooding her sight. She casts the vision away behind her, into the waiting forest. Her hands shake.

Beyond, on the external road Marie can hear the voices of the interlopers, possibly drunk, they are chopping, laughing, their horses snort. Her women wait in silence. A swift slender nun runs back to Marie and signs that the group is twenty-one strong, and there are only four horses. Some arrows, some armor, mostly clubs and swords. Then the shadow nun dissolves again back to her watch. Wulfhild frowns at Marie when the one road out has been broached and there are sounds of closing in through the woods.

Between the roads, Asta and her crew have made a kind of gulley with digging and rockwork, hiding their traces with shrubbery and moss, which to any rational mind would offer an easier way through to the next road than laborious cutting and thrashing. The gulley narrows to single file near the road, and bends sharply so that the bodies that have passed before are hidden.

Closer. She waits. Closer.

Marie at last brings down her hand and the villeinesses crouched in wait in the ditch are able to silently swarm, noose, gag, and bind four before a fifth can understand and shout a warning.

Now seventeen remain, Marie thinks grimly.

There is a crashing backward, a conferring in voices that are low but still carry through the silence. Marie has an urge to laugh. The shadow nun returns and signs that the horses are coming first this time.

Marie nods and looks up at the canopy, where she can't see in the darkness but knows the young nuns are ready with their nets weighted by stones. She raises her fist. The nuns obey and wait, wait, wait, until Marie can see the moonshine in the eyes of the first horse, then she opens her fist and the novices throw their nets, and they fall with a gorgeous slowness downward, and strike true, the stones tangle in two of the horses' feet and the horses fall and the villeinesses swarm again out of the shadows like the shades of the dead.

Now out of the trees, a silver rain of stones, the melon sound of stones striking skulls, and bodies tumble and now there is shouting and wild confusion and Marie gives another hand signal and up the road to the north the novices pour into an opening where there are no trees so that the girls shine bluish in the moonlight, their hair loosed and gleaming and all so beautiful, so distant in the bright opening along the dark road.

While down the road to the south, lit in equal brightness with torches, stand the stoutest of the field nuns and the servants, grim with their hoes and threshing flails.

And onto the road pour the remaining interlopers, twelve or so Marie thinks, and in their uproar, half of the group turn toward the novices, and they begin to run, outstripped by the two horses, and the other half turn toward the field nuns, and there is a great whooping of voices as the feet thud upon the road.

Up and down the road, the novices and field nuns stand firm and ready; oh my beauties, Marie thinks, oh my brave good women.

Then the catgut strung in the shadows in the novices' direction catches the riders and one horse screams, a cut spilling blood across its neck, and the horse stands on its hind legs, and falls backward, crushing three runners; and the other horse gallops on, but the next catgut does what it is meant to, and with awful slowness a head lazily bounces off toward the novices, spraying them with blood, and the girls scream and the horse slows and stops when it feels the corpse riding it tilt and slide off.

Down the road, the field nuns are shouting, roaring, the angry tide of six or seven is coming close, and Marie braces for the clash; but the layer of sticks hidden under a powder of dust at last cracks and gives, and bodies go tumbling down into the deep pit set with spikes and now there is a bloody screaming of the wounded. The villeinesses take down the rest, hollering.

There is a pause, a moment of peace before the cries of pain rise and fill the air.

Finished? Marie thinks. Already? The battle itself took not even thirty breaths. Her sword and staff gleam, disappointed. She has not touched or been touched. There has been no arrow to the throat. Her end will be elsewhere, at another time.

Wulfhild says, oh, well, that went well.

Rather satisfactory, Marie says drily.

But a woman is screaming in English, and Marie sends the mare trotting forward, and in the light of a pitch torch she sees one of her villeinesses, the mother of six under the age of ten, writhing in the road, the massy gleam of entrails slipping wet through her fingers and into the dust. Nest swears in Welsh, then puts a leather bit in the villeiness's mouth and shoves handfuls of guts back inside her until her eyes roll white and her mouth hangs open, the woman either having fainted or being fully dead.

Marie says to take her to the abbess quarters, take her children there also, and Nest sends Marie a look full of anger and betrayal, and turns her back on her old friend.

The villeinesses put the two dead and nineteen injured interlopers in the road. The horses, which have now become abbey horses, are loaded with three bodies each, and the rest are carried arm and foot back to the inner field, where there are wagons waiting, and hoods of doubled cloth to keep the secret passage back to town a mystery. Nest flits between the bodies, putting on salve and bandages and setting bones. For even though these sinners rose up against a community of holy virgins, in all things, nuns must be merciful.

Marie has to rescue the severed head from the novices, who are taking turns playing Judith with it.

The abbess says a prayer over her nuns and servants and villeinesses, her voice loud in the dark field. I am proud of you, my daughters, she says after Amen. Their moonlit faces are happy. Together, laughing and talking, they go up the hill to the hot wine and honeycakes awaiting them.

Marie on her horse leads the wagons into the sleeping town. In the cathedral she has the stone pulled away from the ossuary, and the injured put in the musty chilly room among the dead. Before she leaves, she pulls off the hoods one by one and stares grimly down; she wants her face to be the thing remembered when they think upon their death-beds of their most grievous sins. She herself pushes the stone back, and can hear the groaning and the attempts to shout through the gags. They don't know that someone will come along before morning and they will be freed. She hopes the pain and darkness and fear of being interred alive these hours will be a second lesson.

And the dead she delivers herself to the estates she knows well, where she has sat with the women drinking ale and eating nut tarts. Now the same women silently reach up for the bodies. They cannot look at Marie. They are not angry. They are sorrowful, guilty. Marie wants to shout at them. But she does not. She rides off.

She knows before she arrives by the keening coming from the huts near the brambles that the hurt villeiness has died. Perhaps one dead to save many is not a sacrifice too rich. But still this needless death will weigh upon Marie's soul, she knows herself that there is no solace for a mother taken too young. Well, she will do her best. The older girls will be oblates, the tiny ones taken by the dead woman's sister. And through the countryside, the women will tell stories, woman to woman, servant to servant and lady to lady, and the stories will spread north and south upon this island, and the stories will alchemize into legends, and the legends will serve as cautionary tales, and her nuns will be made doubly safe through story most powerful.

4.

It is after the Octave of Epiphany.

The world is coated in a fine shining ice a thumb thick. The wind blows in knives of cold.

Marie is alone in the cloister, walking fast to think. She has trod a black streak into the ice there.

All her nuns are bent to their tasks. In the infirmary, Nest and the novice she is training in the healing arts, Beatrix, grind herbs with a pestle in the infirmary's enormous mortar. Since Beatrix has come to the abbey just after All Saints' Day, something wordless has been unfurling between her and Nest. They think it is invisible to the others, but Marie can trace it with her eye. Marie feels both warmed and suffocated by the understanding that soon, for intimate affection, the infirmatrix will put a stop to the expression of built-up humors in the other nuns, and that Elgiva and Marie and the anonymous others who quietly go to her will return to their bodily suffering for the lack. Marie has already begun to grieve.

The scriptrix nuns are bent over their manuscripts, the spinster nuns are spinning their yarn, the webster nuns weave the cloth, the baxter nuns are baking the good fine bread of evening meal. And all around there is industry: the kiln has baked bowls and cups all day, broken things are being mended, habits are being sewn, stockings knitted, gossip and stories drawing the nuns closer. Out in the distant wide world the Angevin banner flaps over the dust and heat of the Holy Lands, but Marie can sense that before the year is over, the third crusade will come to an awful, disastrous end.

Eleanor's favorite eaglet is now full-fledged, bloody-beaked, savage in talon and temper.

Stories are told of Eleanor that make Marie burn with rage. They say she is promiscuous, insatiable, she sleeps with whole families from the doddering ancient down to the least servant. There are murmurs that Eleanor can only get her satisfaction from a horse.

When Marie writes of these things, warningly, Eleanor laughs them off.

The queen moves so freely out in the world, now, she goes where she wishes with arrogance; she doesn't understand that she too carries around her own abbey with her, an invisible wall-less abbey of people known to her, very large indeed, but still enclosed by the body and the mind. All souls are limited in the circles of their own understanding. At least Marie understands the limits imposed upon her; Eleanor in her great arrogance believes herself to be free.

Marie looks up and out to find the shearing wind stopped; the trees in their shining shells of ice have all leaned toward her, the dim light of winter is pulsing in the air.

In her fingers starts the holy fire that whips and sears through her limbs and gathers in her throat and splits her sight.

And fast descends upon her the third vision that Mary, Blessed Mother, has thought meet to bestow upon her faithful daughter.

Clear over the stone walls of the potager garden she sees the naked tops of the apples and pears and apricots; and with the vision Marie's sight rises into the air to the height of the dortoir and she can see the whole of the orchard, the ladder left forgotten leaned against one tree, the piles of pruned branches awaiting the spring bonfire upon the long flat rise beyond it. And in that place the ground begins to thrash and shake and roll as though it is not earth and stone and a thickness of sod but rather the water of the seas, and the tremors reach even Marie's feet fixed to the stones of the cloister. Now a black hole falls into the ground, of a perfect roundness and incredible depth, and out of the hole a strange and coppercolored sapling grows upward. The tree grows swiftly, it unfurls ever larger until its roots have reached to the boundaries of the edge of the flat land, and the trunk pushes up toward the heavens and from it grow swift fat limbs and boughs of silver and gold and copper and bronze, and the shade of the tree covers the walls of the abbey and stretches down the hill toward the pond, the sheepfold, the pigsty. Out of the final fingerlike branches that are the fatness of Marie's own arm, there push vast leaves like sails and each leaf has a white cross pressed into its central vein. Now the tree begins to flower, huge white bells greater than the greatness of tall women, and when they open they hold in themselves naked girls held pendant by the ankle with hair flowing down to the ground like stamens. And some of the flowers stay and others blow, the petals rain to the ground, and the girls curl their bodies back up in fruiting, and around them there grow ovules fat and round and the red of carbuncles and the green of emeralds. When they have grown so great they bend the branches and at last break them with a snap, they fall to the ground, where they split upon falling, and reveal faceless women who struggle in the snowy pulp to sit up.

Then all the frantic growth pauses, the fruit women and the girls in the flowers turn their heads to the east, listening; they leap back into the tree, the tree retracts its boughs and flowers and fruit and leaves, it sinks into the hole it grew out of, and with a low rumble, the hole closes, the world stirs itself again, the wind blows in its chill sharpness, the noise of the movements of nuns inside has returned. Novices are practicing in the choir. And with the voices, the last of the vision has gone.

Marie runs lightly up to her small, glowing abbess chambers where Prioress Tilde is writing renter letters and Subprioress Goda is making the family trees of the abbey beasts to avoid incestuous breeding. They speak to Marie but their voices are dissolved into the air. She takes up the book, and even as she is writing she understands.

The Virgin is directing Marie to begin the construction of the abbess house, though the labyrinth has impoverished them again. Within the vision, she has been shown the way forward. With the greater quarters for the abbess and the larger brighter room for the business of the abbey, there will also be apartments for corrodians, rich ladies come to live their later lives in a more holy way, giving to the abbey a handsome dowry. There will be a large light room for more manuscript copying, for this is the most precious income stream, begun by Marie herself when a young prioress; though in the beginning it was whispered about only among the women of the world, for many consider it unmeet that women be scriptrices, especially of holy works; they doubt their ability to write at all. In the new building there will be a better schoolroom and separate dortoir for the little-girl oblates and it will be large enough to take in the noble girls of the countryside for a goodly sum to teach them to read and to write and to know languages; to seed the countryside with literate girls and women, who through their lives will remain loyal to the abbey. Marie can beg for enough to begin construction and can finish the building on the strength of the silver from the corrodians and schoolgirls alone.

Perhaps, she dares herself to think, if it is beautiful enough and comfortable enough, it will tempt Eleanor to retire here and not at Fontevraud.

Then, oh hush, Marie, she tells herself angrily, you would die of such close proximity to that blaze.

Prioress Tilde is looking at Marie with a face knotted in anxiety. She tells Goda in a low voice that she fears it is another project.

To this, Goda says oh but she misses the forest work, such as she was allowed to do, for often she was left back with the defective nuns, which she thought was deeply unfair, but of course nobody could take care of the chickens and pigs and goats and kine and geese and so on like Goda, who, everyone says, has a bit of a genius for animals. Such a pity the nuns are now eating the freemartins one by one. Goda herself holds their great heads in her hands and whispers a prayer in their ears when she touches their throats with a knife. She believes it is a solace to them that it is the hand of no less than a subprioress that takes them from the worldly plane. She juts her chin proudly.

Marie finishes her writing. Words seep back to her mouth. She says, low, to fetch Asta and Wulfhild.

Goda looks at Marie and her medlarfruit face is changed by what she sees there. She, a great respecter of mystics, leaps up and runs off. Tilde clutches her hands to her chest and says to herself a despairing dear, oh dear, oh dear, oh dear.

Later that morning, after the meeting, Marie goes into the warming-room off the kitchens where her nuns are sitting upon their stools with the books they are meditating over in low murmurings. Among the nuns at the abbey only Marie practices silent reading, and every time she does, it makes Goda shiver and protest shrilly at her witchy magic. Yet if there is no inner reading, how can there be any inner life? Marie thinks and imagines the cold blowing desert that must stretch inside her subprioress.

The obedientiaries sit closest to the fire in order of rank, and the child oblates shiver, farthest from the fire, nearest the cold. Marie closes the door behind her and does not move to take her seat in the place of greatest heat, but feels the chill wood against her back. When she will step forward, the nuns will hear of the new plans, she will share what she has been given; for now she savors the vision inside her. The light through the windows is watery and angled so that it shines through the breath of the nuns as they read aloud, the rising breath silvering, the streams of word made visible, word transformed to ghost as it rises from these mouths. The noise in the room is a low sweet hum without pause, the voices mixing so beautifully that the impression is not a tapestry of individual threads but a solid sheet like pounded gold. With their heads bent over their books like this, their words palely shining, she understands that the abbey is a beehive, all her good bees working together in humility and devotion. This life is beautiful. This life with her nuns is full of grace. Marie sends a prayer to the Virgin in gratitude. And then she steps forward; they are stirred from their reading to look up at her; they see the remaining radiance of this day's strange woman-tree vision shining out of her; and it casts itself like the light of a fire upon their raised faces. She begins to speak of her newest vision.

Prioress Tilde weeps in her bed in the night, she thinks she will die if she has to do all the work of the abbey again, but she is silent so she does not disturb her sisters.

Asta dreams of pointed arches, buttresses like the ones she saw going up as a child, the bold and shocking building on the island in Paris with its vast windows, its magnificent height, the facade, they said, that would be thick with statuary in brilliant paint, in her mind she balances and hefts and figures weight against weight and is too thrilled with the planning to sleep for a week. She once ran away from her nurse when she was nine or ten and spent an enormously satisfying afternoon wandering the building site of the cathedral, asking questions of the workers and gaping, and getting herself filthy with stonedust and dirt, until she was caught by the ear and hauled out to the street by her hysterical nurse, who had been pinched and fondled and had fallen down in the rotten pig muck of the street while she looked for her charge.

Wulfhild stays up most of the night doing abbey accounts. She is exhausted, she rides out six days a week to the abbey's landholdings and cajoles and thunders all day on Marie's behalf, she is the abbess's voice within the town and beyond so that when Marie does at last visit in person, she appears to all eyes as greater than mere woman, she appears as myth; some say saint, some say witch, the rumors mix and muddle; descendant of the fairy Mélusine with the rages and the power to bend nature to her will, kin to royalty, too-huge woman on her warhorse, crusader, abbess of unwomanly face and body and knowledge and force of will.

Wulfhild swallows her prudence and sighs, because she has no power against the visions of the Virgin. The nuns can do a great deal of the work—scaffolding and small mortaring and thatching and carving and plastering and painting—but there is not one who can teach stonecutting. They are almost self-sufficient, but in this they do not have the skill.

The next day, she comes up to the abbess chambers. She leans toward the abbess, and they touch foreheads for a moment. Marie kisses Wulfhild affectionately on the bridge of the nose. Then Wulfhild tells Marie her plans, that she will take a team of a dozen of the best worker villeinesses and build a stoneworker encampment over the hill beyond the sheep meadows. There must be no contamination between sexes; she does not want to afford the nuns or servants or villeinesses any sight that might offend their chastity or tempt the weak. She will work out a system of blindfolds to bring the strangers in, give extra pay for swifter better work. She will take it on herself to keep trouble from imposing itself on Marie's tender nuns.

Practical Wulfie, Marie says aloud. Inside, she says: heart of my heart.

Done in a year, perhaps, Asta believes, having her own glorious visions.

Marie writes and her letters are so clever and charming; to the queen, she sketches the plans, thinking she is seeding the idea to come here in retirement; but in return the queen sends no money, she is hoarding it all behind her own seal at a loyal cathedral, but she does send Marie a warning. When Marie opens the letter, the queen has written only that Marie must be careful, that she risks making her abbey so fine that Eleanor will tax her double next year.

Marie's breath catches in her sternum at the thought.

The field nuns and villeinesses make a better road to the quarry; easy work over the treeless meadows, with the great pressing wheel to use. Stoneworking strangers are brought in blindfolded during the night and installed in comfortable huts.

The snowdrops press up through the frozen mud.

The work of the new abbess house begins.

Early March, after midday meal. Distant noises of stone falling on stone, the groaning of the ropes upon the wooden cranes.

Full and sluggish with bread and parsnip pottage, Marie is dreaming of lintels. She thinks of lintels carved with wheat and apples; lintels of grapes and sheep; lintels of honeycomb with bees like spangles through them.

She slides a knife beneath a letter's seal; she sits forward and reads silently and a smile flicks over her face.

Goda peers at her. She asks sourly if there is something of interest. Goda smells of placenta and sheep shit; she has been helping three ewes lamb all morning and has forgotten to take off her smock.

Marie considers telling her to bathe; rejects saying so because Goda would not take it kindly. She says that in three days, they'll be getting new sister named Avice. Urgent, it seems. Excellent family. A dowry promised so generous she'd be a fool to refuse.

Goda asks hopefully if the girl has a vocation, or better if she's a mystic? She is envious of another abbey a day's ride away that has a famous anchorite to whom pilgrims flock to wring holy advice through the window. It is hard to compete with a holy loner.

Marie says no, that their newest sister it seems has been too liberal in her affections. Multiple times. Caught in flagrante. Whipped. Remains unrepentant. The abbey it seems is the family's last hope.

Tilde snorts, then blushes and pretends to keep working.

Marie looks at the prioress and her mouth twitches as she says that in fact, the girl is Tilde's own kinswoman. Third cousin? One Avice de Chair.

A musical name, Marie thinks, old Abbess Emme would have liked it, would have sung it under her breath over and over.

Tilde groans, dropping her pen. She says that it is impossible, Avice is wild, she cannot be contained. She once held her own sister's face into a pile of manure until the girl thought to feign death.

Drily, Marie says that, well, she can only attempt to contain her, but it is god who will or won't choose the ultimate containment.

Tilde says that mere mortals upon the earth cannot possibly succeed in keeping Avice in a nunnery.

Marie says that they have no choice but to try. And that is the end of that.

She has business in the town on the day of Avice's arrival; and since the rain is spilling down at a windblown angle, when she is finished with her duties, she goes to pray in the cathedral. The prioress and sub-prioress have spent all morning praying; now they wait out of the wind, in the doorway, for the novice to appear on the street.

Later, after their return to the abbey, Tilde will shut the abbess's door and tell her with strain in her voice how roughly Avice spoke to her retinue of kinfolk, how she stormed and raged and would not allow them to dismount, but screamed abuse until they paled and turned away without meeting with the prioress or subprioress. And when the girl could only see their backs, she shrieked at her family that now they've slaughtered their sacrificial lamb, they can go to the devil. Then Avice saw Tilde frowning at her, and called her a terrible vulgar name and demanded the abbess. But when they told her the abbess was in the cathedral and she saw Goda running to fetch Marie, Avice ran faster, passed the older subprioress, and ran up the steps of the cathedral first.

And this is what Marie sees when she hears the great heavy wooden door slam open and looks behind her: in the narthex there is a girl with pale hair plastered to her cheeks and neck and chest, in a dress far too thin and pale for propriety, soaked through so that every sharpness of her body is clearly drawn, and it is as though she is walking naked in the day. Not beautiful, no; features bunched and a forehead so shiny and large it is an egg, a gleaming Romanesque window.

But with the sight of her, something in Marie, something awful, rises up. It says softly, hissing, that this girl might be worth burning the abbey to the ground.

Now the girl is running toward Marie, her eyes hot, and the wetness on her pale sharp face is anything but tears.

Marie watches her coming fast, and she keeps herself in stillness. She keeps her hands folded in prayer. When Avice reaches her, the girl spits that they can go to the abbey, her prisoner is here.

Marie looks up at the girl for a long while as she pants, impatient, and Goda appears in the door, then withdraws. Marie says Amen and crosses herself. Then, as slowly as she can manage, she rises and straightens her back to make herself as large as possible and now towering over the girl she steps close to enfold her in her arms. The girl struggles but Marie holds her easily. She speaks quietly and at length down into the girl's head; and as she speaks she watches the goose bumps grow upon Avice's cheeks, the droplets fade into the hair, the last wetness drying on her ears and neck.

Through her skin, she feels the girl's rapid heartbeat slow. The cold of her flesh warms under Marie's warmth.

There is a great stirring in Marie that she understands dimly to be a warning; now the inexplicable attraction to this girl, her wild flame, the small angles of her face, the fairness of her hair, comes clear, Marie sees Eleanor as she had been once, young, stretched naked in a tent in Outremer, her lined eye opening, the only bright thing on the whole dark earth.

At last the girl, in something like a trance, murmurs, and Marie lets her go. The girl's face is pale, her eyes nearly closed. She follows Marie down the nave to the door. Before going into the rain, Marie unpins her great thick woolen cloak, and puts it around the girl, and the fabric swamps Avice so completely that when she comes back into the wet day, she finally appears as what she is: a mere frightened and furious girl of eighteen.

After she kneels to pray in the night beside her bed, Marie discovers on her pillow a handful of purple rosemary flowers stolen in the day from the herb garden. An apology. She listens through the antechamber into the nuns' dortoir, and can hear only the sounds of her sisters sleeping, the whistling in the noses and the sighing and the stuttering of farts; there was colewort in the stew in the evening. Not a body stirs but her.

Marie presses the flowers to her face and crushes them so her hands smell of rosemary. Then, disturbed by the heavy sweet scent, she throws the flowers out the shutters and washes her hands in the basin until the perfume is gone.

Rafter by rafter the abbess house grows.

The heat descends, dry lightning branches the night sky.

The Feast of Saint Mary Magdalene, Apostola Apostolorum, who wears Marie's face in the chapel, as painted by mad Sister Gytha. All around her above and to the sides have been painted scenes from Revelation. The whore of Babylon rides upon a dragon painted after Gytha caught a feral dog and shaved its face to see the way the bones of the skull were built beneath; the beast's body is a roasted eel, its wings are extended chicken wings. Worse, the whore of Babylon has two faces, and both faces are the queen's. Gytha had glimpsed her once, when she was painting a mural in the great room of the hostelry and the queen rode through town with her retinue on her way to somewhere else. When Marie first saw that the whore of Babylon wore the queen's face not once but twice, she had the urge to cover the image with her body so nobody else would see it, then she wanted to grab up Gytha's brush and paint quick swipes of black over it. At last, she laughed until she cried, and let the painting stand.

Marie prays desperately in the night when she wakens and feels something shifting loose inside her, she prays for help from the Virgin to make herself unmuddled with carnal heat again.

And she feels dread, darkness rising somewhere, either inside her or outside her, she doesn't know which is worse.

In the thickest hottest part of summer, Marie devises great work to keep her nuns busy. They make enough soap to sell at the fairs, they expand the garden, they weave and make shoes and windows and furniture for the new building, they pluck the fruit and make preserves and they hardly have time to breathe. Nest and Beatrix, faces close, laughing at something on the ground in the herb garden, the touch of Beatrix's hand to Nest's waist. Marie feels sorry for herself and goes to the chapel and kneels on the stone to pray.

A sound of running feet; and Avice for a moment peers into the chapel, her headcloths slipping back and showing the white dazzle of her hair.

It is a sign, Marie understands, and she directs good Sister Torqueri, magistra of novices, that the seven novices will have no free time whatsoever. Torqueri makes them sing and write on wax and learn Latin and Greek and the French of France until they mutiny or cry.

When she can escape her work, Marie prowls the worksite and in the lavatorium before Vespers she scrubs stone dust from under her fingernails.

The complaints of her obedientiaries pour over her: the apples are bad for the cider this year; the bees have fled two hives; the coneys have gotten into the medicinal herb garden and have chewed up the rue, hellebore, savory, sage, pennyroyal, tansy; the smallest sheep has been carried away by an enormous eagle. All omens, mostly bad, but of what, exactly, Marie wonders. Perhaps the noise of building disturbed the bees.

Perhaps the queen bee knew of something evil coming and took her bees to a safer place. But an abbess is no true queen, she cannot take her hive and fly away.

Sometimes in the night, when the wind has stilled itself, low and indistinct voices can be heard singing from the encampment, and this is a sound that makes the hairs on the back of her neck stand, for such voices are unnatural in this place that for decades has known only women, and far more terrifying than the very worst thunder that has ever rolled up from the ocean and echoed between the hills, doubling, tripling, loud as the wrath of god.

Marie spends her time with her obedientiaries only; she is keeping herself separate.

Still, she looks up to find Avice's eyes burning on her at mealtimes. Quick smile, flushed cheeks, eyes cut back to the wooden spoon in her hand.

Avice in an apple tree with two of the oblates, one from a family of alemakers, one from fine candlemakers, laughing down at poor Magistra Torqueri until Marie comes silently and stands frowning up at them and then they climb down, shamefaced.

Avice and the novices escaping to the pond to swim in their linen underthings, because it is hot. For this they each receive three lashes and kneel on unhulled barley between Terce and Sext in the misericord.

Marie did not see them swimming but the image is so bright in her imagination that she is haunted with it.

Avice and the six other novices running through the golden wheat grasses with their hands extended to feel the pelt of the field soft on their palms. The girls gather in a knot and swiftly disappear beneath the surface of the field. Marie feels their giddy happiness in herself until Torqueri runs out with a furiously red face toward them; and then the girls stand, most bowing their heads, repentant. But Avice has her headcloths off, and her hair is out in the open, waving in the hot breeze. And the hair that Marie had first seen transparent and clinging to her pink skull in its wetness is now nearly blinding white in the full sun, and the other novices have braided thin plaits into it that they have studded with small blue flowers like jewels. The wind licks the fine ends of it at the girl's hips. Danger, something whispers in her. This girl could crush everything in her hand. Marie is shaken. She has to turn away.

Cellatrix Mamille complains; an entire milk-dried heifer must be bought every single week to feed all the hungry mouths at the stonecutter camp.

Her face, without its nose, so like a skull already, vanishes. It is replaced, for a moment, with an actual talking skull. Memento mori.

Marie blinks and the woman is fleshed alive again. One more month, Marie promises her, and then the nuns will be by themselves again. But her voice quavers with the foreboding given her by her brief vision.

The night is unbearably hot. In the solitude of her cell, Marie dares to take off her headcloth, her clogs and stockings and scapular, and she sleeps in her shift, in what hot air stirs through the window. And that night she wakens from inside her early dream, in which she sees, confused, a shadow detach itself from the deeper darkness against the wall, watches it come near. A pale face gleams beside her own, a mouth is pressed lightly upon her mouth. And as Marie believes herself asleep she presses back, and upward against the dream mouth. Upon her hand, which she thinks is a sleeping hand, she feels hair so soft it is indefinable like water, silk on her face, on her chest, and now there is a weight upon her body, a hipbone shifting against her, sharp; she moves in her pleasure against it. She smiles against the mouth and it smiles back and Marie slowly comes to understanding as the pleasure builds within her that she is not asleep, that she is awake, that there is a woman of flesh in her room lying and moving upon her. But, in horror, she cannot stop herself. She gasps and releases and when her heart calms and she dares to open her eyes, the other has vanished. Marie is alone in her cell, the sweat dampening her bared legs, her back. It is uncomfortable, it feels like shame.

She descends to the chapel to lie in a cross upon the cool stone but her body needs movement and she stands and prays as she walks in the cloister. She goes barefoot to make no noise. Out in the fields the glowworms cling to their stalks, flickering, a million blinking eyes looking upon her. Too soon, far too soon, the bell for Matins rings. She looks up into the window on the night stairs and there is a shuttering of the blackness there, the flickering bodies of her nuns descending, one after the other, toward prayer.

For seven days Marie sleeps with her body on the ground in her chamber, pressed to the door so that it cannot open, and on the eighth day, she returns to her bed.

She awakens to the same pleasure, the same lightboned moving succubus, the silence and swiftness in the dark, the rush and wild and pulsing release. Better than wine. As shameful as drunkenness.

After Prime, Tilde's eyes rest on Marie's face as the women go over the accounting books. She asks hesitantly if the abbess finds herself well, and when Marie asks why, the prioress says only that she has a darkness to her these days.

Marie says that she is well, and isn't sure if she's lying.

She returns to her sleep on the floor, blocking the door; penance, avoidance. September passes.

Marie hears someone calling urgently for her, Abbess Abbess Mother please wait, as she's crossing the orchard toward the unroofed building, but she knows that voice and dreads it; though she is over fifty years old and of a great bulk and height, she hurries faster with her long legs until she is running. The voice pleads, there is hysteria in it, there is anguish, but Marie loses the voice in the trees.

On the rise, the crane of wood and boulder and rope shifts, groaning, as, in the bleary sunlight, the last of the great stones is laid. A roar goes up; Marie lets it die and thinks soon, soon, the abbey will be at peace again.

That night, Marie sends a tun of good Bordeaux wine to the encampment for celebration but also for the confusion of drunkenness, and walks out in the dark before dawn to say a blessing; there is vomit on the ground, a miasma of sour exhaled breath. Then the blindfolds, the carts trundling off, the delivery of the abbey back solely to women before the sun's first finger touches the earth. Oh blessedness, relief.

It is the bathing day, and the children go first, then the novices.

The tubs are drained and refilled for the obedientiaries. Before Marie is called to her own fresh tub, Magistra Torqueri stands in the abbess's door. She wears a rictus that the abbess has only ever seen on the faces of the newly dead. Torqueri says quick and low that there is a terrible problem.

Marie says softly to Goda to shut the door. But already, somehow, she knows what the calamity will be. It was the vision of Eleanor when she first held wet, shaking Avice in the cathedral that had put the certainty in her.

Marie calls the obedientiaries to the abbess chambers.

Prioress, subprioress, cantrix, sacrista, cellatrix, subcellatrix, almoness, kitchener, subkitchener, abbess's kitchener, infirmatrix, subinfirmatrix, hostellerix, scrutatrix, mistress of scribes, magistra. There is no room in the old chambers, so they stand along the walls.

Though the bailiffess is not an obedientiary, Marie calls Wulfhild; she is at least as loyal and wise as any learned highborn lady nun.

Then, when all are assembled and are waiting quietly in the solemn room, Marie calls Avice.

The girl enters with a face full of contempt. Her chin juts. Torqueri was correct; the girl's belly is enlarged. Someone sighs, someone begins to cry. She places the girl in a chair at the center of the circle.

The abbess's sitting room is close with all the bodies of the nuns and soon it warms even without a fire.

Marie says calmly that their dear novice is with child. Some nuns gasp, others count on their fingers and see that Avice could not have arrived pregnant. Marie cannot look at the girl; at the sharp bones of her cheeks, at her delicate mouth, at the betrayed expression she is surely turning on Marie, who, if she had wished, could have saved her.

Avice says angrily that no she is not pregnant, but all the nuns' eyes are upon her swollen belly, and she covers it with her arms.

Goda says it is a scandal, it is infamy, she is a wicked girl, the devil has taken her.

Ruth cries out in sorrow. She asks how did it happen; Goda looks at her with her pinched face, and opens her mouth to explain the process, and Ruth blushes and says hurriedly, she understands how it happened, but how did it happen here?

Marie waits for the girl to speak, and the moments slide past and grow heavy with expectation and the girl at last bows her head and says, low, that, yes, she is with child, but you see it is a miracle, the angel came and spoke the Word in her ear.

Cellatrix Mamille's face falls in astonishment, she crosses herself.

Marie cannot believe that she has to tell her grown nuns that this too is a lie. Avice laughs nastily, and Goda sighs and Prioress Tilde looks as though she would leap up in a moment and scratch her kinswoman on the cheek.

Magistra Torqueri begins to weep and, striking herself, says mea culpa, mea culpa. She says she is sorry but she sleeps heavily. She has often noted grass on the novices' clogs at Lauds, but thought she was imagining things. She has failed in her protection of these poor girls.

There is a moment of shocked silence, and then Marie asks if she meant to say girls, plural, or just this one girl.

Avice says nastily that oh it wasn't just her. She looks mean, cornered. Marie thinks of a badger caught by a dog against a wall, claws out.

Another silence as this sinks in.

Nest and Beatrix share a look and Marie tells them that they will examine the others as soon as the council has decided upon this poor miserable creature. The question is now what to do with Avice.

Whip her before the other novices. Bread and water in the misericord until she has her wretched bastard. Goda is the one to say this, though she would not suffer such treatment of even the least of her animals.

Wulfhild, the only mother of the flesh in the room, says angrily no, that the girl needs healthy food and milk to keep herself strong for the babe.

Prioress Tilde says that they must return her to her family in scandal and shame. She is red, and it has taken her great courage to say this, because Avice's family is her own.

A chorus of voices shout No, for if the larger church were to sniff this out, the consequences for the abbey would be so severe, they would be punished by the church superiors, all their carefully built power and wealth would be stripped from them, it is not unlikely Marie would be cast out of her position, and how could they survive then?

Kind Sister Ruth suggests they keep Avice in the misericord with ample food and milk until she gives birth.

Oh but the misericord is so cold and drafty. Nest says she can keep her in the infirmary with the dotard nuns. It would be a punishment but not a painful one. Nest's shoulders are up to her ears with anxiety. Beatrix squeezes Nest's hand and she consciously lowers them.

Goda blazes with this, saying that the girl needs a severe punishment as a lesson for the others, that they should whip her on the bared back, that each nun of the abbey should whip her once. It is not too much to ask that Avice bleed for her sin.

But Cantrix Scholastica with her crystalline voice says that there will be no whipping a pregnant girl. It is simply cruel. The girl would give birth to a stillborn or a calf or a goblin.

Goda says fine, they can lash her hands and knees with an ash switch. It hurts just as much. And rules exist for a reason.

They decide on twenty lashes on the hands and knees, and for the girl to be kept captive in the infirmary until the birth. If the baby survives and is female, it will be an oblate given to the abbey. If it is not female, they will give it to a villeiness to raise until the age of sending it away. If Avice survives, her family will be told that she has run away, in language so careful it will not be a lie, and she will be sent to be a servant in one of the houses of the loyal donors, they cannot give such a sinner to another house of holy women, and if they were to excommunicate and banish her to the world without a penny, it would be condemning the girl to a brutal short life of begging or, more likely, whoring.

With this word, a shiver goes around the room.

Nest says in her gentle Welsh voice that it shouldn't be long. The poor child has kept her condition wondrously hidden. It is a marvel they only discovered it now. Nest's face is no less lovely, pale and stricken as it is.

And Avice, in whom anger visibly built as they spoke about her, now bursts into a horrid screeching so shrill it is without words.

Nest says that is enough: the council has been merciful and if Avice does not silence herself they can change their minds. And she escorts the girl out and down to the misericord to await her lashes.

Soon from the window the obedientiaries watch all the white veils of the novices being driven like lambs into the infirmary. Beatrix comes out, and with a face loosed into relief, she shakes her head: none else have been so terribly compromised as Avice. And when the novices come out again, pale and wobbly, Marie calls the nuns of the abbey into the refectory and gives a short speech.

Then out into the chill November evening, and Avice is brought into the cloister with no headdress, in her thin shift, and is made to kneel. In the last light the fabric of her shift is translucent and her sin is obvious to all. Her pale hair grows filthy at the ends where it touches the dirt.

The scrutatrix gives the rod to Marie, as it is her duty and right as abbess to punish. But Marie's resolve fails, she cannot hit this girl who is a mirror of the queen when young, that rebellious blaze, she looks about her for another to do what she cannot. It cannot be Tilde or Goda for their fury, not Ruth for her sweetness, not Nest for her goodness and mercy. And so she hands the rod to Torqueri, hoping that the magistra's failure to protect and guide the girl will stay her hand from great severity.

Marie forces herself to watch when it does not.

The walls of the vast new abbess house are being plastered and painted. The roof is on. Teams of nuns work on the inside.

The house sits grandly on its rise, elegant and strong, with the new arches, great windows, high ceilings. The rooms are full of light. It is where the oblates and novices live and it is filled with their young voices raised in laughter and singing, it is where the scribes have located their desks, where the new corrodians have their apartments, rich ladies come to live out their retirements at this abbey, and such ladies are used to finery, little dogs, birds, music, secular servants. With all these women together, the abbess house is a place rich in spirit. At last, a building worthy of its abbess, Marie thinks as she looks from the cloister up at the smooth stone building. A building worthy of Marie.

A holy rite: the edifice is asperged with lustral waters.

There comes to Marie's dreams a dark foreboding: she is galloping on her horse down the hill toward the forest, and clouds and thick darkness are all around her, and lightning lights up the world and the earth trembles and behind her she hears the sound of the abbey's stones cracking and falling in thunderous disaster, the screams of her nuns as the roof falls upon them, but Marie cannot look behind her for now she feels pressed against her back a shivering warmth, thin arms tight around her. She awakens lonely.

Avice goes early into labor. Screams rise from the infirmary. In the garden, the nuns gathering the last of the coleworts and the turnips and parsnips from the cold dirt draw into a circle, kneeling and folding their hands to pray. Choughs sneer, perched in the medlars.

Even beyond the orchard in her chambers on the ground floor of the new not-yet-finished abbess house, which smells of plaster and paint, Marie can hear the screams. At last, she rises and Prioress Tilde tries to talk to her but the abbess cannot hear a word. She goes out into the cold and walks first into the sheepfold but the sheep stare back at her with their dumb, astonished faces and say nothing. Then she turns along the stream and begins to run and comes swiftly through the cloister and into the infirmary.

It is close and hot in there and smells of rust and sweat. Avice is panting with her hair slick and eyes feral in the dark of the bed. Goda is feeling between the girl's legs. She is saying that the human body appears to be more delicate and far more poorly constructed for birthing than the bodies of the beasts she administers to; that she has often wondered why human females so frequently die in childbirth, but now she has discovered it's because their hips are so small and the babies' heads so disproportionately large, and why god would make the human beast so unfit for birthing is a mystery. Or perhaps not, she sighs, I will multiply thy sorrows, and thy conceptions: in sorrow shalt thou bring forth children.

Nest says in a tight voice that Goda should probably keep such observations to herself.

Beatrix snaps when she sees Marie, huge in the doorway, that they do not need the abbess's help, but Nest tells her to hush, that it is good and right to have their Mother's light with them.

And Marie carries a stool to Avice's side, and lets the girl squeeze the blood from her hands. She prays to the Virgin, fervently.

Terce, Sext, None pass. It seems a moment in the huge suffering of the girl.

Avice's breath is shallow and her face deathly pale. It is a relief when she loses her conscious mind and her screams silence all at once into sleep. She bleeds so heavily they spread a cloth impregnated in oil beneath her to save the third pair of sheets.

And in her sleep, Avice's body convulses and the head of the child emerges, purple and horrible between the thin thighs. Another convulsion and it is out, slick and dead. A little girl.

There is no one to shrive Avice, Marie looks toward the door with anguish but no one comes, and she is indignant, this is a terrible sin of withholding mercy; and in her panic, her weariness, Marie does not think to do it herself.

In the new gush of blood from between Avice's legs, Goda is painted red up to the shoulders, red on her forehead, and Nest and Beatrix press cloths to the flood but in moments the cloth too grows red. Avice's hand in Marie's gives a twitch. Her breath sighs out of her body and does not enter into it again.

In the evening, Marie calls the obedientiaries to her. A ring of faces grave in the candlelight.

She says that they will decide together what to do, and she does not lend her voice to the disputation but at last calls for a vote.

Goda stands after the vote is taken and says righteously, her face flushed with her victory, that they take this action only as a warning to the other nuns who may be swayed in weakness and commit the sin of lust. Oh, Marie thinks, she will never again make the mistake she had with the stoneworkers, she will never again allow anyone but a woman to set foot here. But Goda needs to punish someone, and so the grave is dug in the unconsecrated ground outside the churchyard, under the farthest arms of the malevolent yew. In the morning, without ceremony, Avice is lowered into it in her shroud facedown with her babe at her feet, so that in the Revelation her bones will never be able to rise to the hands of the Angels of the Resurrection. Such pitilessness, Marie thinks, for a sin of the flesh.

Avice, dead. A garden shut up, a spring stopped, a fountain sealed.

They had agreed upon no rite of committal, but Marie cannot stand the silence and she steps forward and says the short prayer aloud, her voice too quiet and swift for the first words to be heard but growing louder with . . . whence pain and sorrow and sighing have fled away, where the light of thy countenance visiteth them and always shineth upon them. Amen.

The other nuns' faces flare into anger with her for praying over the disgraced sister, and for their abbess, a woman after all, saying such words. When the dirt falls on Avice and her little babe and obscures the shroud, they turn their backs and go away to their work. And a great coolness rises between the more vengeful nuns and their abbess, which no intensity of light from Marie could ever burn off.

Eleanor writes. Her letter is an act of extreme delicacy; she writes about the abbey's fruiting fields, how she had heard that blight was found in one. Beware, the queen says. Should word of your blight get out, your best fields may be seized by the greater church.

Marie replies that it is true, but that the field burned down and did not infect any other, and that she relies on Eleanor to praise the abbey's harvest and not spread news of the blight of one tiny, inconsequential field. It is in the nature of some fields to be blighted. Eleanor, with her wise understanding of agriculture, knows this better than anyone.

The queen's fields, Eleanor writes snippily, have never been blighted, despite what Marie may have heard. The richer the harvest, the more false news is spread by those looking to drive down the price at market.

Of course, Marie writes back, this was not Marie's implication, but rather a gesture of solidarity, Eleanor's fields are rich, as are Marie's, they both know how it goes, they both work against the old carrion-birds Gossip and Rumor. Perhaps someday Eleanor can visit the abbey and they can ride Marie's fields together. Marie has made the most beautiful apartments, with a tapestry of a unicorn woven by her own nuns, and is reserving it for her regent. Perhaps the queen would like it so much she would come here when she wants to retire from the world.

Marie feels as though she is unable to breathe during the month she waits for the reply.

Oh, dear Marie, Eleanor writes at last. Even now, when both are so old, Marie is up to her tricks. Can she not remember? They are not the kind of friends who love each other best when they are in the same place, riding the same fields. They, the queen writes, must be friends at a distance.

5.

Letters fly to Marie's hands, letters like flocks of starlings, wild commotion, stripping the grain.

In the letters of her spies and friends, Marie sees evil settling on the world, an evil overcoming the goodness in the hearts of even the holy.

The brightest and best of Eleanor's children, that royal warlike lion, is seized and held against the laws of Christendom. Crusaders, by holy dictate, should be exempt from kidnapping. If there is no ransom set and accepted, the Angevin empire is finished, shriveled and feeble and easily overcome. But the ransom asked for is staggering, four times the English royal income.

Eleanor's letters are now signed Eleanor, by the wrath of God, Queen of Angleterre.

The queen sends Marie her demands. When Marie reads the sum required of the abbey, she gives a single wild laugh, and Tilde looks up and wonders if something in the flesh behind Marie's face has caught fire.

In a tight voice, Marie reads the letter to the prioress and subprioress. Goda blanches and says doubtfully that she supposes they can sell the new lambs, what a shame, they were so remarkably fine this year, Goda herself went three nights without sleep to yank them from their mothers and thought at the very least she'd get in payment a bite of lamb with mint but alas, as always, her efforts will go unrepaid. And Tilde thinks and says that perhaps they can sell their farthest estate, for it is great enough to bring in that sort of coin. Marie will not even look at the prioress when she tells her not to be stupid, land is power and no one is less powerful than a woman religious, and it would be madness to sell what power they have slowly and painfully built in the world. Her words are so unaccustomedly savage that they strike Tilde like a box to the ear.

Marie thinks, then stands, and finds the staff of the abbess Emme and her predecessors, which is fine silver filigree and horn and could be bought by a patron to bestow upon another, lesser, abbey. Tilde watches it go with sorrow in her face. Marie sees her expression and is struck to the center of her that there lives in the prioress expectation of her own eventual elevation to abbess. Tilde's arms of course are too feeble to lift Marie's heavy staff. From the chapel, Marie takes a recent gift from a family of crusaders, the elbow of Saint Anne in its little reliquary chasse shaped like a cathedral and glistening with chalcedony and onyx. Goda cries when she sees it will be leaving the abbey; she has spent long hours on her knees praying to the saint, the mother of the greatest mother of all. And this still will not be enough to pay the abbey's part of the ransom, so Marie goes heavily to the trunk she brought with her so long ago, which is empty save for a very ancient Byzantine ring of jacinthe, which had belonged to her grandmother. It can only fit on the final joint of Marie's pinkie. When she wears it she sees golden birds diving through fields, a muscular river, and a springy gray-haired woman with no face but a soft voice, her grandmother. A thickness fills her throat that she cannot swallow away.

She will go to London alone; she will be faster this way, because she needs no rest, and can fight easiest and best if beset in ambush, and she can trust no one to get the prices she can. Her horse groans softly when she mounts her before dawn, and Marie scolds the mare in a stern voice that she must be very tough because Marie will be asking quite a lot of her. The horse reconsiders and stomps at the ground. They move off at as quick a pace as the horse can sustain, a shattering pace for any frame less solid than the abbess's.

Marie is famous in the countryside, the huge abbess with all that inherited magic in her, all that radiance given by the Virgin, and when the workers in the fields see her riding by they kneel and bow their heads in fear.

But she feels her power waning the farther from the abbey she goes. Her letters do influence the most powerful in the Christian world; yet to these commonfolk beyond the abbey lands who do not expect to see the famous warlike abbess, she is only an enormous nun on an enormous horse, stern and strange and old.

Before twilight, Marie arrives in London, into smoking stinking fog that permeates the skin and lungs, the babel of voices shouting and arguing disembodied out of the close tight alleys, the milch goats leaping suddenly at the horse off dungheaps in shadow, the barges on the river tangled dark and high with osier wattle. A headache of constant overlapping bells. Straight to the shop, where she wears her majesty so hugely it presses all other bodies in the room to the wall. She uses silence; she is bestowing a tremendous favor by choosing this place to sell her precious goods. She negotiates like swordplay and leaves the shop having bled everyone in it with fine stinging swipes that show how precisely she can cut, how lucky they are that she restrained her hand. She does not show on her face how pleased she is, for she is very pleased, there will be some coin left over for future emergencies or perhaps the projects to fortify the abbey that have begun to brew in her. She sweeps into the dark and walks the horse straight to the exchequer house and pounds upon the door with her fist and enters pushing past the yawning servant girl, waking the household in their nightshirts and confusion. She is immobile, gracious, wearing her Angevin face, she frightens all. She will not leave until the book of levies is taken down and Marie's entry—more generous than the queen had demanded—is entered into it.

Now it is late. She feels light, divested of money and duty. Above the river, a sick wan moon hangs its yellow head. She is supposed to sleep at a patron's house where there will be rest for the horse and good food and a fine bed for Marie, but she cannot take this seething city into her anymore, being in the proximity of so many of the far worser sex is filling her with aggression and fret. She thinks she is taking evil into her very body with each breath. So she whispers to the sainted horse who holds her eyes closed against Marie's chest in weariness for a time; then opens them and is ready also to go. Back through the black stink of streets, and at last into the open fields at the edges of town, where the free rebellious wind strips the devils of the city off Marie's exposed skin.

A voice in her says that she will never again see the city that burns so darkly at her back. She is glad of the release of it. Aging is a constant loss; all the things considered essential in youth prove with time that they are not. Skins are shed, and left at the roadside for the new young to pick up and carry on.

There is a fine polish of near-morning upon the abbey, so distant on its hill, when she comes out of the final tunnel of the labyrinth's secret hidden underpass. She feels nearly weak in her relief; the mare's skin shivers delicately with fatigue and she walks with her head low.

How glad her nuns are to see her safe again, they are radiant. Their faces, needing no shell in this place that Marie has made safe for them, are so vulnerable Marie feels she could wound them by looking too closely. She asks gently for a bath to be made ready and in the meantime food to be brought out to the garden, where she wants to let the good sun burn through her skin, to warm the chill of travel out of her bones.

Already at so early an hour, the old and feeble nuns are sitting on the bench beside the great spilling coins of echinacea in their full yellow. Wevua who snarls at Marie like a dog and kicks at her with a mangled foot, Amphelisa whose stroke has sadly recurred, Burgundofara who has begun falling everywhere, her bones so brittle she has broken her hip, and Edith who no longer sleeps but ranges like a ghost in the night, calling for her mother. Brainless Duvelina claps when she sees Marie and stands and then something shifts in the nun's face, a slyness slips across it. There is the sound of a small rain upon the damp dirt and Duvelina lifts her hem and she is pissing hard on the ground where a puddle grows around her clogs. And because Marie is so tired she can do nothing else, the abbess laughs along with her laughing mindless nun as all the other aged or decrepit nuns leap or shuffle or creep in horror from the growing puddle beneath them.

It is in deep summer when the rains come, and a miasma breathes up out of the too-damp soil and ditches and puddles near the pond, and the bad air sickens half the nuns. Marie herself is made so ill by it she is moved to the infirmary, where she lies for some nights among the dying and sometimes the dead.

She hears the rain stop, she hears in her long fever as all the moisture wicks out of the earth and leaves it dry, dry for days, for a full hot week.

Her fever rises so hot it makes her convulse, and she wakes to a small shiny blue demon squeezing the tip of her tongue with fire pincers. When she comes back into her own mind, Nest and Beatrix will tell her that she bit off the very tip of it in her fit.

The infirmatrix nuns speak softly in a corner but the awakened part of Marie's mind hears them and understands that they are worried she will die. And with their words, Death steps into the infirmary and stands a bad vigil in the corner of the room.

In the night she wakes again to see Death bent over Sister Sybilla, who had been old even when Marie came to the abbey, a hard worker and uncomplaining but perhaps because she had been born without a voice to speak, and Death is pressing its lips to her mouth and breathing the life out of the old nun.

Then Death, still thirsty, splits into two and its second head bends over young Sister Gwladus, a Welsh princess stripped of her insurrectionary family and given to the abbey as punishment, for if she had not been given to god, she would have bred great strong intelligent Welsh nobles who would also inevitably chafe against the English crown.

And both nuns rise out of their bodies through their gaping mouths to join the black shadow of Death sucking upon them.

Later, when she can sit up and grip a quill without her ague knocking it from her hand, Marie will write of what she sees, in her Book of Visions.

Though death did not take me, she writes, I was like a feather carried on a current of water. I was carried behind my good dead sisters as they ascended toward heaven.

We rose and we rose through the firmament and toward the warmth of the hand of God. And it felt upon my body as a hawk feels when the tiny invisible gusts of wind carry the bird upon its current with no flapping of wings, only a glorious floating.

At last, I found myself in a plane of clouds as they left me behind in their ascent; and in that vast plane above the clouds, for as far as one could see, there were seven towers, some closer to where I lay upon the wind, and some nearly invisible to the eye.

The closest tower was near at hand and I came toward the window and looked inside. And I saw my very own long-dead sisters, some in vestments of gold and some in shining light and some like the abbess

Emme with great crowns of thorns about their heads and they were all praying aloud together.

And below my feet fathoms deep upon the ground, I saw the four beasts of the apocalypse: the lion, the she-ox, the eagle, and the woman-faced one; all with wings and all their bodies covered in blinking staring eyes. And the beasts were slavering and howling and climbing the sides of the tower with a slithering like that of a newt under a rock; and they came so swiftly upward they stopped my blood in ice.

As the beasts came, my sisters' prayers within the tower became louder and more fervent and soon they broke into divine song. And in singing they came closest to prayer, for singing is the very heart of the heart of prayer, and their voices mixed and melded. And under their voices there was a great earthquaking, and my sisters' singing caused the stones of the tower to shake and tremble.

And the beasts gnashed their teeth and they howled, but their grasp faltered on the tower and they began to slip down the long slick stones. And one by one they fell, the lion, the she-ox, the woman-faced one, the eagle, and despite their wings they were dashed to the earth.

As I watched, my sisters fell back to silent prayer. But there was no safety from the beasts, for springing up out of the bloodied corpses of the beasts, smaller versions of the same were birthed, and began their terrible wailing upon the ground, and they grew even as they climbed.

When I woke, my fever was gone.

Darkness had fallen upon the abbey and all the sounds of sleep were deep in the infirmary, and I held as a gift this vision given to me in my illness.

For it had been revealed to me in my vision that this abbey of saintly women is one of the seven great pillars of humankind built to keep the raging gnashing violent bearded beasts of the Revelation far from the tender lambs of God; and though the six others are yet unknown to me, this seventh is equal to all.

It is the brightness of my sisters and their faith and their piety that are as a great fire keeping off the terror of the night.

And I, in whose protection this abbey grows, must stand firm as the tower of stone and strong and tall, to hold them safe and high above the ground.

It was in the morning of the night my fever broke that I heard the news that, over the rim of the labyrinth, out in the city, in the night, the wind blew at a small fire from a tipped lantern in a barn and it soon became huge. It spread so swiftly through the houses of the western part of the sleeping town that there was hardly time for shouting or for running for water from the river and wells. And though it spared the pilgrims sleeping in the hostelry and our sisters caring for them there, it devoured the other side of the road, eating the wood-and-thatch shops leaning against the cathedral, and, far worse, the entirety of the church's house behind it, with all the holy inhabitants sleeping within, all those poor pious souls devoted to the church. Sister Ruth the hostellerix and almoness woke to look across the road, and she saw there a charred plain with smoke rising from it, and in the ashes they found the bones of twenty dead in their beds.

And with this disastrous conflagration, there was not a soul left alive in the town whom our superiors have qualified to come through the secret passages and say Mass at the abbey, none to give my daughters the solace of confession. Save, of course, for me.

And with this news, I at last understood the vision and the order that had been given to me within my fever.

I will take upon my own shoulders the abbey's sacerdotal duties.

For I, as abbess, am the mother of this place, the parent of my daughters with all the authority of a parent given by god. And like Mary Magdalene, Apostola Apostolorum, who preached and converted many, I have been called to preside over Mass and confession for my daughters.

Two weeks pass before Marie can rise to her feet and stand and move about. She has lost some of her muscular weight and her habit flaps upon her. There is still a charred-meat smell when the wind blows from the northeast, an ash that collects on the wind-side of the apple trunks.

On the cheery faces of her nuns, darkness has fallen. They have lost guidance, they have not been shriven or taken communion since the conflagration, they are mourning the lost souls who, though they were aged and fumbling, had tried with goodwill to give the nuns their comfort. Though every day Tilde annoys Marie about it, the abbess doesn't write to summon anyone new.

At last when she is well enough, Marie calls the holiest of her sisters to her, cantrix Scholastica, whose goodness is a pure and humble light, and confesses to her, as the nuns often confess their sins to one another according to the Rule. The cantrix smiles, holds Marie's hand, but she does not dare give penance. And when they are done, it is time for Mass. Marie goes to the little room off the chapel and puts on the vestments. The fabric smells of other bodies, onions and skin, bodies that lived so recently and that died in the fire.

She has the missal, she has prepared the bread and the wine with her own hands. Marie watches the faces of her nuns as she comes out into the chapel wearing the vestments and all her largest authority, and on some faces there is shock and on others a sort of wild hilarity barely suppressed. On the faces of the oldest nuns, the ones who had known the abbey before Marie came and took it in hand, there is dismay and anger and fear. Goda looks so appalled, Marie would not be surprised if she left her earthly form here and now.

Wevua stands, her stick clattering to the ground. She bellows as though she is wounded, a deep loud animal sound. In the uproar and confusion, Ruth stands and leads the old nun away, throwing Marie such an acidic look that Marie knows this is the end of their ancient friendship, she has lost Ruth, perhaps she is gone for good. Marie bows her head to let the pain send its wave through her, then looks again upon her many other daughters, commanding them with her sternest face to stay where they are. They, so used to obedience, remain. Confusion roils in their faces, for which is the lesser sin, to leave Mass, or to hear it presided over by a woman? Time flows on and decides for them. The introit begins. Marie smiles; she offers the cup, the bread, she blesses. The recessional. Her nuns stand and silently go to their work.

There is a great deal of angry muttering all day.

Goda is waiting in the abbess's chambers, shaking so hard her clogs chatter on the ground. She says that it is wicked, wicked, it is against the church, against god, for a woman to preside over Mass.

Marie wills herself to love poor Goda. It is not her fault she was born like this.

She says to Goda to please tell her if she believes that women are the lesser sex?

Goda snaps that of course women are the frailer and the more sinful sex. Corrupted and weak.

Marie asks what her proof is, knowing that Goda knows little scripture by heart.

Goda gapes. She has large holes in her gums where she has lost teeth. At last she says, uncertainly, well, isn't this the lesson of Eve?

Marie tells the subprioress to look at her and sits beside her and takes her hand. There is something in Goda that craves touch; perhaps this is why she attends to the animals. She resists, but then she lets Marie unclench her fingers and slowly begins to lean her body against the abbess's. Marie says, Goda, do you not think the Virgin Mary, though born a mere woman, is the most precious jewel of any human born to a womb? Is our Virgin not the most perfect vessel, chosen so that in her own womb the Word can become human?

Goda says angrily of course. But but but.

And Marie says, wait a moment, let's look closer at hand, and she knows Goda and she have had their fights in the past, but please be truthful, daughter: has Goda ever met a person Marie's own equal, of any sex? And she waits as a terrible struggle takes place in Goda, and the subprioress at last says a very quiet no. She is sour and shortsighted and in thrall to hierarchy and authority, but she is pure in her way, she cannot lie, the poor old nun.

Marie says to remember that the abbey will have a visit from the diocesan just after the Feast of the Nativity of the Virgin. If a woman saying Mass is still so wrong to Goda, she can unburden herself with her private interview then.

And poor Goda is so wrenched inside, she stands and informs Marie that she has to vomit, and runs out, leaving Prioress Tilde and Marie alone.

Tilde evades Marie's gaze. Her cheeks are purple with rage. Marie looks steadily at her.

Tilde says at last that all of this is a terrible blasphemy, a terrible sin. If Marie persists, there must be an election for abbess.

Oh please, if there were an election today, Marie says, she herself would easily win.

Tilde says no that is not true.

Marie says only that Tilde should count, and watches as Tilde sorts through the nuns in her mind. At last Tilde sighs. She breaks her pen into pieces in her hands.

Tilde says that if there is a faction against Marie, she will—but Marie is glad to see that her prioress is too savvy to finish the sentence.

They hear Goda still retching on the ground outside. Tilde says that now that she is at last standing against Marie, she has long wondered why Marie keeps Goda as subprioress. Goda is an excellent mistress of the animals but her Latin is bad and she is no help in the business of the abbey. And she is simply wretched with the personal issues among the sisters. She has no understanding of feelings.

Marie says that it is true. In those matters, it is best to hear Goda's advice and do the opposite.

But Tilde says that this is not an answer, and why does Marie not put in her place the sacrista or cantrix or mistress of scribes, all of whom are intelligent and subtle thinkers? They could be at least useful.

Marie says that, along with her duties with the animals, Goda's position as obedientiary keeps her busy. High constant emotion mixed with rigidity is dangerous. A busy Goda poses no threat.

Marie understands what Tilde is doing; the prioress wants to install a new subprioress as payment for her silence. Marie bets on Tilde backing off first. Between the two, Marie has the far greater force of spirit. After a long span, the women frowning at each other across the room, Tilde's eyes flood and she hurries out.

But Marie's answer gnaws at her, and later in the afternoon she has to stop in her reading to consider what she said to the prioress. It is true that she keeps Goda near because the woman's venom disperses swiftly with small easy obsequies to her dignity. She looks at Goda, her fingers mottled with ink as she murmuringly accounts for the ewes and the heifers and the hens on the back of an old letter, and then crosses out, bites her pen, scratches marks again and counts these aloud, scribbles again, and licks her lips that blacken with the tip of her tongue, which itself is black with ink. Perhaps it is her very barnyard reek and her vulgarity and her loud voice and her proud stomping upon the emotions of her sisters that draws the subprioress to Marie. Perhaps in loving a sister as difficult as Goda, Marie can be more sure of her own goodness.

And so it is as a sinner herself that Marie goes to hear her daughters' confession.

The dam has burst. Most of the old nuns are furious but they do not dare to speak their fury aloud, they mutter it, they pray, they turn their shoulders to Marie.

At first only the novices and oblates and young nuns flock for confession, but after some weeks, Marie is kept sitting for hours. She listens; she hears them.

Suscipe sancta Trinitas has oblationes quas tibi ego peccatrix offero, they say, and often they cry.

And over the years that she will be the abbey's confessor, what she hears will make her burn hotter in anger for them. Not the small things, the praying with no true prayer in their hearts, the lying, the stealing a bit of roasted chicken off the spit, the small lusts and the special friendships—how many feel themselves polluted with an impious kiss!—these she sends off with small penance and there is a smile in her voice and they are reassured. But she sorrows for her daughters in their lives before, the secret invisible weights they have dragged behind them into the abbey. For the way this novice of eighteen is weeping because she is no virgin, because she had discovered a shadowy form sitting upon her bed each night from the day she turned eight years old, and how she has swallowed the sin, which is not hers, and taken it into herself as her own. The secret pregnancies; the sudden fists in the gut, the kicks in the head. The faces held to the dirt and the skirt pulled up. One young hesitant voice tells of the knife waiting in her hand for she knew a particular evil was planning to come stealing into the girl's room on the day of her sister's wedding, and it did happen like this, and she was ready, and then suddenly there was blood everywhere and bellowing and the death of internal rot afterward and her sister a widow almost as soon as she was a bride. Such murder heavy on the poor nun's heart. And she could not bring herself to tell any confessor until Marie, there could be no ears for this but a woman's. Until Marie became confessor, if she died, she would have burned in hell for this.

This is Sister Philomena, a quiet, pious nun whose nose often flakes with dead skin and whose eye is never bright with anything.

Marie says that, as the dear child knows, it was defense. The true murderer was the one who chose to come through the childhood door with evil intent.

But in the silence, Marie hears that this answer would never be enough. Philomena needs to hurt, to find catharsis through bodily pain, she will not be satisfied without it. Marie hates corporeal punishment as penance, but sighs and tells the nun to go to the misericord and flagellate herself until blood rises to the skin of her back. Stay on her knees in the cold there until the bell for Vespers. Pray as she kneels, pray with her whole soul. When she rises, her pain and her prayer will have washed her sin from her, and she can leave this sin on the floor of the misericord and go with a heart unburdened into fuller prayer.

She watches Philomena all the next day. Something under the young woman's face has quickened, her shoulders are straighter, a warmth has seeped into her where her unhappiness has lain these years as cold and heavy as a stone.

As confessor Marie has come no closer to god. She feels disappointed by this. She had hoped to discover the root of her vocation here.

And yet as consolation, with each secret shared, she feels her nuns' love of their abbess growing, she feels it warm and bright as a sun circling her days. They cannot revolt now, she thinks. She knows too much of them.

And when their sadnesses weigh so heavily upon her that she cannot sleep, Marie likes to go down to the scriptorium and change the Latin of the missals and psalters into the feminine, for why not when it is meant to be heard and spoken only by women? She laughs to herself as she does it. Slashing women into the texts feels wicked. It is fun.

Eleanor writes Marie that she has heard from her little spy that Marie has assumed for herself another heretical role. Not simply confession but also Mass? She is putting her hand in the fire. Marie should not be surprised when her flesh burns.

As ever, mention of the spy nettles Marie. Appalling that Marie could not discover the traitor among her daughters. A chink in her armor that lets Eleanor's arrows in; and this one lands true, for she knows of her own risk. But also of her own rightness.

The queen drops her archness, and writes gravely that she cannot see how Marie will evade punishment for this, and from this place where the queen finds herself, she cannot protect Marie.

The letter comes from Fontevraud, where the queen is considering retiring for the rest of her life. Still, she exaggerates her feebleness. Everyone knows that she pulls the strings of her royal and papal puppets from there. So much war, so much money flowing out of Angleterre to defend Normandie, Anjou, Poitou, Aquitaine from uprisings. Siphoning from Angleterre to protect other distant lands cannot be sustained; the English will revolt, and Marie believes the revolt will be soon. And there remains the question of succession.

It is wearisome, the queen writes, but Marie feels behind her words an unwritten energy; the queen is a great and subtle political mind. It is not surprising to discover that all along, Eleanor had been the force behind the Angevins, this empire just now on the verge of falling.

Later in the letter, the queen writes: And it was quite a surprise to find the cellatrix here at Fontevraud was Marie's twin in body. She thought she was dreaming or was imagining things when she saw Marie's great massy bulk and heard her deep voice in the French abbey, and not in that queer little English abbey hiding behind its maze. At last, the queen was able to hunt down Marie's double and discover that, no, this tall muscular nun is none other than Marie's aunt Ursule. Oh, the queen says, she remembers Ursule young on the crusade. So beautiful in her face, with those golden boots, one of the greatest huntresses in her Ladies' Army, nearly everyone was in love with her, but back then she was even less tractable and civilized than Marie had been, great rustic gallowsbird, when she came to Eleanor's court! And how shocking what time does to the beautiful and young, now Ursule was as massive and broody and plain-faced as her niece. That two such unthinkable viragoes exist in the world! In any event, the queen writes, Ursule has prayed Eleanor to send her love to Marie.

And Marie clutches the letter and presses it to her, because she believed her aunt must have died long ago, she is at least sixty-five years old, and it is an unexpected gift of god to find she is not alone, that there is someone else on this earth alive who knew what it was to swim in the willow-hidden bend of the river, what it meant to gallop after a doe's tail springing through the forest, to love the great calm intelligence that had been Marie's mother.

The day of the diocesan's visitation arrives; there is pomp, solemnity, there will be a whole roasted sow with her roasted piglets at collation, the good meat smells are already seeping about the buildings. The blindfolding of her superiors was tricky, but Marie moved so smoothly and swiftly she did not give the opportunity for protest and so there was none.

The abbey has been made to shine everywhere for the visitation; atop its hill it is a thing made of abalone.

There is a play the novices and young nuns have put together: the Virtues and the Vices. In their innocence, the Virtues show the beautiful flesh of their plump arms and chests, and swim in masses of unshorn hair loosed from cloth and binding, and Marie knows, without looking at the faces of the visitors, that she will have to spin and spin over their shared meal to make this entertainment at last seem not only acceptable but holy.

Later, after eating, Marie watches from her chair in the refectory as the nuns, starting with the child oblates and progressing through the novices, the sisters of the fields, the sisters of the choir, the obedientiaries, singly go in for their interviews. One hundred eighty sisters in all. And when they exit the room, Marie can read the Omnia bene written on their faces. All is well. Not a single soul, not even those who still refuse confession, have told of their abbess's presiding over the Mass. Some are loyal. Some are frightened.

But then it is Goda's turn. The subprioress goes with her hard step toward the door. She slides a knotted look toward Marie and thrusts her chin out and the door closes behind her.

Marie thinks that now there is nothing to do but wait and see.

And when Goda comes out, embossed upon her face too is Omnia bene. She has faltered at the last minute. Her small eyes water, pink-rimmed, her shoulders slump.

Tilde rises and looks slightly in Marie's direction. No; the prioress poses no threat. A sad Omnia bene is on her face when she comes out.

Marie herself stands, goes in.

She says Omnia bene in her deep grave voice, and her heart is clear because it is not untrue, all at the abbey in her firm grasp is indeed very well.

6.

One day, Marie looks at her hands and sees them spotted, knobby. She is old, she thinks with surprise.

To keep the wolves that come down from the hills from stealing the lambs, Marie has her nuns build a wall of stone around the sheep's meadow, so tall it is unleapable. This takes a lazy autumn.

Elgiva, passing through the kitchen with a bushel of onions, comes too close to the fire and her habit goes up in flames and she is mostly consumed by it before the kitchener can put her out with slopwater. She lives until just before Sext, and it is Marie who closes the woman's blistered eyelids. She touches her red and swollen hands, but under the pressure of her fingers, the skin slides off as easily as the skin of a roasted beetroot.

The fields are scythed, her dark nuns spread out and swinging.

The winter is a sheet of parchment that the small feet of birds, of vixens, of hares, write upon.

Simple Sister Duvelina, out walking in the fresh tilled spring furrows, hears a tiny noise and kneels to discover a nest of baby rabbits, half of them mashed to pink pulp, the other half trembling, naked. For weeks afterward she moves her body with extreme care; until one day in the lavatorium, Cantrix Scholastica holds Duvelina back while the other nuns hurry away, and looks in her pocket to find in the darkness there four twitching noses, eight brilliant eyes. Such tenderness, Scholastica thinks. How warm it must be for these orphaned babes against Duvelina's body. And then it is as though she is held inside Duvelina's mind for a breath, a wordless place full of wonder, sharp beauty, a love so pervasive it can only be felt bodily, a breathing heat, a thrumming joy. Scholastica pretends she has seen nothing. And when in the night, not long after her discovery, there's a thump then four tiny bunnies sleeking down the night stairs, and Scholastica rises out of her bed to run after them, she can tell by the barely contained smiles of the nuns pretending to sleep that although others, perhaps all, knew Duvelina's secret, not a single one told.

A hot summer, and Asta has built, with the blacksmith and carpenter nuns, great strange spinning things that they then embed at each end of each row of vines. Even with small wind, these contraptions spin and catch the sun, which they throw dizzyingly back on the vines, and make a constant woman-voiced singing that the cantrix with her perfect pitch has modified so it sounds like voices raised in unending song, a song low and comforting even in the night. Some nights Marie sliding to sleep has the impression she is a child on her mother's lap, rocked into drowsiness. And these singing and light-flinging structures are meant to frighten the birds, and they work so well that the grape harvest is nearly too vast for the nuns to handle, and the carpenter nuns are busy making wooden tuns, and even Marie comes down to the wine-pressing vats where there is general hilarity when she takes off her clogs and sinks her feet in the luscious sweet ooze of burst grapes. The villeinesses sing, clapping their hands, and Marie removes her dignity and dances with the other nuns, young and old, slipping and laughing until she is weak in the stomach, and must be helped, covered in the guts of grapes, from the press.

She bathes and comes clean and happy into her chambers to find a letter from Eleanor. It is a strange letter, a frenzy beneath the calm surface of her words.

The rumors that the spies have sent along are correct: The queen's favorite child, at last ransomed and freed and rampaging in royal wrath against those who took advantage of the long absence, has been killed by accident, an arrow returned to the English at random and finding the royal spine. A great lion brought down by the lowliest worm. The queen's favorite daughter, Joanna, former Queen of Sicily, has died penniless and abandoned, a hasty nun, vows taken even as she died in childbirth. And shortly before Joanna went to the hand of the Holy Virgin, the queen's two eldest daughters died, whom she left behind when she fled the bed of France for the bed of Angleterre, but whom she cherished.

Of the ten children born of Eleanor's womb, there are only two remaining, and those two by far the least beloved. And the very worst of them, the eaglet with no scruples or strength or love of god, is the inheritor of the great English island. It will be disastrous.

The old queen will see her last living daughter, Eleanor, soon; she is nearly eighty but is being sent south to Castile, where her daughter reigns, to choose one of her own granddaughters to be the young queen of France. Redoubtable old Eleanor. Only she could pull this off.

But Marie sees so much sorrow in Eleanor's words that she shivers with them.

Eleanor is nearly broken; nearly but not quite yet.

How human the queen has become in her age; or perhaps only in intimacy to Marie. Once she was radiant as the face of the sun, impossible to see; now Marie can see through her face and into her. She had sought Eleanor that she might feel her way toward her and find her; but Eleanor is actually not far from Marie.

This is what Marie wanted. It strikes her as a loss.

Eleanor writes in a hastier hand at the end of the letter that she has dreamt that she will die on this journey, that she will be captured again and die of the grief of it, she begs holy Marie to pray for her queen, tell with her blessed insight if her dream will come true.

And Marie looks down the long corridor of her vision, and sees no death for the queen on her trip to Spain or back. She writes this to the queen, but sternly, telling her to buck up and do her duty. She makes a joke designed to infuriate Eleanor with its stupidity. Eleanor is named after her own mother, Aenor: alia Aenor, the queen whom no woman has ever equaled has, as a birth name, the Other Aenor. Marie calls the second Eleanor the Queen of Castile—Eleanor, Eleanor's daughter—Alia Alia Aenor in her letter. Better an irritated queen than a desperate and panicked one.

Finally, Marie says that she does see that the obvious granddaughter, the elder and more beautiful, is not the one to choose to bring back to France with her. Urraca is too fine; she would die of all that would be required of her. The girl who will birth generations of royals and saints will be the lesser sister, Blanche, who is not the obvious choice, but who has inherited the queen's spirit and wisdom.

She does not say that this is not a vision; this is what she has been told by a beloved friend, a girl she'd educated at the abbey and who married well in Castile, and who knows both royal girls intimately.

And perhaps Eleanor sees this in the girl herself, because it is in fact Blanche and not Urraca whom she brings northward with her, whom she sends on to Paris to become the queen of the French. Then, feeling weak, the old queen returns to the abbey of Fontevraud.

But too soon, Marie's aunt Ursule writes, saying that the queen has ordered her to do so. Only Ursule must write and not the abbess, for the queen is preparing to die, and her mind is beginning to slide in time. She believes in some moments that Ursule is Marie. Ursule had been unaware that there was such a great friendship between little Marie and Eleanor, how strange that it might be so. In fact, the queen told Ursule the other day in a strange voice that she loves her too, but only like a sister, and this is why she has to send her away. What hidden things there are in Marie, in Eleanor, in the relations between them. Ursule wishes Marie were here in her own place, her aunt says. She wishes they were sitting together at the pond before dawn, so young, waiting for the animals to creep forth in the night to drink.

And something is cutting off the air to Marie's lungs and she briefly considers getting up and running to the stables and riding off and hiring a barque to take her across the channel and riding swiftly down from Normandie to put herself at her queen's side and serve her as handmaiden unto the great woman's death.

But then she looks up and sees Tilde waiting with the manuscript commissions to approve of; Goda impatient with the news of a mysterious murrain in some of the cows, heat rising out of them, abscesses on their thick, damp gums.

And a bee with sidesaddles of pollen bats its body against the wall.

Marie sighs and passes a hand over her face. She sends her love home. She keeps her body in muddy Angleterre.

Marie waits for the queen's death. The waiting is terrible.

She comforts herself as much as she can by luxuriating in the space and whiteness of the plaster in the abbess house, her fireplace to warm her even on nights with a slight chill, the excellent kitchen and her own staff to feed her at her will, the sweet voices of the oblates and school-girls singing where she placed them, in the classrooms directly below her apartments. From her glass windows, frightfully expensive, she can look down upon the cloister and gardens and spy upon her little nuns.

But her appetite leaches from her. She stops eating the larger part of the meals her kitchener sends up, and her muscles begin a slow collapse against the bone. She is still tall but no longer massive, and her habits need hemming because they drag against the ground.

In these years of waiting, there comes to the abbey one Sprota, a novice of remarkable beauty: her lips are full in her round face, her fairness a gold seemingly touched with pink, both skin and hair, her eyes enormous and a blue so pale the irises hide themselves; they bring to Marie's mind yolks whipped into their whites. When Marie first meets her at the cathedral in town, she is moved by the girl's astonishing beauty and the delicacy with which her family weeping and lamenting bade her goodbye. A bolt of anxiety runs through her; all these years, she has been afraid of another Avice arriving, another shock to the foundations she has so patiently built at the abbey. But the way the girl receives the love of others with jutted chin and calm expectancy, lifting her pale hand and holding it in the air until they each in turn kiss it, something about the girl begins to grate upon Marie, and she soon sees this is no echo of Avice, but its own thing entirely, a different kind of threat. And when the girl's mother, a woman with an avid face and enormous bosoms, dares to come close and whisper in the abbess's ear that her daughter is blessed, holy, likely in time she will be proved a saint, she must above all be treated with the respect due one blessed by god's hand, she must be treasured as the very pearl of the abbey, something still darker moves within Marie's spirit.

Marie looks from the mother whom time has coarsened to her fresher likeness in the girl, and does not say that beauty is the great deceiver, that it is harder and not easier to become saintly when one has been born with it, that ordinary women become more holy only when the dew of youth has passed from their bodies and the small humiliations and stamps of age have pressed themselves through the skin and into the bone.

She says only, drily, that, yes, Sprota will be treated as well as all the novices are treated. All holy sisters at Marie's abbey are treasured as pearls.

Now that Sprota has taken the white novice veils, she speaks little, in a high breathy voice and only in phrases from the Bible. She wears a constant smile; sometimes Marie sees a hardness there, the very fleeting edge of mockery. Young nuns and schoolgirls and her fellow novices follow her, clinging. When Magistra Torqueri sets her to scrubbing the refectory floors with the other girls, or going early to the heifers to milk, the servants have been seen to take the work out of Sprota's soft hands. And when in punishment for this laxness, Torqueri gives the girl harder work, and she wears the yoke on her fragile shoulders to carry buckets of water to the lavatorium and trips and spills half the water—perhaps, Torqueri will say privately later, not so accidentally, perhaps meant to lighten her load—the other novices see her suffering and protest at how the lovely reed of a girl staggers under the weight. But Sprota raises her soft pale hand and says that, no, she delights in weaknesses, in insults, in hardships, in persecutions, in difficulties. For when she is weak, then she is strong.

Light shines into the novices' faces; and Marie, overhearing Sprota's words in passing, is struck by the fear that a cult is springing up at the abbey. Some of the old strength returns to her. Marie is always at her best when there is someone to fight.

And then one afternoon, Sister Pomme, still head gardener though so old she is bent outward from her hips, hears the girl quietly preaching to the bees. She speaks of the desert, of the smoke of aromatic spices and all the perfumes, she speaks of lilies among brambles. Of all things, she's preaching from that wicked old song, Pomme tells Marie, breathless from climbing the hill.

Oh but it is a very holy song, not wicked in the least, Marie says. It is my favorite of all holy texts, the Song of Songs.

Well, it makes my stomach feel strange, Pomme says. And that strangeness is the wickedness of my body. And I do not like it.

I feel this way also, but I very much like it, Marie does not say.

From her window Marie sees Sprota with her arms outstretched and palms open to the sunshine, the hives, the massing of Sprota's followers behind her, only five, but they are clutching each other's hands, their shoulders together, in adoration of the girl.

Marie comes down to the garden and stands on the other side of the wall from Sprota and listens. The girl is an excellent speaker, clear and calm, her message hardly revolutionary, to love the world in work the way the bees love the meadow flowers, but she uses her voice like a lute, drawing emotion out of the listener. When Sprota is finished she drops her palms, and seems to awaken from a trance, blinking and smiling shyly when her followers crowd her, pet her, saying oh dear the last she remembers she was in the bleachfields, she does not know how she arrived at the honeybees, what it is that she has done.

But Marie can see, as clear as her sight extends, that in time Sprota will have her own visions. And her visions will have as object her elevation, for surely the rumor of the beautiful girl with visions will spread, it will bring strangers to try to come to see the holy girl, and to keep them from finding a way into the abbey, the girl will have to be brought to town to speak, she will blaze before her listeners and her name will become louder in the world than the name of the abbey that holds her. When Sprota has gained enough power from her fame and the money brought in from the pilgrims, her visions will begin to war with Marie's visions. The abbess bends and touches the spiky purple heads of the rush leeks, considering what to do.

Patience, she tells herself. Strike in rage, and all that you have built in this place could collapse.

At supper a week later, Sprota will not eat. She sits still and silent.

When her fellow novices sign, asking if she is fasting, she signs back with her hands to say, No meat of four-legged beast. Against the Rule.

The next night, the spiced mutton in almond sauce goes untouched by the entire novice table, as well as by some of the younger nuns. Swan-neck, Marie's old friend, protuberant eyes closed in praying, is also abstaining.

This is certainly a blow. But Marie might have taken this new development in her own slow time if she hadn't looked out at her nuns' silent faces and seen the smiles suppressed, the insolent glances at her, Sprota gazing at her with eyes narrowed.

Marie gazes back, testing, but Sprota does not look away, and Marie sees that her will is a wall, high and strong, one that Marie's more liquid will must surround if she is to overcome it.

Worse, the next day when Marie goes out to the garden to tell the kitchener her plans for the week's meals, she watches the kitchener glance at Sprota, who is pretending to pick the spinach, and who gives a tiny nod. Only then does the kitchener rise and come to Marie and show her a plan entirely devoid of meat.

Pity that the oxtails will rot, Marie says, raising an eyebrow. The kitchener is pale with fear, her hands shake, but she whispers, Ah, but you see, Sprota has been preaching more adherence to the Rule, she finds it all so frightfully lax among these supposed holy women. She foresees a great punishment if we do not correct our ways.

Clever, Marie thinks. Any bad thing that will inevitably befall the abbey will be made Sprota's proof: the hay struck ablaze by lightning, a lamb swallowed down by a bog, a hole in the roof to let the rain in. And bad things happen constantly; it is the reality of such a vast estate.

Marie summons the servant to saddle her horse and rides to town to confer with Ruth, almoness and hostellerix. Ruth is wise, but also furious enough with Marie to speak plain. Marie finds her old friend sitting in the sun under the blazing red roses that have grown up over the hostelry's wall. Ruth's belly has usurped her lap. Her face is so full it is extruded from her wimple.

Ruth does not seem to see Marie. Marie stands closer, until she is nearly touching the other nun. She lowers her face to Ruth's. Ruth gazes calmly at nothing. At last, Ruth mutters to herself that something is blocking the sunlight from her cheeks, she came out to breathe the fresh air and watch the people passing on the streets, but a witch must have cursed her, or perhaps the black cloud of the devil is hanging invisibly before her and stopping the light.

Marie checks her smile and says that, no, she is no black cloud of the devil. Rather Ruth's mother and a friend who loves her dearly. How strange that Ruth was not even so childish when they were novices together and Ruthie made secret little poppets of thistledown and rags to cuddle in the night.

Ruth's eyes snap to Marie's face and she says, Oh, well, childish, if the abbess wants to speak of childishness, there is nothing more childish than dressing in priestly vestments and serving one's sisters false sacrament, as though Mass were merely a play and not utterly vital for the eternal soul. For shame. She is trembling with fury.

If Ruth felt so strongly, Marie says mildly, she should have written letters to the superiors—

But Ruth interrupts her, saying that, as Marie knows very well, she did write letters, many letters, and somehow every one came to Marie with seal intact. It seems even the most unlikely people are in Marie's pay. That even the ones placed directly in the intended hands went awry.

Then perhaps, Marie says, Ruth must find her solace in prayer. In fact, perhaps she would sit with Ruth and they would pray together that all evildoers receive their eternal reward. Or they could save the prayer for later and just enjoy the pleasures of the day, the warm sun upon their skin, the roses, the company of an old friend. For such enjoyment of earthly delights is a form of prayer also.

Despite her anger, Ruth smiles at Marie's heresy.

At last she says, It's always strange to find such carnality in such a renowned holy woman as the abbess.

Marie sits beside Ruth and together they breathe in the fragrance of the roses.

Marie begins to talk of Sprota. Though Marie can feel Ruth's spiky anger, she can also feel the other woman listening. As she speaks Marie sees the slow movements of the street: the white goose marching forth with her retinue of goslings, the child crouching to shit behind a bundle of sticks, the carts loaded with turnips and rags, the horses intent on their own forward movement, the massing of those seeking alms at the almonry gates. In the alley at the edge there is a brown movement, which Marie fixes on, thinking an enormous rat or perhaps a swarm of rats, then when it moves into the light she sees it is a pair of lepers crouched to hide, the mother advanced in her illness, her fingers and toes shortened, her nose dissolved, and great lumps upon her face, the child with an eye whitened in blindness and the eyebrows gone. They cling, human heaps. A woman in fine black linen, passing upon the street, sees the pair now creeping into the sunlight and spits a great gob upon them, and behind her the two small girls trailing in tiny copies of their mother's dress also spit as they pass.

Marie goes silent, watching. Ruth, in whom long friendship has built a window between them, can briefly see inside Marie's mind. Suppressing a smile, she says that this inspiration of Marie's seems more devilish than divine.

Marie says that she cannot doubt it is divine, for how else does one explain the abbey's difficulty in finding a good renter for that little house with its gardens on the far side of town? It is providence. She has been shown their path.

And the women stifle their laughter with solemn faces, and watch the alms being given out, and the lepers, the last to creep to the gate, holding out their bowls and bowing.

Before Marie returns to the abbey, she leaves instructions with Ruth. She embraces the other woman, who does not embrace her back. When Marie has swallowed her hurt and mounted her horse, Ruth at last says, carefully, that she loves her friend Marie, but she hates the devil that has possessed her abbess with all her eternal soul.

At evening meal Marie can look with calmness again upon Sprota, who glows with the conviction of her own inner divinity.

In the morning, Marie calls for a special gathering. So many nuns, Marie thinks, looking at those faces arrayed before her; perhaps the abbey has grown to touch its limit. More nuns will have to die before she accepts new ones. Well, if anything, death is a constant here.

She rises, they hush. She speaks. She tells movingly of what she has seen in town, the poor mother leper and her child, the spitting, the human life lesser than that of street bitches with their teats scraping the earth. How in the Bible, the lepers are healed with love. How it is the nuns' duty to care for the most wretched of the earth.

Her nuns' faces blaze with goodness, oh how she loves them.

She says at last that after much prayer she has been given a vision to found a house of lepers with its own gardens at the edge of town, and that the abbey shall undertake to care for these most wretched souls. And with this news, the faces of her nuns are eager, for most are truly women of god, devoted to their faith.

Marie goes on. And after the vision, she prayed all night to seek guidance to choose the one who will be installed as the mistress of lepers. She knelt in the chapel and by morning, she was given her answer.

She pauses to build tension.

She says that new mistress of lepers will be the dear novice Sprota.

Marie watches as the pink drains out of the girl.

The girl stands. She says in an admirably steady voice what a great honor the abbess has laid upon her head. But alas, Sprota finds herself still but a novice and has not yet taken the veil and has so much to learn before she has made herself equal to her holy sisters. She is devastated that she must stay and learn for years more to come before she could deign to pick up such responsibility.

Marie says that she has prayed about this too and it was told to her that Sprota's special radiance will allow the nuns to overlook the depths of her ignorance. Everyone here has seen it, has seen the way Sprota ministers even to the insects of the earth. Because of such godly radiance, she will receive her profession this afternoon.

Sprota demurs, oh no, but she is but a worm, she is a dung beetle, she is not worthy of this great honor. Perhaps a nun who has already proven her strength should be Mistress of Lepers. Surely, Subprioress Goda would be fittest in holiness and propriety for this position.

Goda juts her chin proudly at being spoken of with such fervor.

Marie thinks, smiling, of the sudden vacancy of the subprioress role, and the election that would need to be called to fill it. She admires Sprota's wiliness, the chess pieces she moves in her head.

Well, doesn't Sprota's modesty reflect well on her, Marie says. Such humility and grace! But they must remember: For all those who exalt themselves will be humbled, and those who humble themselves will be exalted.

And because there can be no further protest, the girl's eyes fill with tears. Those who love her read the tears as pious and are moved.

Before None, a cart is loaded with ale and wine and flour and other foodstuffs, linens and ticking mattresses, the girl's followers gathering around overjoyed to see her elevated, and so quickly too. Beside Sprota sits a skinny dun servant who after the announcement leapt at Marie, pleading to go along, and now trembles and flushes in waves to be sitting near the beautiful girl.

The servant will later report to Ruth with a face drawn that as soon as they arrived, Sprota closed herself in the back room—to pray, she shouted through the door—and when the servant was making the pottage in readiness for the first lepers to arrive, she found the girl's window open and the horse gone from the shed.

Swan-neck comes to Marie weeping, furious. She could not shout if she wanted to, but her whisper is worse. You did this, her old friend says. You and your ungodly pride. You could not have another prophetess here. You had to rid yourself of competition.

How silly, Marie says lightly, I did not open Sprota's window and kick her horse to walking.

Marie writes to the family in sorrow about their apostate nun. The one glimmer of fortune is that Sprota is not infected with leprosy;

alas, however, she has been instead infected with false ideas of her own holiness, which have been proven to be ideas sprung into her mind by the devil.

The silence she receives in response is evidence that they are harboring the fugitive, as well as forfeiture of the handsome dowry, which Marie dedicates to the maintenance of the leprosarium.

It is Swan-neck, plain and quiet and old now that her anger has left her, who volunteers to be mistress of the lepers in Sprota's stead. Privately, she says she had a sister who died of the disease. It is an ugly thing to be tormented as one's body rots. It is far worse for most lepers, cast out into the elements and hungry and hated, than for her sister, who was cherished and loved until her death. She will keep their lepers clean and fed and beloved and safe, she says.

Marie says that Swan-neck is truly good, touching the woman's hands.

Swan-neck smiles. Alas, she says, of course she is no saint. Only an old woman with pity in her heart. A rather common form of goodness.

Marie tells her gently, so as to take away the sting, that such goodness can seem common only to those who see holiness in places where it is not.

On the Kalends of April, Marie wakes to a hush—it is like the stillness of the air just after a bell has rung into silence—and she knows that Eleanor has died in the night.

Everything spins; and Marie is falling. Out of what? A hand that had long held her. Moonlight daggers in. All around, her sisters are rising, praying, baking bread, she can hear she is not alone in the world. She is terribly alone.

For some days, meaning takes leave of the world. Marie lies in the abbess's bed and thinks, absurdly, of her body as a feather mattress with the down pulled out in handfuls.

She never did discover who Eleanor's spy could be; and this lapse now fills her with rage.

A week later Marie finds herself at her desk. The letter confirming the queen's death is open before her. Tilde squints at the account books but Goda stares at her from across the room. She raises her head and sniffs. Something of the hound in Goda, smelling out invisible emotion.

All people are like grass, the subprioress says suddenly, and their glory is the glory of the field; the grass withers, the flowers fall, but the Word lasts eternal. Her voice quivers. She rolls her eyes to the ceiling of the abbess's study, which Marie hates just now for being so perfect, so high and uncracked and white.

Thank you, Goda, Tilde says, surprised, but Marie doesn't bother to answer.

Perhaps, Marie will later think with wonder, after the queen dies, her grief drives her a little mad.

She is told she lifted a table and threw it, scattering manuscripts, candles, ink, but this she does not remember. In crossing the cloister, her foot reaches out independently and kicks a cat over the wall. She feels no remorse. She has always hated a cat. Once, she stops reading to her nuns and stares above their heads unblinking for a slow count of a hundred, and they wait, for this is how she looks when visions overcome her; but instead of shining the intensity out at them and proclaiming, she closes her eyes and falls over like a tree.

When, suddenly, only a few weeks after Eleanor dies, Wulfhild is made a widow—and a tragic story it is, a bird's nest in the eaves, a rickety ladder, a fall into the street, a trampling by a dung wagon passing at speed—Marie rides to her and takes the weeping woman in her arms and kisses the crown of her head, feeling sorrow redouble the grief of this child of her heart. Wulfhild's daughters crowd around. She prays with them, for them, until they all fall asleep upon her and Wulfhild speaks all night of her loss, her dearest companion, the gentlest soul the earth has seen. Marie listens, though a small piece of her is comforted that Wulfhild knows something of what Marie feels, that she is not forced to bear her own desolation alone.

She takes to riding between Sext and None every day, no matter the weather. Through the constant rain of April and the fogs of May, through the fields and around and around, wishing she could broach the forest. She dreams of days-long hunts, following a trail of blood to where a wounded beast hides itself in its exhaustion, the frenzy of the kill, the hot blood on the hands. The poor horse plods on.

She tries to touch her sorrow in words, but it is like grasping at a cloud.

Instead as she rides, she thinks of god. It strikes her now that god must be most like the sun in the sky, which rises for the day and sleeps at night, endlessly renewing itself; and it is warm for it pours out its warmth and light, and yet at the same time it is coldly remote, for it continues on even as humans who equally fill the earth with life live and die, and it does not care either way, it does not alter its path, it does not listen to the noises on the earth beneath, it cannot stop to notice human life at all, it shakes off what absurd stories we try to pin to it and exists in calm as only itself, radiant and distant and meaningless.

It is up to saints and angels to intercede for those humans embroiled in the dirt of the earth beneath, filthy small creatures that must seem to them in their grandeur as little writhing insects crying out in words too muted to hear.

June passes, July. On one of these rides she sees how the brook that feeds the brewery and carries the shit away from under the garderobe has dried up in the heat of August. She rides it thoughtfully upstream to where it disappears into the forest. Even over the dry bed, a great deal of berry brush tangles itself and rakes at the horse's skin until the poor creature bleeds in tiny ruby beads.

At last, beyond the berry bramble, she finds the close forest, and beyond this she finds the nearest road of the labyrinth.

The stream here is so well hidden in tunnels beneath the road that one would not suspect it runs there. Across the road, she plunges again into the brambles, into the streambed, and pushes through to the other side, and through forest so thick she has to lie flat with her legs behind her and her fat horse has to suck her gut in and twist and groan to squeeze her body through the tight trees. And up again to the road. The horse, who in her life has faced down bloody battles with a valiant heart, balks at the third plunge into thorns, but Marie coaxes her and curses at her until the beast concedes to the abbess's larger will. Four more strips of thick forest, four more roads, then she is outside the labyrinth.

The trees here are shrunken, the ground sloppy. This must be the crown's land, she tells herself as her horse's feet slip in the mud. She ties the horse up, and kicks off her clogs, and keeps walking on though the bog pulls at her bare feet and shins.

At last she comes into an opening so broad and strange she rubs her eyes and looks again. It is marshland with stunted swamp trees like hands scratching at a low sky, and great tufts of green and brown reeds and sickly grasses. Her eye snags at last upon the strange blue bowl of stone that circles all the way around.

She feels the fire in her fingertips; but the fire withdraws itself from its spin through her body, and it is unclear, she will write later, if what she sees is a gift that the Virgin has let fall from her hands or simply a vision her own mind has brought forth.

But what she sees is that this moisture will be stopped up in the place where she is standing. Where the marshland's wet seeps into mud and finally becomes the stream, there will be wooden locks with iron wheels raising and dropping gates, so that the great bowl of stone will fill with water and become something like a lake. And when it has been pent enough, the stream could then be let to flow no matter the time of year. In the hot months, the sheep would drink fully from the water and no longer find themselves thirsty, they could stand to their knees to cool themselves, the music of the flowing waters would fill the abbey's summer sounds. The stream would slide calm and constant in its path under the brewhouse so that the abbey could have fresh ale and mead even in the summer, when now they content themselves with old ale and last year's wine. It would carry away with it the stink of the nuns' excretions.

And this vision is good, though it may not be holy. It fills her with her hot old ambition.

She will make something useful, a lake, out of something useless, this bog of mud and stink, this swamp. And if it is not her land to drown, there is something angry in her that feels ready to flex her might against the crown that dares to still exist, even though the one who best filled it has been taken to god. She would crush the crown in her hands if she could.

Asta says that indeed, such a project is possible, and she says it with her old quickness, her thin face older only in the fine webs of wrinkles by her eyes. She quivers with excitement. She bounces.

Tilde protests, they cannot, they cannot flood land that is not theirs, it is stealing, but Marie is drawing her plans to demonstrate, and nobody is listening to the prioress.

Wulfhild frowns at the idea of another building project. She says it is a heavy burden. And why do they need to grow ever larger? Why must this abbey eat more land? Marie won't rest until she controls the whole of this mushy island, she says. She is shouting now. Already, Wulfhild is worked off her feet, already the nuns are so rich their wealth is drawing ire; the alms of clothing this winter were woolens so good that well-off housewives could not afford such stuff, and they complained that the poor should not be given for free what honest folk could not buy.

Time has been unkind to Wulfhild. There have been decades of constant travel on behalf of the abbey, of conflict, of receiving anger and bitterness and abuse, of seeking money, of the sun beating down upon her face; her new grief has aged her even faster. Deep black bags hang under her eyes, and there are strange pouches of flesh by her mouth, under her ears, under her jaw. Since her widowhood, she has brought along her two eldest daughters—Young Wulfhild, and Hawise—because the girls have become their mother's lieutenants and have taken on the excess work their mother can no longer do. All three smell a bit gamy, the shining leather of their garments impregnated with the odor of their bodies, their horses, the sour weather, the peat and damp of the countryside, the huge dogs they keep to protect them. When Marie looks for more than a glimpse at Wulfhild's daughters, her breath is knocked from her: they wear their mother's face from when she was young, those clotted black eyelashes, those rosy cheeks.

Marie says as though it were obvious that they are making the abbey impregnable. If drought comes, if the wells dry up, the abbey will still have water. The nuns can remain inviolate within themselves. She reminds them of the Rule: self-sufficiency.

Asta says not to worry, it's not a large project, really. A mere fragment of the work of the labyrinth or the abbess house.

Wulfhild leans forward. There is a moment, a sense of building; the will of the bailiffess gathering itself to rise against Marie's. The other women in the room hold their breath, seeing what they did not imagine, that even redoubtable Marie might be matched by another.

But into the tense room Goda clumps, flexing her hands. She just had to drown three litters of kittens, pity, but serves the cats right for being such lusty little sinners. She chortles. Then she looks around and asks what's wrong. The sense of power gathering in Wulfhild vanishes.

Wulfhild nods. She says heavily that she will do as Marie wishes.

Tilde says a little more loudly that even stealing from the crown is stealing.

Marie snaps that they are stealing nothing, that the land will remain where it always has, that the nuns are only making it useful. Tilde opens her mouth, shuts it, opens it. Her courage fails. She keeps it shut.

They begin. Blocks are chipped from the quarry walls, carted, trees cleared, stumps removed, a platform built over the marshy ground to enable work. The first blocks laid are swallowed by the mud. The heartiest nuns in their dozens move across the ground like ants, for all is being done in swiftness and silence. It is unlikely that any of the agents of the crown would see what they are doing, for it would entail trespass into the labyrinth, or looking up from one tiny place on a rarely used footpath across the bowl of stone with sharp hawk's eyes, because a step forward or a step backward and the trees there shield all glimpses of the wall. Yet it is not impossible for someone to glimpse it and tell, Wulfhild told Marie quietly; and though the abbey is more beloved than the crown in all the lands about them, there will always be royalists in this place.

The edges where the dam will grow up each side of the bowl's opening are built first; and back in the abbey, the blacksmith and carpenter nuns crouch and consider their drawings in the dirt, then the forge rings, the hammers peck all day, the echoes fill the chill air. Snow begins to sift out of the sky, and melts upon the bodies of the working nuns and soaks through their habits. Marie rides out daily to cheer them, to bring them hot food. She prays with them and sometimes stays to bend her body to fitting stone to stone for the external staircase to access the top of the lock, because even old she is strong and her body longs for this form of hard work of the muscles. And when the nuns gather to work in the morning after Prime, Wulfhild urges them to be ever faster, saying with her pinched face, her hands shoved into the warmth of her tunic, that they must finish before full winter. The water is calf high, now waist high, now it has already climbed against the temporary wall blocking where the gates will stand; so much has already been swallowed under the surface, the grasses, the nests where the rare marsh birds live, the snake dens, the beaver dams. The last living exemplar of strange red salamander found only in this damp place is chased away from its hibernation nest and perishes, its guts pecked open by a bird. The twisted trees, small but ancient, having seen Romans and Danes, watch the waters close up over their topmost branches. There is a shimmer of ice at the edges of the new lake. To carry the lock gates to where they will be installed requires four draft horses straining, shoulder to shoulder, but the nuns have had luck, the ground has frozen and makes the pulling vastly less onerous than it would have been even a month earlier. There is a great snowstorm that halts all progress, the nuns return to the dark, close abbey, and at first it is a relief, it puts them in mind of weary workhorses brought back to the comforts of the stable, but soon comfort becomes a feeling of captivity and they long for air. They watch the icicles grown downward off the roof and think of spring.

At last, with delicious relief, a break in the weather, a shimmering cold day and the snow made such firm ice they can walk upon it. The nuns finish the staircase, working fast to stay warm, the lock gate is sturdily in, the gates themselves rise and fall easily and quietly with Asta's clever design. Asta has the horses chained to the temporary wall that has held the water back, she shouts for them to pull, and they break the wall, and a great roar of water churns brown out of the lock, until Asta lowers the gate and makes it into a steady flow. Even in the thick of winter, the water rushes merrily down the streambed, as wild as if it were swollen by spring melt and rain, rushing under the roads and into the fields.

Leagues away, in the abbey's sheepfolds, the shepherdess nuns will hear a thundering and look up to see water in a foamy charge coming over the distance through the dry streambed, and they will think of a herd of riderless horses galloping at full speed, and will shout with joy.

Wulfhild stands beside Marie atop the dam, looking across the great gray matte lake.

Marie considers all around her. She did this. She made this, she blocked the bowl and filled it with water. She feels the radiance in her hands, her feet, in her belly.

She feels royal. She feels papal.

But beside her, Wulfhild wheezes. She has had a cough these months of work and it has deepened, has begun to rattle. Marie looks at her bailiffess, and takes her arm, seeing the paleness beneath the sun-browning, the thinness in her sturdy body. Marie asks, worried, if Wulfhild is well, but now she feels the heat rolling off her skin.

Wulfhild says that she's just a little ill and tries to smile. There is something the matter with her lungs.

She has worked so hard, Marie says. She must go home and take a little rest. And she orders someone to fetch Nest, to have the infirmatrix attend to her at her house in town to make sure the bailiffess obeys, because Wulfhild is not happy unless she is riding out on abbey business.

Then the nuns retreat, fixing the cut-through of the roads of the labyrinth as well as they can before they are able to come back to plant saplings and bushes in the spring; they walk home to the abbey alongside the streambed. The younger nuns, thrilled by the wild, churning white water of their efforts, dance and sing, and the older nuns laugh at them and clap their hands for the beat.

Cellatrix Mamille, knowing this day means the end of the work, has plotted with the kitcheners and together they have had a fat pig slaughtered and roasted and there are also buttery leek pies and, most deliciously of all, a soup of milk and fine herbs.

For two days, Nest sends wary messages: Wulfhild is quite ill but the illness is only in her lungs, it is not progressing.

On the third day, when Marie rides out to Wulfhild's house, Nest runs down to the courtyard, her face looking old in her weariness. Without Beatrix beside her to relax her, her shoulders have returned to their tense place near her jaw. Oh Marie, she says, and tells the abbess she is sorry that she cannot see Wulfhild, that more than anything, Wulfie needs sleep.

The earliest sheep have begun lambing, and Goda and her helpers stay for the night in small clever rolling huts in the sheepfolds. Ah, well, it is not uncomfortable, Goda tells her when Marie comes to visit, and at least it doesn't smell of feet and flatulence like the dortoir. With a rope, the subprioress ties the still-wet, still-bloodied stripped fleece of a stillborn lamb to an orphaned one, and the trembling baby touches the nose of its new mother, who gives a cry on smelling it that sounds nearly like a woman in pain.

The air is damp with mizzle that increases until it becomes a hard and sleety rain. Marie walks back through the mud, thinking of the lamb in the dead lamb's skin, thinking what it might mean as an omen.

She dries herself in the lavatorium, then on considering twice, orders a bath for herself, thinking of Wulfhild, how nice it would feel on Wulfhild's aching body to have a hot bath, knowing she cannot extend this comfort through her own body, but still believing that perhaps her old ancestress Mélusine's magic extends like this, through the air, for the fairy was one who also loved a bath. Who is to tell what invisible paths such magic takes.

Because of the rain, the night falls too soon and Compline comes on the heels of Vespers. Marie is alone in her bed before she has tired herself out. Something is seeping, a dark mist over the land, something large and dark skulks beyond Marie's vision. The rain lashes against the windows.

She lies in bed until she hears feet running outside and the bell ringing wildly and she rises knowing that what she dreaded at last has arrived. She puts on her ancient sealskin cloak that she wears on business outside the abbey and runs swiftly out and through the orchard to the yard. There is a commotion in the dark, someone shouts the stream is overflowing, the villeinesses are yelling in their difficult English, one comes close and says to Marie with her face dark in her hood that ach the wantsum lambru die in such wet. Marie thinks of Goda and her nuns sleeping in the fold and it is as though a cold hand has reached into her chest and stills her heart. She sends Asta and three strong villeinesses on horses to the lock, then takes one of the torches being hastily lit and plunges on her fastest legs into the dark sideways rain into the fields toward the sheepfold. She runs and runs and her running seems endless, the ground sucking at her heels.

At last, she sees a clump of darkness on a rise that, when Marie nears, reveals the sheep saved, nuns running into the sodden fields waist deep to save more. Palenesses floating in the dark are drowned sheep. Marie wades out into the icy water to her waist, to her ribs. Cold seizes her and the wet habit grasps at her legs. She finds a ewe standing upon a dead sister, paddling with its front legs in panic, and though the beast is twice the size of an ordinary child and thrashes in her frenzy, Marie picks her up in her arms and carries her to the rise. In the dim all is dark, until a torch burns closer out of the distance and shows the sudden gleam of pale fleece, the sheep pressed together in a cloud at the height of the hill. More torches streaking forward now and she sees that the water has risen too high for most of the nuns to go out safely and they cling to each other weeping in a knot. Marie is not as strong as she once was. Still, she goes back out, chest deep, brings back two ewes under each arm. Again, again, again, again, the water is to her neck, she holds aloft a lamb that is limp though it still breathes.

But now Goda's face is heaving forward through the dark, her headcloths lost, rain pouring down her cropped skull, eyes narrowed to slits, she is shouting that this is enough, that is enough, they have lost enough, they cannot lose an abbess, also. Enough. Marie hears herself audibly shuddering, a groaning rising up from her gut and through her throat and she can't stop it, or stop her teeth from chattering. She puts her head on Goda's shoulder and the subprioress cradles it in her arms.

Oh now, she says to her in her native English, calm now, calm your heart, my dearest, my abbess, as though Marie were an unsettled heifer, and the cold rain pours down Marie's neck.

Morning reveals the size of the devastation: three dozen sheep drowned, and a calf too small to swim to safety, a nun with water in her lungs. The lock has been forcibly broken and it needs, Asta says gravely, three days to repair. The poor sodden sheep are put into the orchard for safety. Dumb creatures with no memory; they are happy nosing among the roots for rotten windfall apples. The lamb dressed doubly in lambskin has been miraculously saved. It gambols as though it has not already tasted loss.

Wulfhild's three eldest daughters come to the abbey unbidden. Young Wulfhild, Hawise, and Milburga. They stand before Marie, each grave and pale, and she wants to gather them in her arms in her sorrow and guilt. If god had given her grandchildren, it would be these daughters of Wulfhild, whom Marie's pride is now leaving motherless.

Marie waits for the angry words from them, the recriminations for letting their mother work herself into her sickbed, but the young women press close, kiss her, she does not know why they still love her, she does not deserve their love. It was Marie's violent grief for her love that sickened Wulfhild; Marie's vast pride and arrogance.

They say they have examined the broken lock and it was clearly the work of the agents of the crown. And that this fight will continue until it's far worse, unless they hunt who did it to the ground. They ask that Marie let them do this work. It is unfit for holy women and will give the girls solace because the dam and the lock will be the last of their mother's efforts. Wulfhild's labored breath fills the house day and night; she is swollen, wild-eyed. They are glad to escape the house, or they will go mad, they say. They will find the people who broke the lock and ensure that nothing like it will happen again.

Marie warns them that if she lets them do this, she is allowing them to commit sins on the part of the abbey.

Young Wulfhild smiles and her eyeteeth are sharp, like her mother's. Here she is, Marie thinks. The darkest piece of Wulfhild is alive in this one.

Young Wulfhild says isn't it lucky, then, that Marie is their confessor.

A fever falls on Marie in the middle of Vespers the next day, and her linen underclothing is soaked through by the Magnificat. She feels the crown of her head steaming. Food revolts her. She stops a servant who is rushing by with a bucket slopping with dirty water and tells the frightened child to warn the stable hands to saddle her horse, she needs to ride to town.

The fever, she trusts, is drawing her to Wulfhild.

The cool air feels good upon her cheeks as she rides. The town is quiet in the dusk, all have gone home to their families to eat and rest for the night. Someone gallops by whose face Marie cannot see in the dark.

She throws her reins to whoever will catch them at Wulfhild's house, and runs inside to the room that shines above with candlelight. As she runs up the stairs, she hears a rasping like a metal file upon an anvil, and knows it is her poor Wulfie's breath.

In the chamber, Nest is pressing a wet cloth to Wulfhild's swollen purple face; she looks up, amazed. The abbess must be as magic as they say, she tells Marie, she must have flown there on the wind. Nest had sent Beatrix to fetch her only a few minutes ago.

From her pillow, Wulfhild looks at Marie with panic.

Wulfhild's daughters are in the shadows, they too have just come in, there is a stink of horseflesh and sweat, a dark stain on Hawise's stockings, a spatter across the hem of Milburga's tunic. Marie's eyes flick at them. Hawise nods, grim and pale. It is done.

Marie bows her head. Their attention returns to poor Wulfhild.

Marie removes her clogs, and climbs into bed close to the wall, her huge feet dangling off the edge. She holds Wulfhild, trying to draw the woman's pain into herself. Wulfhild's breaths grow less labored; her bulging eyes close. The daughters come forward, the youngest, small rosy pretty Ydon, brushing her mother's hair back from her cheeks.

Marie looks insistently at Nest. The infirmatrix shakes her head at first, then when Marie does not relent and makes her face into an order, at last in silence Nest bows her head to the abbess's will. She turns to pour out her whole vial of opium into the cup. She holds a white cloth near Wulfhild's mouth to catch the spill, but there is none because Marie brushes Wulfhild's throat and with eyes closed the woman laboring to breathe swallows the whole draft. Wulfhild's rasping slows as the drug seeps in.

Young Wulfhild, her face hard but her cheeks wet, asks that Marie shrive her mother now, and Marie does in as clear a voice as she can manage, the holy water she carried against her skin too hot with her own flesh's fever.

When this is done, Wulfhild's daughters kneel and rest their heads on their mother's body.

There is such pain in the room, Marie can hardly stand it. Prayer helps, but what helps more are stories. She tells the girls that when their mother first came to the abbey as an oblate, there was another oblate who hated her. This girl was twice their mother's age, and much, much bigger. For about two weeks, she would pinch Wulfie during the divine office, wait until she was asleep then push her out of her bed, trip her so she fell in the dung heap, things like that. Wulfhild took this so calmly, and didn't complain even once, that everyone thought she was a paragon of humility.

Now the girls begin to smile; they know their mother well.

But, Marie goes on, in fact, their mother was waiting. Finally, one night when the wind was blustering so loudly that the nuns could hardly hear their own voices, and everyone was on edge because mad Sister Gytha had stood during the readings at collation and confidently said that it was the night of the full moon, when the wolf-people change into their great dog-forms and pant at the windows to watch Christians sleep in their beds. And from her bed in the dortoir, Wulfhild watched the nasty girl get up and light the taper stub to go to the garderobe. She stole behind her outside with bare feet, even though it was monstrously cold. When the other girl was inside the garderobe, Wulfhild quietly took the horseshoe she'd hidden in the weeds for this moment and wedged it into the door so that the girl was stuck in the stinking filthy place. Then she waited patiently in the dark as the other girl kicked at the door and shouted, but the wind was so loud nobody could hear her. And then when the girl's taper burned out, Wulfhild took a broom and beat at the walls, scaring the girl inside until she fainted. Wulfhild went back to bed and slept. The poor girl in the garderobe was set free, half frozen, when the magistra woke shortly before Matins and saw she was gone from her bed. In the morning, when the magistra lined all the girls up to discover who would do such a sinful thing, Wulfhild stepped forward and said in her little voice that she did. Now they were even. And though the magistra beat her savagely for this crime, Wulfhild didn't repent.

The girls laugh. Hawise says it sounds like their mother.

Milburga says that she once watched her mother stand up from nut-cakes and good mead being served by one of the abbey's renters and all of a sudden leap out the window, having realized that they were only trying to waste her time while their servants took half the sheep to a distant meadow to hide their true wealth.

Young Wulfhild says that she was there too that day, and their mother was of course correct.

Ydon asked what happened to the mean girl, did they make friends at last? Because nobody can be mad at her mother for long. Have the girls ever met this nun?

Marie rests her hand on the girl's head and smiles at her. She does not say that it is a sad story, that the poor child was bucked by a horse only months later and died of a crushed head; and that Marie, who forgets none of her daughters, who forgets nothing, has forgotten the name of this child who had so hurt Wulfhild.

The candle gutters and Nest lights a new one, her face weary. Ydon has fallen asleep with her head on her mother's chest when Wulfhild gives a rattle. Her long eyelashes are clumped on her cheeks. Marie holds her breath, waiting for Wulfhild to breathe in again. Perhaps, she thinks wildly, and presses her hands upon Wulfhild's heart, sending her force downward into the still body, every thought a plea. Come back, she thinks. If ever the Virgin has shown Marie a miracle, it must be this, Wulfhild's breath returning to her lungs, the blood rushing into her face, her eyes opening, the great sunburnt chapped hands touching Marie's face again. But the silence stretches. The panic dies out of Marie and she at last removes her hands from the woman's heart. Well, she thinks, it hadn't worked to bring her mother back, either. All this force inside her, and yet her hands are not the kind that can raise miracles of life out of dead bodies. She watches Wulfhild's daughters' faces as the understanding arrives slowly in each, one and then the next, that their mother is gone.

We will see her in the next life, Marie says. The pain is too great for her not to believe it.

Nest returns to the abbey. The daughters go in their sorrow to their sleep.

Marie sits in Matins over the body of the last of the women she has loved with her own heart; not with the borrowed heart of an abbess. All gone: her mother, five aunts, Cecily, the queen, Wulfhild.

Slowly as the night ekes on and her own fever withdraws there occurs in Marie a transfiguration. No raiment shining white as light, no clouds speaking sternly from above; only the death of this daughter of her soul, and the endless dark.

She has known prayer in her life, but before tonight it has been prayer like sending a coin with a wish into a body of water, it was hope dispersed vaguely outward. She sent it not toward the stern trinity imposed upon her, but toward the Virgin Mother who wore her own mother's face. Even in prayer she was rebelling.

She sees now what should have been apparent. She has made her life holy, she has lived sinless, she has said all the right words, but deep within she has coveted her own rebellious pride.

Marie's arrogance brought this final illness upon Wulfhild. Her endless hunger ate up the daughter of her spirit. The need to enlarge this abbey she has thought of as an extension of her own body. Her actions always in reaction to the question of what she could have done in the world, if she had only been given her freedom.

Now, sitting beside the dead woman, Marie renounces the hunger that has always lit her from within. She will maintain what she has been given. She will learn contentment. This repentance will prove to one so ambitious to be an effort of will, a constant wrestling match with the devil who wears her own face.

She will renounce her long struggle against the central beauty of the abbey, she will let ego be swallowed by noes.

Oh, she thinks, she is already so old and weary.

And that very morning, riding in her grief back to the abbey, for the briefest of flickers she sees looming above the trees a great stone eagle the size of a mountain. And though the day is soft and bright in the forest where Marie rides, there hangs over the carved eagle a black and raging thunderstorm veined through with lightning. And under the weight of the pouring rain the bird's carved feathers swiftly melt, the beak and eyes dripping in gray streams from its face as though it is made of loose dust, not stone.

The horse walks on, the vision fades, the blue of the sky seeps back. Marie blinks and breathes again. Her vision is about the empire, the Angevin striving coming at last to its end; very soon, everything that Eleanor had so carefully built will crumble into nothing.

Marie sighs and rubs her weary face with her two hands. Collapse is the constant state of humanity, she tells herself; the story of the flood and the great ark that saved the creatures two by two is only the first refrain of a song that is to be sung over and over, the earth's gradual and repeated diminishment, civilization after civilization foundering to dust, until the final death of the children of Eve with the apocalypse, the seven seals, the seven trumpets, the seven angels, the seven bowls. In the end, the earth will crack and the wicked will be cast into the lake of fire. Marie suspects this fiery end would be the stone and the soil and the waters of the earth itself, through human folly and greed made too hot for it to be willing to bear any more life upon its back. So it will go, and so it would be; and Marie cannot stop it, even if she had the force of will any longer to do so.

7.

Life slows. Time is wheels within wheels.

Postulants arrive tender and young; work and prayer. Nuns escape their bodies in death.

Temporale, the proper of time, the cycle of Christmas, the cycle of Easter. Sanctorale, the proper of the saints. The seasons with their colors: dove gray to green to floral prismatic to gold. The Kalends Nones Ides of the month. The days of the week, the Sabbath. Night and day.

Matins Lauds Prime Terce Sext None Vespers Compline.

In the choir as the nuns prepare to sing a particular psalm, Swan-neck, who has returned from the leprosarium to confer with Marie, can feel the eyes of the child oblates, their just-contained hilarity. At the moment when they sing of the frogs that descend and destroy, she tucks her chin into her chest, blows out her cheeks, bulges her eyes, flicks her tongue. A great fit of coughing comes over the oblates, the novices, even the young nuns. This is Swan-neck's joke with this psalm, decades old; a tiny thing that the young wait for in the cycle of the liturgical calendar, that they love her fiercely for.

Such comfort in knowing all the old cycles will turn again.

Old age falls upon Goda, a thunderclap. She comes to Nest for a salve for her swollen red knuckles. As Nest rubs it in, the subprioress sighs and closes her eyes. Nest looks at Goda's tight small pleated mouth, marveling at the distance between now and when Nest herself first came to the abbey as a grief-blasted young widow, and was cowed by Goda, her snappishness, the authority of her position, her swift English and French, her fine noble blood. But over these years Nest has come to understand that if you minister enough to any adult body, you will discover the frightened child hiding within it. The greater the protestations of power, the smaller the child. Goda, a raw infant. The salve should be working already, but Nest does not drop Goda's hands. She rubs gently until at last the bells for Terce ring.

Now a new darkness touches the island, led by incompetence and madness and greed, and up rises a fight between the crown and Rome.

In 1208, a papal interdict falls over the land. Penance is to be inflicted as well on the healthy as the sick; for in the midst of life we are in death. No Mass can be celebrated, no bodies buried in sanctified ground. Only babies can be baptized, and extreme unction given at deathbed. There will be sorrow, horror, everywhere, and in all the cities the people will suffer, they cannot be confessed, they cannot take communion, the beloved dead will be left to rot and the air fills with the stink of their putrescence.

When Marie reads the awful news—days before the messenger can arrive with it at the royal court, for her network is swifter and better— she puts the parchment down with rage gnawing black at the corners of her vision.

These people who think of themselves as her superiors, how foolish and unnecessarily cruel they always choose to be. Throwing blows at the innocent people to hurt the crown. Thus does power corrode the mind and the soul, she thinks.

Down below in the abbess house, a servant is singing a small sad song in an off-key voice, and Marie listens for some time to the brush upon the stones, the singing, the cows lowing in the pasture.

The old hatred stirs in her, rises.

Well. She will tell none of her daughters of the interdict. They will know nothing of it, it will have no bearing upon their lives, it will not disturb their peace. They will live as they always have, happily, and knowing they are the best beloved of god.

The island of the abbey will recognize as highest authority only Marie.

She finds even herself a little thrilled at this thought.

From the diocesan there comes a letter days later, shaken: Oh, noble virago, you who in wisdom are exalted above all other exemplars of your sex, it begins, then goes on to ask her to set her nuns to constant praying that the anathema be lifted.

She senses Tilde behind her, reading, and though her first impulse is to throw the parchment in the fire, she allows the prioress to see.

We have been under papal interdict? the prioress asks Marie with extreme crispness.

Well. Angleterre as a whole, yes. But the monasteries are still allowed divine office, Marie says, as if that explains all.

The prioress sits and slowly tilts forward until her face rests against the surface of her desk. Marie waits. The rasping brush cleans the stones of the abbey below, the voice sings. But Tilde doesn't stir.

I am the shepherdess of all the abbey's souls, Marie says at last. I am the mother, here to protect and guide all of our sisters and our servants and villeinesses. We are whole in ourselves.

Marie, you are very far from being the head of the church, Tilde says, muffled by the desk.

As the hierarchy see it, perhaps. But holy sisters in our humility and meekness sit nearest of all humans to the hand of god. And our abbey is known as the most powerfully pious in the land. And if there is any intermediary on the earthly plane, that intermediary is me, Marie says. Ergo, I recognize no anathema.

Where is your vision that told you so, Tilde says, lifting her face, and she has such rage there on that soft and timid face that Marie's heart skips. No? No vision this time? Tilde says. Perhaps it is not real, what you're saying.

It is real, Marie says. She has never been more sure.

Tilde sighs and puts her head down again. She says oh well that it is as it will be, but that the nuns all have families out in the rest of the world, suffering under the interdiction. And they should know at least what their families are suffering.

And with a pulse of victory Marie sees that she has won; that Tilde won't stand in her way, that though her nuns will know of the interdict on England, they will not be touched by the dark papal cloud that has descended upon the greater island, they will stay in the bright warmth of Marie's protection, alone, together.

But death, as always, strips even this victory from Marie.

Asta reaches her hands into the workings of a pump in the kine barn, but a rat that has taken up residence there bites her on the thumb. How unexpected, Asta thinks, staring at the bite, growing angry as she does when events of the day fall outside her calculations. She ignores it, continues on. In a week, poor skinny staring Asta slavers and froths and speaks wildly of the devil sitting astride her, and she thirsts so terribly her tongue sticks out huge and black in the hours before she dies. Marie weeps, preparing the knock-kneed body.

Then a servant unhappy to find only women around her flees in the night with a round of good cheese and the finest of the altar cloths, studded with pearls. Months later she is discovered in a tight lobe of the labyrinth, a mess of stained cloth and picked-over bones, having likely died of loneliness and fright. The cheese is gone into the gullets of wild animals and sunk into the soil, but the nuns find the altar cloth has remained as new. A miracle! the other servants say, though Marie hears that some have whispered it was not a miracle, but a binding curse the abbess herself had laid upon the girl when she stole the holy cloth.

And one day when a storm threatens heavily all morning, Sister Gytha goes wild, and instead of Saint Lucy holding her eyeballs, she paints on a manuscript a tree in which the apples are neither apples nor

butterflies but open female sexes. When the pressure building all afternoon ends in a wild summer storm with blustering shrieking wind and
thunder and black howling skies, the mad nun goes into the sheepfolds
dancing and is struck dead by lightning, a small and perfect black hole
running into her skull and out her left heel.

Marie washes this last ropy body herself. How dull the abbey will be
without the mad nun, how sapped of its color and beauty. She does not
sew up Gytha's mouth. Those blue teeth she will leave bared merrily to
death.

But later, through the beauty of the funeral, the voices of her nuns,
she feels restored.

To think: All the hatred so deep inside Marie when she was young
has, through the pressure of time, somehow turned to love.

For this community is precious, there is a place here even for the
maddest, for the discarded, for the difficult, in this enclosure there is
love enough here even for the most unlovable of women. How short
and lonely Gytha's life would have been, an isolate lost in the cruelty of
the secular world. How much less beauty she would have brought into
this flawed and difficult life if she had been forced to be without her
sisters who loved her.

It is good, Marie thinks, so very good, this quiet life of women and
work. She is amazed she ever resisted it so angrily.

It is 1212. Marie is seventy-one.

The papal interdict has hung heavy upon England for years. It torments the faithful outside the abbey.

Her spies in the court of London report that all over Europe, parents are buying good sturdy shoes and clothing for their children, packing a little sack with sausage and hard bread and cheese, and sending their innocents off to the Holy Land on a children's crusade. Marie imagines a rain of innocent children pouring down into Outremer, getting lost on the way and starving, being stolen and used as slaves, being drowned at sea, suffering. And at home the parents feast on their happy sacrifice, sure that by sending off their child, they have bought their seat in heaven.

Once, she had thought a crusade the human fist of god. Now she knows it is shameful, born of arrogance and greed.

Marie shakes, enraged. She puts the letter down and is about to remark about it to Tilde, who has gained a squint in her middle age. But a voice calls from outside and Tilde leaps up and runs to the door. Goda and Marie exchange looks. Marie is reading her letter again in silence when the door opens, and the prioress brings in by the hand an old woman.

Tilde says, smiling with a mouth so full of teeth that Marie wonders what is wrong with her, that here, Mother, is the abbey's newest corrodian.

Marie studies the old woman. It is clear she is supposed to know her. Perhaps a child oblate who never took the veil, choosing marriage, and now in her age has returned. Perhaps a girl educated at the abbey, come back after a good marriage. The woman's clothes are simple and dark but sumptuous in fabric, and the hem and bodice of her dress are embroidered finely.

Then the woman smiles, and breathes Marie's name, and in her wrinkles there is pressed a great handful of dimples on both cheeks. Marie stands slowly.

It isn't as though the age peels off this antique woman with over-large earlobes and drooping eyelids; but that there stands in the same place as the old woman another, Marie's own golden-haired Cecily, her first friend, all round and brusque and loving. In the same form, the girl of memory and the fleshly old woman together reach out their hands to Marie.

Marie finds herself wordless for the first time in memory.

Cecily says she has returned to Marie. At last. Like she promised. Three marriages, each richer than the last, but there is no more marriage in her. No children, a lot of money to give to the abbey for corrodianship. She has come back to take care of Marie.

All this time. And yet Cecily never once wrote, Marie says at last. She thought Cecily had died.

Cecily says well, that is entirely Marie's fault, as the stupid girl had only ever taught her to read, not to write. She begins to cry in happiness.

This has all been arranged with Prioress Tilde, Cecily explains. Tilde says that she has made ready the corrodian chambers for Cecily. But the old servant will never live in them; she bids her own servant instead to move her things into Marie's abbess apartments. Marie does not forbid her. She only holds the other's hands, laughing in wonder.

Tilde tells the other nuns sternly, to forestall gossip, that the new corrodian and Marie were raised as sisters. She says it also to stop the discomfort that has risen in herself.

And for these good last months, Marie has Cecily to warm her bones in bed again.

8.

The swiftest of my visions came to me, Marie writes in her book. Of the gifts of vision that the Virgin bestowed on me, it was the nineteenth and the sweetest because I understood when receiving it that it would be the last.

For I have lived seventy-some years, and am become old, and am as an ancient tree in the orchard whose gnarled trunk pushes out buds and flowers in the spring but all the sweetness of the sap is concentrated in its scarce fruit in the fall.

We were gathered in our prayers in the chapel when the vision came. My nuns were singing Psalm Eight . . . the moon and the stars, which thou hast founded . . . when between the saying of one word and the saying of the next the strange fire touched my skin and before my eyes fell a vision of the beginning of the world.

As this vision was of the radiant immensity of God brooding over the dark face of the waters, a great hen.

And from this brooding there fell the shining eggs of creation. And the eggs cracked and out of the shells there spilled what had been held inside each. And in the first was light split into day and into night, and from the second came the skies. And from the third came the ground and the seas and the fruit of the land. From the fourth came the sun and the moon and the stars, and from the fifth all the beasts of air and water. From the sixth there came all the beasts of the land as well as our first parents.

But the tiny bodies of the first humans lay still upon the ground as though dolls made of mud until the wings of God stirred up a wind that blew over the new land and sea and forests; and this great wind breathed life into the bodies and they stirred and sat and looked about them.

For this was the Holy Spirit, which is like a midwife who kisses the birth from a babe's mouth and frees the babe to breathing.

God laid the goodness into the world with her eggs.

God's Holy Spirit fills us with her breath and makes us live.

And out of the vision, I returned to my body even as my mouth was forming the next word of the psalm.

Beside me the beeswax tapers all at once flickered and extinguished themselves with the breath of the Holy Spirit and it was as confirmation of the truth of what I saw.

And plunged in darkness I spoke to my daughters of the beauty of this world, which I saw that I would soon leave.

And I knew also that this would be the last of my visions. I feel them all gone. For I am all poured out like water. And all my bones are out of joint. And my heart has turned to wax; it has melted within me.

Marie is seventy-two. The fight in her released itself after Eleanor and then Wulfhild died. What is left is a growing dread of those who live beyond the abbey, their badness, their ignorance of god.

She is weary. Between her breasts, she feels an egg slowly hardening. Her mother too had been given this egg; and her mother's mother as well. She remembers how gray her mother's flesh had become in dying, her great bulk whittling to bone.

Prioress Tilde scurries and manages; she will be a good abbess. Uninspired, perhaps, but Marie feels reasonably certain that she will keep what Marie fought for all these long decades on this damp dirty island, in this strange abbey that she has built around her as a shell, a cathedral, a home.

Marie and Cecily sit together in the abbess's antechamber, the window open to the chill April wind. A fine white lock escaped from Cecily's headcloths lifts and falls; her hands slowly pull out of nothing a Tree of Life in gold thread. For a long while, Cecily has been telling a story, but Marie has not been listening, consumed by the hopes for the ginger patch planted in a warm and shady bowl near the birches, by the green insect the size of a fingerbone preening its little face with its hands on the sill, by how the voices of the novices learning the Guidonian hand in the orchard down the hill are weaving fantastically through the rough warm warp of Cecily's story. But now Cecily has worked herself almost to the glorious catharsis of weeping, and Marie snaps to, listens backward to hear the story Cecily has told up to this point. It is an ancient one, which Cecily's own mother the cook loved to tell when she pared apples with her quick flashing little knife; it is about a fine lady so beautiful, with such luminous eyes, that everyone who saw her fell in love with her. The lady was given no peace, day or night, she was hunted when she went hunting, followed where she walked, chased when she rode, sung to at night so she had no sleep and her handmaidens had to sleep with daggers to hand to keep those with evil thoughts from stealing into her bedchamber. At last, driven out of her own mind, she went to her window to where the lutes and flutes played invisibly in the garden below and, in the light of a torch, plucked her own eyes out of her skull, shouting that if they wanted her eyes so very much, they could have them. And she threw her bloodied eyes down upon them.

But Marie hisses before Cecily can finish and allow herself her fully gluttonous weeping, and says she had always thought this story very wondrous stupid, that in the story if the lady is beautiful she is punished for it, when, in life, it is far more true that if a lady is made unbeautiful she is the one who is punished.

And Cecily, irritated, says sharply that Marie herself knows better, that Marie had never been thought beautiful, but instead of being punished for her ugliness, she has been made great, here she sits now the holiest of holy women in the island, venerated and beloved, baroness to the crown, owner of more land than the vast majority of nobles here and certainly the richest abbess north of Fontevraud. That had Marie been beautiful or even just as ugly as she was but bearing a soft and mild femininity, she would have been married off, she would likely be long dead of childbirth and all that would be left of her in the world would be some daughter, a minor noble, so busy she'd hardly remember the lines of her mother's face. In fact, Cecily says, it was Marie's unbeauty that was the making of her.

Marie looks at Cecily with some heat. She wants to wrestle her like they wrestled when they were children, to pull her hair and twist the skin of her arms and hips until it bursts out in purple plums, to bite. She says, low and sharp, that Cecily is mistaken. No one but Marie has ever made Marie.

Now Cecily laughs with scorn and says oh sure, she is self-made! Like a worm birthed out of nothing but mud. No. Since she had been a seed in her mother's womb Marie had been molded by others, her mother, her ferocious aunts, her books, her money; that the queen had more hand in making Marie by sending her to the abbey than she had in making herself. She was given everything, not least a great blessing of ugliness, and she would repeat that Marie would right now be dust and rot with the grubs crawling through her rib cage if she hadn't been so lucky to be born so ugly.

The wind flicks and flicks Cecily's white lock against the dark wool of her headcloth. Her cheeks are flushed, she is a girl again, frank and blunt. But now over her face there slides a confusion and she says with alarm that it couldn't be true that Marie's eyes have grown teary; she has said nothing so severe as to make such a venerable ancient abbess cry, has she?

And Marie says in a distant voice, blinking back the wet in her eyes, that she never realized Cecily thought her so revolting as all that.

Cecily goes painfully down on her creaking knees before Marie and takes her hands and brings them up to her lips, and says Marie may have some accidental royal blood in her veins, but the rest of her is entirely old fool. For when it comes to strength and goodness and brilliance and gentleness and grandeur of spirit so vast that it takes one's breath away, beauty is nothing, beauty is a mote to a mountain, beauty is a mere straw alight beside a barn on fire.

Marie tells her to get up, what an old bumpkin she is. But her face is red and she can hardly suppress her smile. And Cecily, who has always spoken truth when she sees it, looks up at the face with its whiskers and wrinkles and those sharp shining brown eyes, and knows she has soothed Marie's pride all the way to her internal light. She has a lot more sharp things she could say. But, out of love, Cecily holds her tongue.

Now the abbess has begun to sleep a great deal. She sits in the sun beside Wevua, who is astonishingly still alive though surely she must be over a hundred years old. In Wevua's mouth, language is gone; she grunts and makes faces, like the monkeys Marie saw a life ago in the court of Westminster.

Soon Marie is too weak to be brought outside, and she lies in her bed and tries to pray with each heartbeat.

When she is not sleeping, but pretending to sleep so that she can be left in silence, she thinks of her life.

Some of it returns so vivid it is nearly a vision. Cecily, so young in the fields the days they fled the estate in Le Maine to Rouen, a sudden rainstorm, drops thick as spit, the horses urged to a trot as the rain came down hard, a field with hayricks, a tunnel into the dry interior of the haystack, where the girls squirmed out of their soaked clothing and pulled the woolen blanket over themselves, laughing at the closeness of the other body and the way their limbs knocked as they moved and the sound of the rain and the thick sweetness of hayscent. They lay back, pressed close for warmth, and Marie felt Cecily's heart beating along the length of her, the pulse in her temple where it rested on Marie's arm, and her smell was strong, the soap of lemon balm and lavender at the heart of her braid, skin with honey and wild onions and leaf rot in it. They had always rubbed together through their clothes, but they had never been naked like this; they would never have dared. Cecily blinked and her eyelashes brushed Marie's arm. Marie held herself still, counting to a hundred. At a hundred, she would either move away or kiss Cecily. But at twenty-one, Cecily turned her head and pressed her lips to Marie's throat and Marie lifted her hand and touched Cecily's face, found her lips with her fingers, and there was no one there to see or stop them, no need for the breathless pulling away as the stable door cracked to sunlight and a silhouette was framed against the sky, nobody here below on the earth knew where they were, and shy and slow, Cecily's cold hand touching the inside of her knee, trailing up the long shank to the innermost part of her thighs. Let her left hand be under Marie's head, her right hand embrace her. And under her mouth Cecily smiled, Cecily's hand circled but didn't touch Marie where she wanted to be touched, she moved it beyond to the hipbone and the small curve of belly and the ribs and the nipples and at last she relented, slid her hand down again and put it very gentle against the center of Marie, where Marie had never before dared to ask Cecily to touch, and the wall that bound Marie tight inside herself began to fall, she slid out of her own mind, she sank into the rings of pleasure expanding from the center of her, culmination of all the moments in the henhouse, in the stables, the furtive kisses, the wrestling in the river as the small fish nibbled their ankles; and at last she lost the ability to think, there was joy coursing through her, the ecstasy of living within a body that held such riches in it, within the astonishing material world so overfull with beauty. All night, until the day breathed forth its wonder.

Even now a small echo of pleasure rings in the flesh of the sick body.

But not all is so good. There is also pain. Pain like being gnawed or bitten by small invisible beasts, foxes or weasels.

And in this pain there return to her those months after she had come to the abbey, when it was as though she were an apostate angel thrown from the light of heaven to the darkness of hell.

She remembers over and over a night soon after she took the abbey in hand when she woke to restlessness and went out into the thick starless black. A calf had been separated from its mother that day. Both heifer and calf had lowed all afternoon and into the night, had lowed enough to put some tenderer nuns off their feed. When Marie had gently remonstrated, Goda had snapped that separating the cow and calf was necessary unless the nuns didn't want their milk and butter. Marie went silent because she loved her milk and butter, and because she felt personally aggrieved that milk and butter seemed well worth the beasts' suffering. The cow had quieted at dusk, but now Marie's step must have awoken her from her sleep, and looking all around her she searched for her calf again but could not find it near her, and the cow started up again with her lowing, which, from near the beast's body, sounded to Marie so full of anguish that she felt tears flush into her eyes. The cow's suffering was immense and powerful, a wave, and in it the suffering that Marie herself felt was swept away. She went into the paddock and found the mother, and touched her on the flank for comfort. But the cow shuffled her body so her head was facing Marie, and she tucked her broad rough crown against Marie's chest and stomach, and Marie put her arms around the heavy jaw, feeling the mother's grief for her lost calf rushing through her, and like this she lost the outlines of herself in the suffering of the other. And later, as the bells for Matins sounded in the dark and she walked back in the darkness as though blind, she wondered if in fact this had been the closest she had been to god—not in fact invisible parent, not sun warming the earth and coaxing the seeds from the soil—but the nothing at the center of the self. Not the Word, because speaking the Word limits the greatness of the infinite; but the silence beyond the Word in which there lives infinity.

She understood then that it didn't matter that the landscape inside her looked so different from that of her sisters, that they had been taught to crave their own subjection and she had not, that they believed things that she thought silently were foolish, unworthy of the dignity of woman. They were filled with goodness as a cup is filled with wine. Marie was not and could never be. Of course Marie did have a greatness in her, but greatness was not the same as goodness.

And she saw at that moment how she could use this greatness for her sisters; she could give up the burn of singular love inside her and turn to a larger love, she could build around the other women an abbey of the spirit to protect them from cold and wet, from superiors waiting to gobble them up, she would build an invisible abbey made out of her own self, a larger church of her own soul, an edifice of self in which her sisters would grow as babes grow in the dark thrumming heat of the womb.

As she entered the chapel with the single lamp lit and saw in the shadows and the darkness of the habits only the faces of the nuns gleaming, singing, she saw them as tender bare babes floating in the amniotic dark.

And now that she is old and dying in the close herbed air of the infirmary, she thinks of how strange it is that it is not the long good comfortable times of happiness returning so close to the end, but rather the times of briefest ecstasy, and of darkness, of struggle and passion and hunger and misery.

She smiles at the version of herself at that time of pain, so young that she believed she could die of love. Foolish creature, old Marie would say to that child. Open your hands and let your life go. It has never been yours to do with what you will.

9.

Marie sickens deeper.

One night she sees the hounds of hell circling in the darkness over the grounds outside.

She sits up, desperate to warn her daughters.

A sweet voice tells her to hush and gentle hands lay her back down. They take off her headcloths. She knows the warmth of these hands, the smell of herbs. Nest. Oh lovely, nervy one.

When she was young, she had the thickest and most beautiful hair, someone says in sorrow. Now look. White as ice. She knows that voice, she struggles to find the name, she cannot. But the face comes to her; dimpled in golden straw, or hair like straw. Lips like a heart beating. Young.

Why can she not see? All has become pale in her eyes. She wants to tell them, she knows not yet what. It is urgent. She must. She sees her great wings still spread over the abbey in protection.

She hears the baying in the distance. Yes, yes: the hounds of hell, more and even more coming.

Now she can hear them, hear the weight of their paws running over the ground, so swift. Digging holes in her abbey's lands. Killing the sheep. Howling, calling their hellish sisters forth. She longs to tell her daughters to listen, to go out with their crosses and their prayers, drive the hounds away.

For the daughters of this great place have made one of the seven towers of holiness keeping evil from the world.

For their goodness and their piety is what has kept the grace of the Holy Virgin upon the earth.

For their prayers are as buttresses to the heavens.

Someone is saying now that the poor abbess has been ill longer than she has admitted. She has been gasping in her pain and pressing her hand to the space between her breasts for years. Feel now. There is a rock in there.

Ah well, the abbess would not have told them of the pain. She wouldn't want to worry her daughters. That is how her own mother went and her grandmother before her also, it is the family curse, alas. Marie was very young when her grandmother went but she watched her mother sicken. She is gray in the face, as they were then. It will be soon now.

Someone's breath is rasping loud against this paleness.

The pain is eating Marie alive.

Mouth that cannot speak, eyes that cannot see, hands that cannot feel, feet that cannot walk, nor can she make a sound from the throat. It is coming, it is coming.

The end times: seas rise, seas fall, the monsters come roaring from the seas, the water burns, the trees sweat blood, the earthquakes topple buildings, the hills turn to ash, all people flee, the bones of the dead rise, the stars fall from heaven, the heavens and the earth burn, the earth releases the good dead to the heavens to their judgment, yes judgment is coming.

A doe burning white in the steam of the cold water, a mother, a queen, her crown her rack of antlers.

Daughters, prepare, make ready for the end of time.

Breath so painful to take in.

She cannot protect her daughters any longer, she will soon thank the Virgin for her gifts, she will pray in intercession for them, she will soon lie beside her own mother, letting the warmth of her flesh warm this cold body, touching her curly dark hair in love.

Last rites.

Everything possible with everything given has been done.

She sees a woman in a box.

No, she is the woman in a box. She is slithering away from the swords coming in from all angles, contorting her body in the darkness so that she will not be stabbed by the new swords coming so relentless, so sharp, and each sword is cold upon her body where it presses but not a one does cut the skin to blood.

Yes. It was like this, her life.

Sing the canticles.

My vineyard, which is mine, is before me.

Marie longs for it, longs for it, her whole body reaches for it, the gold, the heavenly music, the release. To see god, who is not split in three, but singular. God, sole, female. She has had an eternity of community, it has been enough.

Make haste, my beloved.

So be it, she thinks. And it is.

The funeral is solemn and the feast is large; the mortuary roll will return so thick with their sewn-on tituli of praise for Abbess Marie that it becomes quite clear that no other woman of the realm could be remembered with such veneration. Marie was majestic; great, still, in death, and her renown struck fear in the hearts of even those who had never known her.

There are few alive who remember the poverty of the abbey before Marie took it up, only Goda, as well as Ruth and Swan-neck, who had been novices with her. The three old nuns at the funeral feast tell stories: Fourteen nuns dead of the plague in one week, Goda protecting the last milch cow with her own body from the four starved nuns come with kitchen knives to kill and eat the beast, the meals of sad roast turnips, the child oblates dying of hunger. And Marie huge and gaunt as a crane, rattling forth from the forest on her destrier on that first day she arrived, such an unlikely savior that, in the abbey, watching from behind the shutters, the sickly hungry nuns wept with dashed hopes at watching her near.

But the novices, thinking now of the summer gardens overgrown with vegetation and the honeybees darting through the flowers and the grapevines under their singing sculptures and the pigs and sheep and goats and chickens and cows and the apple trees heavy with fruit, give little smiles, knowing these nuns to be holy and truthful yet not quite believing their tales.

They bury Marie's body under the stones of the chapel's main altar, place of gravest honor. There has been talk of sainthood. Already, the villeinesses come in the night to pray near her and there are rumors of the healing of a wen, a broken wrist, an abscessed tooth.

Eight nights running after her election to abbess, Tilde is disturbed in her dreams and awakens feeling as though her heart is beating to escape her chest; and on the ninth night, when she wakes in the same panic, she rises and goes to the chapel to pray.

She leaves her taper on the altar and kneels in the chancel, but she is uneasy there, and her thoughts fly from her head. She finds herself looking at the paintings on the wall as they dance in the small light: the apocalypse, the judgment, Mary Magdalene with her long hair loosed to her waist and her long plain horsey face. A great intensity of gold flooding down upon the face of the Virgin in the Annunciation. The Revelation, the two-headed whore of Babylon on her dragon.

And then she feels a small chill wind upon her neck as though a breath blown upon her from close by. Someone or something is in the nave behind her. She swallows and sees her hands shaking before her and says a prayer while slowly standing up. She reaches for her candle, but as she touches the holder, the flame is extinguished. The smoke in the darkness spools over her hands.

And she steels herself and turns to look, and sees a distant simmering of light in the place directly above where Marie has been buried under the stones. She knows without doubt that what she is seeing is the old abbess's ghost, though later she will ask herself if it may have in fact been the moonlight shining off the glossy leaves of the oak outside and through the window, perhaps quivering its reflected light in the air.

There had been a great ambition in Abbess Marie, an impatience, often a barely held rage, but never any evil; Abbess Tilde worked beside her for over two decades, she knows this well. And with this thought, she feels the fear seep out of her skin. Inside her mind she becomes calm.

She bends her feet toward the disturbance, and as she goes it seems to seethe and re-form itself ever farther from her step. And she lets it lead her to the outside, the darkness of trees moving in the chill wind, over the path, through the cloy of rotten windfall apples, and back to the abbess's house.

By the leading shimmer she is brought through the darkness to the desk heaped with her unending work. And in the moonlight she sees what the eye skipped past in the day; that the shelves are thick with the bound parchments of the abbey's workings over the centuries, and that so many of the pages have been filled with the hand of Marie.

But when she broaches the door, time peels from the abbess and in the dark a vision comes before her and she sees Marie as she had once seen her, only months before Marie was elected abbess, shortly after Tilde had become a novice and had taken her place as a copyist in the scriptorium, never daring to even hope that the queen would elevate her to prioress. Marie's face had settled into its handsome austerity by then; she had been standing in the orange sideways morning light, smiling at the door where Tilde had come in quailing and so young, with a question of Latin that the other nuns could not solve. When Tilde had knocked, Abbess Marie had been holding in her hand the abbey's seal matrix, and she placed it deliberately upon a small leather-bound book. She said Tilde, and her name in the abbess's mouth gave Tilde a thrill. The abbess answered her question with no hesitation, but a fond smile.

And then the memory fades and Abbess Tilde strikes her taper alight and rummages among the books until she finds the little one that the seal had rested upon in that too-bright memory.

She reads without stopping for Matins and Lauds and Prime, and when she finishes, she rubs her temples. It is a bleak gray dawn, the Ides of November, and in the window the light shines weakly upon the frozen ground. She kneels in the fireplace and starts her own fire, for she has locked the door against disturbance and will not let the servants in. She stares at the fire to give herself time to think.

She had known Abbess Marie to be a brilliant strategist, a thorough and clever manager of the abbey's affairs, a savvy politician with spies and allies everywhere, a friend of the great and the small, and a good and sensible woman within her own faith. She had seen her untangle a butterfly from a spiderweb, to be so moved by the glory in a sunset that she fell to her knees. True, there had been rumors of witchcraft; but such rumors are irrepressible when it comes to powerful women. Still, Tilde had always believed that the visions Marie had been given by the Virgin were not true visions, but rather ideas that she worked up into vision form to sell her building projects to her sisters. Tilde did not truly believe her abbess to have been an actual mystic. Mystics are ethereal creatures, and Marie was the opposite of ethereal. She was massive, fleshly, ruled by her hungers.

Also, there is something that disconcerts Tilde about the visions; something about them that feels less like the word of god ringing with authority in the Bible; something more human; something that, perhaps, if she's being truthful, feels like things that have not been given, but wholly created.

Yet it must mean something that the abbess's ghost had wanted to speak to her.

She thinks hard and in despair, and can come to no satisfactory action.

She rereads and finds herself again and again astonished to her quick, for had such visions as these seeped into the world during her lifetime, Abbess Marie would have been burned a heretic at the stake and all the sisters in the abbey would have been scattered and the richness that the abbey had built over the years lost to the hungry superiors ever circling above, eyeing the wealth of this place for themselves.

In Marie's visions, Eve and the Virgin Mary share a kiss; god is a colossal dove hen laying the eggs of the world; Marie herself is protector well above the power of any woman born to woman. Singly, each vision does not seem so very heretical, but together it is imagery so far from the common that it takes Tilde's breath away. She has the urge to cover her own eyes.

Putting the book into the world would be impossible; she knows this already. It would be easily discovered who had written it, and the punishment of the remaining sisters would be immediate and harsh. Already Abbess Tilde thinks it is prudent to stop saying Mass and hearing confessions herself, to give back that right without fighting to retain it, for she too is uncomfortable with the idea of women holding such authority in their too-small too-weak hands. Simply keeping Marie's mystic book at the abbey feels dangerous to her.

And she thinks she would simply slide the little bound volume back behind other volumes, to stay hidden until she grows the wisdom to handle it, but now she hears Subprioress Goda's heavy step in the hall, her hand trying the handle, and in a thoughtless panic Tilde takes the little book and throws it in the fire, and watches Marie's careful handwriting crumple like the legs of spiders as the fire eats the parchment in swift blue flame.

Tilde is not blessed with mystical sight, she cannot see how much is lost in the burning: the traces of a predecessor, the visions that might have shown a different path for the next millennium. The strong stock for a new graft gone. How slow the final flowering of good intentions can be, the poisonous full bloom taking place centuries beyond the scope of the original life.

The abbey crumbling, the earth warming, the clouds abandoning this place, and the newts and birds vanishing, and in the new dryness of the hot world, the traces of the old dead abbey's buildings are thrown up in seared brown lines upon the grasses of the strange changed place absent of holy women, the lines of the labyrinth buried under the roads and houses of later, even more ravenous people.

No, the new abbess, so good, so obedient, so deeply pious, only feels a terrible sort of dark and tarry joy spreading inside her, and she begins to shake with the feeling, for she has never before known the profound pleasures of destruction.

It is this pleasure she feels in destruction that she would later reflect on, deeply troubled; it feels elemental, human, it must have been this that was first hissed by the serpent into Eve's ear.

By the time Goda enters, all traces of Marie's visions are gone.

Goda bellows that the abbess must not lock herself away from her sisters, it is not allowed, even for an abbess. She bellows because she is very old and has gone mostly deaf.

Tilde says that she will ask for penance in confession. She feels her face is red-hot.

Goda glares at her, then crosses to her desk and sits with a wheeze. She sighs. She folds her hands. She sighs, very solemnly, the pigs.

Tilde looks at her. The pigs?

Goda says that it is with great sadness that she must tell the abbess that three of the new gilts were born with the kinky back and that they will be culled this morning.

Tilde looks at the good subprioress and wills herself to tolerant love. She says that she is thankful that Goda is so very excellent at over-seeing the health of the abbey's beasts.

Goda looks at her suspiciously to make sure the younger woman isn't laughing at her, but at last nods, her mouth set nearly in a smile. She says she has been subprioress for longer than the abbess has been alive. Fifty-six years subprioress. And she has seen the cattle grow from a single sick heifer to a healthy three dozen. Hundreds of chickens where there were four. Swine and goats beyond measure. She is not a proud woman, but she has done a passable job. Better than passable, maybe, even if nobody has ever thanked her for her hard work. Now, she says in a much lower voice, what is that smell? Stinking. Is the abbess unwell? Colewort disagrees with Goda's guts also.

Abbess Tilde says she just now burnt a thing, but not to worry, it is nothing.

And she tells no lie, for she has looked into the fire and seen the whole book burned and even if it once had been something now it has become nothing, not a book anymore but ember and ash. She is free from having to decide what to do with the strange visions of her predecessor. With the burning, all the visions of Marie are as though they had never existed.

Smoke to smoke, she thinks, and feels a pang for failing her old friend, gone ghost.

Such fires, so small in themselves, will heat the world imperceptibly until after centuries it will be too hot to bear humanity.

In the schoolroom, the novices are chanting the imperfect passive indicative, third conjugation: capiebar, capiebaris, capiebatur, capiebamur, capiebamini, capiebantur; and the novice Lucy with the freckles pinches the novice Gwenllian with the great cow's eyes and both girls smile into their hands.

Down in the abbess's kitchen, the kitchener kneads dough with her sleeves unpinned, and the flour has risen to hover like a mist in the air and a servant eats nuts that she cracks with her strong hands and tosses the shells into the fire and gossips about the new abbess, how though of royal blood and for many decades prioress, Tilde yet seems uncertain in her role.

The servant says that, in fact, Tilde could not be more unlike the old abbess. Oh ancient Abbess Marie was the strongest woman she had ever met in her whole life, they say a seraph had lain with her mother, hence Marie's excessive height and the light that leaked from her. No, the old abbess brooked no fools. Made the air of a room go taut as a drum when she walked in. But catlike on those giant feet, nimble as a girl of ten even sickly in old age and creaking. Scared the piss from all the servants more than once.

Ah yes, she was a crusader as well, the kitchener says sagely. They say dozens of infidels were slain by her great lady's hand in Jerusalem, hundreds, even. She made blood pour knee deep in the streets. Awesome, terrifying, the great domina was. Holy, holy. A saint.

But the chit of a new washing girl says that she had heard here and there that in fact there was no woman hid under that great habit of the old abbess's, no woman at all, and that on top of all that she also heard that the old abbess Marie was either a witch or the devil taking the form of a nun, and did anyone look under the headcloths and see the horns?

The kitchener throws a rolling stick at the girl's forehead, shouting that she will cut out the girl's tongue, nobody won't be blaspheming her sainted Marie, who plucked the kitchener and so many of the others from the mud when she was a grub and saved them from their starving families. A better woman the world has never seen. She pants.

The girl mutters she never said nothing about nothing, rubbing the knot on her head.

Out in the orchard, small, quick Sister Petronilla catches up to Sister Alix on her way to the abbess's house with a stack of clean linens in her arms, and darting her eyes about to ensure nobody is watching, she kisses the young blushing nun swiftly on the mouth and runs on.

In the sheepfold, young Sister Rohese hides from her chores with a lamb on her lap, weeping for her sister who is sickly at home and will soon be called to the lap of the Virgin.

Soon a small figure is seen pulling the bell rope to ring all the holy women to Terce. The nuns hear the peals and finish their labors and conjugations and private weeping. They stream out toward the chapel.

Slowly, as they come, their thoughts turn to prayer.

And the works and the hours go on.

ACKNOWLEDGMENTS

Thank you to Dr. Katie Bugyis, whose lecture gave me the first spark of this story, and whose book *The Care of Nuns: The Ministries of Benedictine Women in England during the Central Middle Ages* provided further inspiration. Her intellect and thorough notes kept me on track during the composition of this book; all mistakes are of course mine.

Thank you to the Radcliffe Institute for Advanced Study, for the extraordinary gift of a fellowship, which allowed me the time and ability to begin this book. Thank you to my undergraduate researcher, Patricia Liu, for the excellent work and friendship.

Thank you to the Guggenheim Foundation, for a further gift of time.

Thank you to my gentle friends, the nuns at the Abbey of Regina Laudis in Connecticut, for welcoming me so gracefully to their guesthouse, masses, and work, and for showing me the astonishing beauty of monastic life. Special thanks to Mother Abbess Lucia and Mother Angele for our openhearted conversations. Thank you, J. Courtney Sullivan, for the referral.

Thank you to Dr. Paul Rockwell of the Amherst College French Department, who tutored me for two semesters in ancien français, and who first introduced me to my beloved Marie de France.

Thank you to my readers Laura van den Berg, Elliott Holt, T Kira Madden, and Jamie Quatro, whose notes cracked the book open again and again.

Thank you to my family at Riverhead, especially Sarah McGrath, Jynne Dilling Martin, and Claire McGinnis.

Thank you to Bill Clegg and Marion Duvert and everyone else at the Clegg Agency.

Thank you to my parents for sheltering us in their tiny New Hampshire utopia while the pandemic raged on in the wider world.

Thank you to Rebecca Ferdinand and Maria Clevenger, for taking care of us.

Thank you to Clay, Beckett, and Heath.

Thank you to my readers.

This book is for my sisters, those of the flesh, and those of the spirit.